LEXINGTON
Heart of the Bluegrass

Copyright 1982
Lexington-Fayette County
Historic Commission

*All rights are reserved, including
the right of reproduction in whole or
in part, in any form whatsoever.*

*Library of Congress Catalogue
Number: 82-082604*

*This publication was made possible in
part through financial support provided
by Kentucky Central Life Insurance
Company and subsidiary firms.*

Christmas-time on Main Street in the 1930's, looking east from Limestone Street. Photo courtesy of Burton Milward.

Fayette County's fifth and present courthouse, erected 1898-1900.

LEXINGTON
Heart of the Bluegrass

By JOHN D. WRIGHT, JR.

Lexington-Fayette County
Historic Commission
Lexington, Kentucky

Visitors to the Bluegrass enjoy a carriage ride at the new Kentucky Horse Park. Photo courtesy of the Kentucky Horse Park.

Table of Contents

Foreword

Cities are not static. They are constantly changing in response to social and economic pressures. Lexington, Kentucky, is no exception to this process, as history amply attests.

While looking to the future, we can often be guided best by taking stock of the past. Lexington-Fayette County has an illustrious history and our knowledge and understanding of it can help determine how we influence the community's future goals and directions. It is our hope that by arousing an interest in the special history of Lexington, we will generate additional citizen support for activities designed to preserve the distinctiveness of this remarkable metropolis, set down amidst the beautiful Kentucky Bluegrass Region.

Recognizing that it has been a century since the publication of William H. Perrin's *History of Fayette County, Kentucky* in 1882, the Lexington-Fayette County Historic Commission concluded that it was an appropriate and desirable time to sponsor a new history of this community, which has been of such significance in Kentucky's development and which today is confronted with the challenge of unprecedented change and growth. The Commission wanted a concise, illustrated account that would interest as many Lexington and Kentucky readers as possible. Also, we hoped it would foster an historical awareness, especially valuable in a community in which recent arrivals outnumber the native-born.

Lexington: Heart of the Bluegrass is, then, a carefully abridged history of the over two hundred years of this community's life. There was no intention of making it definitive and comprehensive, and therefore many individuals and events necessarily had to be omitted. We hope that the interest created by this volume will encourage Lexingtonians — scholars and lay persons alike — to undertake further research, writing, and publishing with respect to those facets of the city's history that justify further attention.

We are most grateful to the scores of local residents and institutions from whom we borrowed the photographs that enhance this publication. In particular, we are indebted to the photographic files of the Lexington-Herald Leader Co.; the J. Winston Coleman Kentuckiana Collection at Transylvania University Library; the Special Collections of the Transylvania University Library; and the Photographic Archives, Department of Special Collections and Archives, University of Kentucky.

Many of the comtemporary photographs that appear in this volume are the work of Mary Rezny, Lexington photographer. Invaluable assistance also was provided by Lloyd Beard, of Stone Photography, who copied many of the pictures made available to us by local archivists.

It has taken a great cooperative effort to put this book together. The Publishing Committee of the Historic Commission; John Wright, our author; Charles H. Thomas, of Kentucky Central Insurance Companies, and Bettie Kerr, of the Historic Commission staff have worked in harmony and with enthusiasm to see the project to completion. My contributions to this undertaking have been rewarded beyond expectation with this important publication.

Richard S. DeCamp
Executive Director
Lexington-Fayette County
Historic Commission

Higher education had its beginning in Lexington in the late 18th century at Transylvania University.

John C. Breckinridge's statue presides over Cheapside and the Courthouse lawn today, as it did in 1887 when it was erected.

Preface

To research and write a 200-year history of Lexington and Fayette County has been a most rewarding experience. There is a wealth of information to be learned about the remarkable past of this distinctive community. The restraints imposed in writing a compressed historical account, however, necessitated the omission of a number of colorful and intriguing individuals and events. There is a bit of the story-teller in most historians, and the obligation to edit out many a fine tale was painful.

It is my hope that this historical sketch, which is primarily a social history of the community, will stimulate other researchers and writers to fill out the uncompleted canvas. If this account informs and interests the reader in Lexington's past, and broadens his appreciation of its rich historical heritage, I shall feel my efforts well rewarded.

This particular project, conceived and executed in the short space of two years, necessitated an unusual team effort. I am pleased and grateful to acknowledge my obligations to numerous institutions and individuals.

First, let me express my appreciation to the Lexington-Fayette County Historic Commission for inviting me to undertake this task, to Transylvania University for granting me a one-semester sabbatical in which to write the manuscript, and to the helpful staff members of the Margaret I. King Library at the University of Kentucky, the Transylvania University Library, and the Lexington Public Library.

My special thanks go to Mr. Burton Milward, who provided untold assistance in opening to me his voluminous files of Lexington and Kentucky history, sharing his encyclopedic knowledge of the city's history, and painstakingly editing and checking the various drafts of my manuscript. I wish to express my appreciation to Miss Bettye Lee Mastin, another fount of local historical information, for her willingness to read and edit the manuscript, and for her numerous articles on Lexington's people, buildings, and events, published over the years in the *Lexington Herald,* which are a treasure trove for the historian. My thanks also to Dr. J. Winston Coleman, Jr., for his encouragement and guidance in reading portions of this work. The data compiled for the Historic Commission by Walter Langsam on Lexington's architecture,

architects, and the history associated with them proved of inestimable value, and I wish to express my appreciation for his editorial suggestions on a number of the chapters of the manuscript.

I also wish to extend my heartfelt thanks and sympathy, based on long experience, to my co-workers who labored for endless hours at the microfilm machines, scanning and evaluating decades of newspaper articles: Mrs. Jean Gossick, Miss Kim Knight, Miss Bettie Kerr, Mrs. Margery Broomell, and Mr. Burtis Franklin.

Mrs. Kathryn Johnson, the City Clerk, was most helpful in making official records and reports available to me. Mr. Joseph Heidenreich, the City Traffic Engineer, who has served this community well in making sure that invaluable early records of this town were preserved, generously shared his knowledge and files.

I appreciate the assistance given me by Mr. Charles H. Thomas, of the Kentucky Central Insurance Companies, whose editing experience and enthusiasm for this project proved most valuable, and to Dr. James E. Klotter, of the Kentucky Historical Society, for his insight and suggestions. I wish to thank Mr. Burtis Franklin for his extensive research in the history of public education in Lexington and Fayette County, which was especially valuable for this past century and the recent period.

My thanks, too, to Mrs. Marilyn Carter for her fine typing skills and helpful editorial suggestions.

My wife, Fran, not only researched portions of the black history of Lexington, but assisted me in so many ways that I cannot imagine how I could have completed this project without her.

Finally, I would like to thank Mr. Richard S. DeCamp, Executive Director of the Lexington-Fayette County Historic Commission, for his overall guidance in this project and for his frequent and timely reminders about deadlines.

The above-named individuals and organizations, however, are not to be held accountable in any way for the end product, for which I assume full responsibility.

John D. Wright, Jr.
July 1, 1982

Portrait of Robert Patterson, leading figure in the founding of Lexington. The painting hangs at Transylvania University.

Chapter I

1775/1799

Emergence of a Pioneer Town

In the pleasant June of 1775, one of many groups of landseekers, hunters, surveyors, and speculators exploring Kentucky and staking out land claims, gathered by a bubbling spring on the middle fork of the Elkhorn, later to be identified as William McConnell's Spring, and talked about creating a frontier settlement which they decided to call Lexington.

It was an act of commitment to the American Revolution to name this site after the Massachusetts town where, on the morning of April 19, 1775, the Minute Men first confronted the British Regulars in a bloody encounter on the village green. News of that battle only gradually seeped along the rivers and trails leading into the trans-Allegheny West, reaching these explorers weeks later. The mountain barrier would seclude them from the major battles of the Revolution but the West was not immune. The British commanders urged their Indian allies, who needed little encouragement, to intensify their attacks on the white men coming in increasing numbers into this western treasure house — Kentucky.

The British government acquired the vast tract of land between the Mississippi and the Appalachians from the French by the Treaty of Paris in 1763, ending the long French and Indian War. By the Proclamation Act of that same year, Britain, in an attempt to avoid further conflict with the Indians, prohibited the colonists from funneling over the mountains into this area, but the colonists were not to be denied, and the Act was ignored.

Of all the land west of the mountains, Kentucky held the greatest appeal. Early explorers, who had ranged along the Ohio River border of this region, tentatively moved down the many tributaries into Kentucky's heartland. Others, like Dr. Thomas Walker, had penetrated the mountain barrier at Cumberland Gap and wandered along the eastern Kentucky mountains and streams. All brought back accounts of a lush and fertile region exceeding anything they had ever seen. Great forests of virgin timber, numerous rivers, rich soil, open savannahs covered with cane, waiting for the scythe and the plow, or as pasture for herds of cattle, and an abundance of pure water from limestone springs — all were there. And the game! The forests teemed with deer, elk, wild turkey, bear, and all kinds of wild fowl. Most fascinating of all were the herds of massive shouldered, shaggy bison pounding out traces to the abundant salt licks in central and eastern Kentucky.

Writers had raved about this Eden of the West, so that a mythical quality about the region began to emerge. Gilbert Imlay wrote:

> Flowers full and perfect, as if they had been cultivated by the hand of a florist ... decorate the smiling groves. Soft zephyrs gently breathe on sweets, and the inhaled air gives a voluptuous glow of health and vigour, that seems to ravish the intoxicated senses. The sweet songsters of the forests appear to feel the influence of this genial clime, and ... warble their tender notes in unison with love and nature. Everything here gives delight, and, in that mild effulgence which beams around us, we feel a glow of gratitude for that elevation our all-bountiful Creator has bestowed upon us.

While most commentators did not indulge in such exaggerated flights of fancy, continuous streams of enthusiastic praise of Kentucky's giant forests, fertile soil and abundant game flowed back into the settled areas, inspiring established families as well as newly arrived immigrants to push their way into this new Eden. One traveler from Maryland wrote to his relatives back home in 1787 from near Danville: "I have often told you that no one could conceive a proper Idea of this country but by sight, to discribe [sic] it would therefore be vain for the Beauties of this country which every now & then strike the Eye with such a sensibel [sic] degree of Pleasure can be felt only by the Beholder ... what would I not give to show you Nature & Nature's works in perfection."

But this only partly explains the reason for the ever-increasing numbers of migrants moving into Kentucky, especially after the Revolution. For most it was land hunger — to own, to farm, to sell, to speculate — somehow to reach out and grasp a part of this rich region to improve their condition.

In 1775 permanent settlements in Kentucky were few. Harrodsburg, settled a year earlier, though vacated for a few months, was the oldest. The legendary Daniel Boone, acting as an agent for Colonel Richard Henderson and the Transylvania Company, established Boonesborough in April 1775, and other scattered stations were carved out of the wilderness in central Kentucky. These were extraordinarily dangerous times for the new settlers. The forests were alive with Indians, especially the troublesome Shawnee from Ohio, for there were no permanent settlements of Indians in Kentucky at this time. Boone had already lost one son on an earlier trip to Kentucky, and he took considerable risk in bringing his wife and family to Boonesborough.

Despite these obstacles, the Edenic appeal of Kentucky and the exploring spirit and land hunger of the pioneers brought many from Pennsylvania, Virginia, and North Carolina into the region. Kentucky, however, was under Virginia jurisdiction, and the whole area was then part of the western Virginia county of Fincastle. In December 1776, it became Kentucky County, and the County Court was located at Harrodsburg. Virginia's laws dictated how lands could be claimed, and those provisions were so diverse, imprecise, and confusing that land claims, titles, and deeds

became the main grist for the Kentucky courts for decades.

It was a party from the Monongahela region in Pennsylvania, under the leadership of William McConnell, along with his brother Francis, a number of McClellands, and others, who came down the Ohio River, and traveled up the Kentucky River to the Elkhorn in the spring of 1775 to the future site of Lexington. They were joined by others, including John Smith, John Maxwell, Hugh Shannon, William Lain, and Cyrus McCracken, building cabins for several members of the party on the North Elkhorn as they came. While they were camped at the sinking spring near the Middle Fork on land later granted to William McConnell, the famous incident of the naming of Lexington occurred. A letter bearing news of the battle at Lexington, Massachusetts, had arrived in Boonesborough on May 29, 1775. The McConnell party heard of it and was inspired to use that name.

A Man Named Clark

Part of the company returned to Pennsylvania to make final preparations for leaving their homes, committing themselves to a future life in Kentucky. In the fall of 1775, equipped with the necessary provisions to survive in the wilderness, they embarked once more for the new land. This time they were joined by Robert Patterson, cousin of the McClellands, and the leading figure in the establishment of Lexington. They spent the winter of 1775-1776 at McClelland's Station (Georgetown).

Kentuckians were engaged in a desperate struggle to survive. Indian attacks on the outposts of McClelland's, Harrod's, Logan's, and Boonesborough persuaded a restless, vigorous, charismatic individual by the name of George Rogers Clark to strike at the source of these Indian attacks in Illinois, Indiana, Ohio, and the British control center at Detroit. With a modicum of support from the Virginia government, he recruited troops and undertook the incredible expedition that resulted in the capture of Kaskaskia, Cahokia, and Vincennes. Governor Henry Hamilton was taken prisoner, having left Detroit to command his British troops and Indian allies. Clark's success greatly diminished British influence in the West,

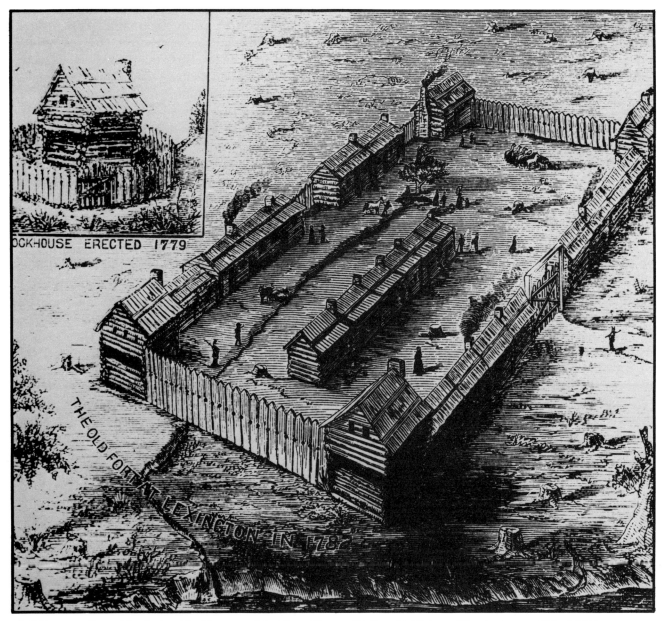

Artist's conception of Lexington blockhouse and fort from George W. Ranck's History of Lexington, *published 1872.*

created dissatisfaction among some of their Indian allies, and reduced the pressure of Indian attacks on the Kentucky outposts.

Among those in Clark's troops was Robert Patterson who returned to Harrodsburg shortly after the victory at Vincennes. Born in Pennsylvania in 1753 of Irish parents, he was barely twenty-one when he enlisted as a ranger and served six months against the Indians on the Pennsylvania frontier. Shortly afterwards, he joined the party coming to Kentucky. Spending the winter at Georgetown, he started out for Pittsburgh with a few others in the fall of 1776 to procure much needed gunpowder. On the way they were attacked one night by Indians who severely injured most of the men

before being driven off. Patterson barely survived. Shot twice, his right arm broken, a deep tomahawk cut between two ribs near his spinal column, he endured agony until rescued. It was nearly a year before he recovered, but Patterson's stamina and willpower enabled him to return to Kentucky and enlist in Clark's campaign.

While at Harrodsburg in early 1779, Patterson was made an Ensign in Captain Levi Todd's company, and in April was ordered to lead a group of twenty-five men from Fort Harrod to establish a garrison north of the Kentucky River. On the evening of April 16, 1779, the party arrived at the Middle Fork of the Elkhorn, soon to be called the Town

Branch. No one knows exactly why this particular spot was chosen. Though adjacent to a pleasant stream and a number of good springs, the location suffered from being on a flood plain with a sharp rise on one side and a more gradual slope on the other. This made any settlement or fortification subject to easy enemy surveillance and musket and light artillery fire. Also, the site was vulnerable to periodic flooding since it was confined to a small flood plain between two slopes, which acted as natural dams.

These handicaps notwithstanding, work began on April 17 on the blockhouse, located at what is now the southwest corner of Main and Mill streets near a good spring. The blockhouse, typical of the type built at Fort Harrod and at Boonesborough, could hardly accommodate many individuals, and some of the men returned to Harrodsburg. About a month after the blockhouse was finished, the men helped John Morrison build a nearby cabin for his wife and children. As this was the crucial planting season, about thirty acres of cane and trees in the immediate area were cut to plant corn, the fields being worked in common.

A number of this small garrison volunteered to campaign under Colonel John Bowman and the Kentucky County militia against the Shawnee centered at Chillicothe, Ohio. Only twelve men and Mrs. Morrison remained in Lexington during the summer of 1779. She stayed in her cabin and although she occasionally heard Indians prowling about outside at night, they did not attempt to break in, nor did she seek shelter in the blockhouse.

When some German newcomers arrived in October, there were only four cabins and the blockhouse. By April 1, 1780, a stockade described as a "strong fort," had been erected and most of the cabins were enclosed within it. Meat supply was plentiful that fall as bison passed close by, but the heavily protein diet doubtless caused some nutritional deficiencies.

With a limited corn supply and jammed together in crowded living conditions, these early Lexingtonians endured one of the worst winters ever recorded. The so-called Hard Winter of 1779-80 started with snow in November, and the ground remained frozen solid until well into March. Game became scarce, and although a number of animals were found frozen to death, their meat was dehydrated and almost inedible. Nerves were rubbed raw under these confined conditions, but the drive for survival forced accommodation among the inhabitants.

Despite the brutal winter, the political organization of Lexington began. On January 25, 1780, acting on the request of the County Court of Kentucky County at Harrodsburg to all Kentucky residents to remain in compact groups in fortified areas and to choose judicious individuals to serve as trustees of their communities, the settlers signed a "citizens' compact," in the prevailing social contract tradition of that day. The compact provided that the town was to be laid off in so many "in lotts" of a half-acre each and "out lotts" of five acres each, the qualifications for ownership being detailed in the compact. Random choices were drawn for the land. A few months later, Levi Todd, Robert Patterson, David Mitchell, Henry McDonald and Michael Warnock were elected as trustees and held office until early 1782 when the townsmen selected a new board including William McConnell and John Todd.

The first Trustee's Book contained a plat of the town and names of the lot owners. The overall plan for the new town followed the traditional grid pattern similar to that used in Philadelphia and New York. However, rather than utilizing compass headings as guides to establish Main Street, the Town Branch was used, and thus all the streets ran roughly parallel or at right angles to this stream. A town commons was also laid out along the Town Branch. The early boundaries consisted of Mulberry (now Limestone) Street on the east, Locust Street (now Tucker) on the west, while Short and High served as the northern and southern limits of the in-lots. A cemetery was set aside on Main Street beyond Spring Street, extending from Main to Short.

A number of outlying stations were established in the Lexington area in 1779, the most important being Bryant's Station, five miles northeast of Lexington. The ablest leader of the Bryants, William, was killed in 1780 by the Indians and the Bryants returned east, although other settlers came to keep the station well occupied.

The slow growth of Lexington in these early years was due primarily to the consistent recruiting of men by George Rogers Clark and other leaders for almost yearly attacks on the Indians. This separated the younger men from their land, preventing both extensive farming and building. But the Indian menace was ever present. Successful attacks on Martin's and Ruddle's stations alarmed the Lexington settlers. Under the leadership of Colonel John Todd, a strong and well-designed fort, defensible against artillery, was constructed in twenty days in March and April of 1781, by recruiting a large number of men from the whole area and guaranteeing their pay himself. Friendly competition and liquor, Todd also noted, were effective incentives. He sent an impressive bill of 11,341 pounds to the Virginia Assembly, hoping for restitution. This sturdy fortress, far stronger than the flimsier stockade though not as large, doubtless enhanced the morale of the residents and apparently scared off the Indians and their British advisors who never attempted to attack it.

Indeed, the only incident of a settler being killed within sight of the fort occurred in early March 1781, when a work party gathering logs in the vicinity of where Central Christian Church on Walnut Street is located today was surprised by Indians. Running as fast as they could to the stockade for safety, the settlers hoped to elude their attackers but the older and slower John Wymore was overtaken and shot. As an Indian stooped down to scalp him, one of Wymore's comrades fired at the Indian, the bullet grazing the Indian's skull and stunning him. Before he could recover, men ran out from the stockade and tomahawked him. "The Indian was scalped," recalled Wymore's son Martin, "and his scalp hung on a string on a pole so that the wind could blow it about to mortify the Indians."

The most alarming attack in the region occurred near the end of the American Revolution. Captain Caldwell and the infamous

Memorial wall around Bryant Station Spring commemorates the heroism of the pioneers in the defense of Bryant Station in 1782. Photo courtesy of Transylvania University.

Simon Girty led a large band of Indians from Ohio into Kentucky in mid-August 1782. They reached Bryant's Station, hoping to take it by surprise. The inhabitants, forewarned of the Indians' coming, lured them into believing that they were unaware of their prepared ambush by sending some courageous women to the spring outside the fort to bring back precious water. The ruse worked. When the Indians attacked, the pioneers inflicted heavy casualties on them.

Lexington and the surrounding communities sent reinforcements to help the beleaguered station. The attackers lifted the siege and the pioneers vigorously pursued them. Unfortunately, the impatient Kentuckians, ignoring Daniel Boone's warnings, rushed into a deadly ambush at Blue Licks. A substantial part of this band was killed, including another son of Boone, Colonel John Todd, and many other Lexingtonians. The impact on the town was traumatic. This disaster was commonly regarded as the last battle of the Revolution, but the Indians continued to threaten Kentucky settlers into the 1790's.

Laying the Foundations

Despite the Indian threats, the determination of Lexington settlers to develop a permanent town resulted in a petition to the Virginia Assembly in April 1782, to establish the town officially. The legislators responded by passing an act in May recognizing the Town of Lexington, and assigning some 710 acres to the trustees in fee simple. This acreage was composed of a patchwork of grants, including an original 200-acre tract warranted on April 19, 1774, by Governor Dunmore to James Buford for services in the French and Indian War, which eventually ended up in the hands of John Todd, who donated it to the Lexington trustees. Other land was obtained from John Maxwell, William Pendleton, Francis McConnell, Robert Patterson, and John Floyd. By granting the land to the trustees in fee simple, the state allowed the trustees to grant deeds to the owners of the various lots already assigned.

As in most pioneer communities, growth in the first few years was slow. Five years after the first blockhouse had been built, only about

Log cabin originally built by Robert Patterson in the 1780's now stands on the Transylvania University campus.

thirty cabins had been erected in the vicinity of the fort. A typical log structure erected at this time was that of Colonel Robert Patterson. Made of square-hewn logs, these buildings were generally called log houses in contrast to the log cabins with their rounded logs. The stick and mud chimneys, sometimes with rock foundations, were usually constructed outside the cabin itself, which made them easier to put up and easier to pull down when they caught fire.

Stumps still remained in Main Street and hogs rooted freely in the area. The need for various products not available from local sources was met at first by itinerant peddlers. At the risk of their lives, they drove their pack animals, laden with wares from Philadelphia and Baltimore, over the Indian-infested traces and trails from Limestone (Maysville) to Lexington, after having drifted down the Ohio River from Pittsburgh. When they had sold their goods at some temporary stand on Main Street, they would return east for more.

Among the first resident storekeepers were Peter January and James Wilkinson, who established their stores in Lexington sometime in 1784. Although January and his family became permanent and distinguished residents of this town, General Wilkinson was by far the most visible, dramatic, and controversial figure to appear in Kentucky and Lexington at this time. A native Pennsylvanian who married into a good family, Wilkinson had created something of a reputation as an officer on the staff of General Gates in the American Revolutionary Army. From all accounts, he was a man of great personal charm but a rank opportunist, entirely without scruples. That he had a daring, if not a gambling spirit, was borne out by his willingness to cut loose from his secure footing in Philadelphia and strike out to build fame and fortune in the rapidly expanding but highly unpredictable conditions of the trans-Allegheny frontier.

With a few partners, Wilkinson engaged a party to transport a sizable inventory of goods down the Ohio, some of which went overland from Limestone (Maysville) to Lexington, the rest to Louisville. But Wilkinson was an entrepreneur, not a clerk, and the day-to-day operation of his store was left to his employees while he bought and sold property in the area and in Frankfort. In 1787 he initiated a remarkably profitable trade with New Orleans, by buying large quantities of bulky Kentucky agricultural products, not easily transportable across the mountains, and floating them down the Ohio and Mississippi to the bustling marts of Spanish-controlled New Orleans. Here, Wilkinson not only made mercantile bargains but also engaged in political intrigues.

In order to enhance his own political and economic fortunes, Wilkinson conspired with the Spanish to attempt to persuade the Kentuckians, by bribery if necessary, to ally themselves with Spain in return for opening the port of New Orleans to Kentucky goods.

Other merchants like Alexander and James Parker, George Gordon, John Coburn, and Robert Barr came in 1784. Hard money was scarce; barter was the normal means of exchange. Furs, butter, tallow, cheese, eggs, chickens, cured meats, home-woven cloth, hemp and tobacco were taken in exchange for finished products and articles such as tea, coffee, and spices. Beaver skins provided the most popular standard unit of value. The Continental currency, printed with much abandon during the Revolution, was almost worthless.

Prior to Alexander Hamilton's efforts as the first Secretary of the Treasury to standardize and stabilize the new U.S. currency, foreign coin was all that was available to the pioneers. French, English, Dutch, German, Portuguese, and especially Spanish coins, found their way into Kentuckians' hands. To make these valuable coins go farther, they were, as in the case of the Spanish piaster, literally cut into quarters or into even smaller "pieces of eight." Weighing them became the only way to gauge their value.

As the Indian threat was gradually reduced, farms in the outlying parts of the county began to expand and greater production of grains, hemp, tobacco, and livestock followed. Certain grains, too heavy to transport profitably to distant markets, were converted into whiskey for export. The process of distilling was mastered by most of the early settlers who included distilling equipment among their most prized possessions. The clear liquid produced at this time was not the famed bourbon of later years that resulted from aging in charred white oak barrels, imparting the color and bouquet associated with one of Kentucky's most famous and profitable products.

Early Taverns and Inns

That Lexington as early as 1784 or 1785 had become the center of a growing network of roads radiating into the surrounding country, thus attracting not only merchants and artisans but many new settlers, is shown by the number of early taverns and inns that began to appear in this frontier community. The earliest of these was apparently that of James Bray on Main Street between Main Cross (Broadway) and Spring streets. Other taverns included that of Captain Thomas Young on Upper Street, 1786, Henry Marshall on Main Street, and the "Sheaf of Wheat," a two-story log building operated by Robert Megowan. "The Sign of the Buffalo," which opened on Main Street under John McNair's management, was later run by his widow. A favorite of the town trustees was John Higbee's tavern on the southwest corner of Mulberry (Limestone) and High streets where they occasionally held their monthly meetings.

The numerous taverns indicate their importance as sources of strong drink, rough conviviality, and news from recently arrived travelers. Conditions were still basically frontier-like. People wore deerskins or linsey-woolsey, the diet was plain and limited, mortality high, and professional medical aid practically non-existent. The Indian menace lurked on the margins of the settlements, and the need to clear the land of cane and trees and build and plant was incessant. As early as 1785 these conditions began to change. Migration to and through the town increased, attracting those seeking new land, and the merchants, artisans, and professional men who, in the next decade or two, would quickly convert this primitive community into a thriving urban center, representative of what is now called the urban frontier — an urban West that included Pittsburgh, Cincinnati, Louisville, and St. Louis.

What made Lexington's early progress more remarkable was that the city was not located on a navigable river. This fact would prove burdensome following the war of 1812 when the steamboats began to push up the Mississippi and the Ohio to reach St. Louis, Louisville, Cincinnati, and Pittsburgh. But in the 1780's and 1790's, Lexington grew the most rapidly as the crowds of migrants streamed through the town, bought their supplies here, and later used Lexington as a market for their goods, either consumed by the residents or shipped elsewhere.

Fayette County Formed

In November 1780, the Virginia Assembly had divided Kentucky County into Fayette, Lincoln, and Jefferson counties. Named after the Marquis de Lafayette, France's most dedicated and influential supporter of the American Revolution, Fayette County embraced a goodly portion of Kentucky north and east of the Kentucky River. This extensive domain was considerably reduced as county after new county was carved out of it: Bourbon (1785), Woodford (1788), Clark (1792), and Jessamine (1798). Lexington became the county seat and Governor Thomas Jefferson of Virginia appointed John Todd as Colonel, Daniel Boone as Lieutenant-Colonel, and Thomas Marshall as surveyor of this county. Although the Lexington

trustees set aside land for a county courthouse in the public square, the first courthouse, built in 1782, was a two-story log structure on the northwest corner of Main Cross (Broadway) and Main Street. Six years later, a two-story stone courthouse was built on the site of the present courthouse and this second one remained until 1806 when it was razed to make room for a third.

Being designated the county seat enhanced Lexington's importance, and brought people to town to conduct business with county officials as well as to make necessary purchases, or to gather for the colorful and occasionally rowdy court days. These occasions were sometimes highlighted by such dramatic events as public hangings. Needham Parry, recently arrived from Pennsylvania in June 1794, recorded in his diary that

> Lexington is a fine, stirring town, containing about 350 houses ... and is the greatest place for dealing I ever saw ... This day, about 12 o'clock, the condemned prisoner, Mr. Wilcox, whose sentence was to be hanged for knowingly passing ... counterfeit bank notes, was bro't from prison, & drawn to the gallows in a wagon ... guarded by about 100 foot, & 50 horsemen, & attended by a numerous concourse of people ... When he came there, his wife and children met him, which to be a spectator of was a very moving scene. However, after he was under the gallows, while a sermon was being preached, he rec'd his reprieve from the Governor, to the satisfaction of many of the spectators, tho' not near all.

It is remarkable that as early as 1783, John McKinney, a schoolteacher, should have begun classes for a motley assortment of pioneer children, reflecting the concern of some parents and town trustees that, remote from civilization as they were, literacy was a necessary ingredient for a free citizenry and a prosperous community. This schoolmaster would long since have been forgotten had it not been for his famed encounter with a wildcat one June morning. McKinney was alone in his rough-hewn log schoolhouse located on the public square when a wildcat entered the open door and leapt almost immediately on the schoolmaster, burying its fangs into his ribs. Though McKinney cried out for help, he exerted himself sufficiently to strangle the cat, before women, hearing his cries, brought men from the fort to assist him. The cat was dead

The Adam Rankin House, one of the oldest existing houses in Lexington, was built circa 1784 at 215 West High Street. This two-story structure, later covered with clapboard, was moved in 1971 to 317 South Mill Street. Photo courtesy of the University of Kentucky.

but it was difficult and painful to extract its teeth from McKinney's side. The schoolmaster was so shaken by the incident that he called off school for the day.

The Early Churches

The early settlers had brought not only their concern for education into this wilderness, but also their religious faith, and while the primitive conditions in the blockhouse and stockade the first few years made it difficult to establish independent churches and congregations, those who brought their Bibles with them might have shared them with others in informal readings or prayer sessions. A layman might have served as a substitute minister on the Sabbath or read appropriate scriptural passages at the burial of young and old in the town cemetery on West Main Street.

Formal church organization began with the arrival of Elder Lewis Craig in Fayette County in 1783. This indomitable Baptist leader, who had been imprisoned and buffeted in his native Virginia for his outspoken espousal of his beliefs and denunciation of the Established Church (Episcopal), had gathered a valiant band of Spotsylvania County Baptists, and trudged over the mountain passes in mid-winter toward new opportunity and freedom in Kentucky. Eventually reaching the Bluegrass region, he organized one of the earliest Baptist congregations on the South Elkhorn.

In 1784, the Reverend Adam Rankin, called by Lexington Presbyterians from Virginia, gathered his flock together and built a small church on the southern border of frontier Lexington on what is now the site of the old University of Kentucky Agricultural Experiment Station on South Limestone Street, south of Washington Avenue. Rankin's two-story log house was built on Hill (High) Street in 1784. A frame addition was added about a decade later and the entire dwelling was then clapboarded, a rather common practice by many owners of sturdy log houses throughout the region. Now one of the oldest structures in Lexington, it has been moved from its original site to 317 South Mill Street.

Called the Mount Zion Presbyterian Church, this original congregation unfortunately became divided over Rankin's views on Psalmody "as many of the pioneer Presbyterians would never sing Watt's version of the Psalms." Though in retrospect the issue seems a minor one, it was sufficient to provoke Rankin's opponents to create a separate church. They purchased from the Lexington trustees part of the west end of the public square bounded by Cheapside, Main, Mill, and Short streets and constructed a meetinghouse facing Mill Street.

Rankin's group meanwhile had abandoned their original church site on South Limestone and acquired property on the southeast corner of Walnut and Short streets. The minister's controversial career finally resulted in his departure from Lexington and his congregation dwindled, but later some of the members became the nucleus of the Second Presbyterian Church.

The Mill Street Presbyterians, who eventually became the First Presbyterian Church, left their downtown location in 1808 and moved to a new church on the southwest corner of Broadway and Second streets.

In addition to forming a Lexington Presbyterian church, Rankin also assisted in establishing the Pisgah Presbyterian Church just across the county line in Woodford County in 1784, and served as pastor of both churches for a few years. Later, James Blythe served as pastor at Pisgah for several decades, while teaching and serving as acting president of Transylvania University.

The Walnut Hill Church, erected in 1801, is the oldest Presbyterian Church building in Kentucky. Non-denominational services are now held regularly at the church.

Some miles southeast of Lexington off the Richmond Road, at the intersection of Walnut Hill Pike, stands the oldest Presbyterian church building in Kentucky. The Reverend James Crawford organized the Walnut Hill Presbyterian Church in 1784 in Fayette County, and Levi Todd conveyed land to the church on which the present structure was erected in 1801.

Frontier Methodists were served by the famed circuit riders of their day whose physical stamina must necessarily have equalled their spiritual endurance. They traveled, frequently alone, along the wilderness trails from cabin to isolated cabin, hamlet to hamlet, subject to the rigors of the weather and encounters with wild animals and Indians. May 13, 1790, was a significant day for the Fayette County Methodists when Bishop Francis Asbury, with a

well-armed escort, arrived in town to attend a two-day conference at Masterson's Station, some five miles west of Lexington on the Leestown Road. Yet, the practice of assigning circuit preachers for Lexington delayed the establishment of a permanent Methodist church. Although a small cabin had been purchased as early as 1789 on the southwest corner of Short and Back (now Dewees) streets, regular services were not held until 1819 when they moved into their new church, a two-story brick building on the north side of Church Street between Limestone and Upper streets. Apparently one of the reasons for the slower growth of Methodism in Lexington in the 1790's and early 1800's was its opposition to slavery, which influenced some proslavery residents to attend other churches. Some Presbyterians and Baptists had also adopted antislavery positions in the late

18th and early 19th centuries, as evidenced by the Reverend David Rice's vigorous opposition to the introduction of slavery in Kentucky at the 1792 constitutional convention. But their position shifted by the 1820's, as did that of the Methodists.

First Priest Ordained

Catholics had been regarded with suspicion and hostility by the British colonists during the colonial era in America because of their identification with the Spanish and French enemies, who had been such a persistent threat up to 1763. Relatively few came to Kentucky in these early years, yet Bishop Carroll in Baltimore sent a priest to the state as a missionary in 1787. It was not until the learned and energetic Father Stephen T. Badin came to Lexington in January 1794, that the Fayette County Catholics were brought together. There were so few Catholic families that not until 1804 was an attempt made to establish a church. They met for a few years in a small cabin on West Main Street, just east of the present First Baptist Church, before moving to a brick building on East Third with enough land for a Catholic cemetery. Father Badin, a native of France who had escaped the "Terror" of the French Revolution in 1792, was perhaps the first priest ordained in the United States. In 1821 he left Lexington to return to his native land.

Lexington Baptists, meanwhile, had been attending Elder Craig's South Elkhorn Church. This was some distance from town, so a few members met in their cabins until Elder John Gano, a chaplain in the Continental Army during the Revolution, came to Lexington in 1787. Gano, with the assistance of Edward Payne and others, erected a Baptist Church on the Main Street site deeded to them by the town trustees in 1789, now the location of the First Baptist Church. However, the building on the property seems to have deteriorated and most Lexington Baptists were attending Town Fork Baptist Church on the Frankfort Pike in 1786. An argument over allowing slaveowners to be members led to a seceding "emancipator" group organizing in a new meeting house on North Mill Street in 1819. Dr. James Fishback, former teacher in the Transylvania University Medical Department but now converted to the Baptist ministry, was their first pastor.

Though the first sermon ever preached in Kentucky was by an Episcopal priest under a great elm tree at Boonesborough in 1775, the Episcopal Church suffered from its historic Anglican and royalist image. Although a sizable number of Revolutionary leaders were Anglicans, it had been the Baptists and Presbyterians in Virginia who had led the fight for religious freedom, and Elijah Craig's Spotsylvania pilgrims had little love for Anglicans.

Indeed, the organization of the Protestant Episcopal Church was not completed until 1789, when it could begin its missionary work west of the Appalachians. An Episcopal Society had been formed among some of Lexington's prominent citizens, which held services at the farm of Captain David Shely. In 1791, young James Moore of Virginia, whose wife, a daughter of the Reverend John Todd of Louisa County, Virginia, was a cousin of Colonel John, Levi, and Robert Todd, came to Lexington with every intention of becoming a Presbyterian minister. He accepted a position as a teacher in the Transylvania Seminary in 1792 while applying to the Presbytery as a candidate for the ministry, but a series of incidents delaying his acceptance persuaded him to look to another denomination to exercise his ministerial talents.

Finding the "Episcopalian Society" and their religious tenets much to his liking, Moore returned to Virginia for ordination as an Episcopal priest. In Lexington he vigorously recruited new adherents to that faith, and in 1796 began to hold services in a small house on the corner of Market and Middle (now Church) streets, the present site of Christ Church.

Convinced that this new Episcopal Church was firmly established, he extended his activities to higher education, accepting the offer to teach at the new Presbyterian Kentucky Academy at Pisgah. When Transylvania Seminary and Kentucky Academy were merged by state law into Transylvania University in 1799, Moore became its first president. After a few years, he resigned the presidency and devoted full time to his ministerial responsibilities, with strong support from William Kavanaugh, a Methodist circuit rider recently converted to the Episcopal ministry, who assisted Moore for three years before moving to Louisville.

In 1803, the frame building housing the Episcopalians was replaced by a small brick church, and in 1808 the parish was organized, including among the subscribers to its pews Andrew McCalla, David Shely, Thomas Hart, John Bradford, John Postlethwait, Henry Clay, and John Jordan. Not all of these pewholders were communicants, as in the case of Henry Clay who delayed his baptism until 1847 when the Reverend Edward Berkley performed the ceremony.

By 1812, James Moore, who had never been a very robust man, had become so incapacitated that he was forced to give up his active ministry. This beloved rector is honored by a plaque on the wall of Christ Church describing him as a learned, amiable, and pious man. Nearly a century later, James Lane Allen would immortalize him in a charming short story entitled *The Flute and the Violin.* He was succeeded by the Reverend John Ward of Connecticut.

In this early period, slaves and free blacks were permitted to attend the white churches, though having no voice in their operation. Baptized along with their owners, slaves might be disciplined for misbehavior or "for speaking disrespectfully of the church." About 1790, a Virginia slave, Peter Duerett, better known as "Old Captain," came to Kentucky and helped to organize the first Negro church in Kentucky, the African Baptist Church.

It is apparent that in the first two decades of Lexington's existence, all denominations struggled to survive due to scarcity of members and lack of religious interest. The decline of

This group is gathered in this late 19th century photo in front of Masterson's Station, where the first Methodist Church Conference west of the Allegheny Mountains was held in 1790. It is now the site of Masterson Station Park. Photo courtesy of Clyde T. Burke.

religion has been noted by historians as a widespread phenomenon throughout the states during the American Revolution and for a number of years thereafter. This situation possibly reflected the intellectual, secularistic influence of the Enlightenment, which had prevailed in Europe in the 18th century and which had significantly influenced the thinking of many Americans, especially the better educated. This changed sharply at the turn of the century, however, as a new wave of revivalism swept the country, particularly the frontier. Some of the most famous revivals occurred in Kentucky itself, starting in 1800 in Logan County and culminating in the famed Cane Ridge meeting of August 1801, which brought thousands of frontier folk from many miles around to this isolated Bourbon County Presbyterian meeting house. Colonel Robert Patterson was among them and was much influenced by it. This intense and explosive religious experience swept away traditional denominational lines and resulted in the creation of groups who called themselves simply Christians, or the Christian Church, ultimately developing into the Disciples of Christ after merging with the followers of Alexander Campbell.

Meanwhile, the Baptist Association was holding a meeting at Higbee's, six miles south of Lexington, at which a similar revival spirit prevailed.

It is remarkable that the Lexington newspapers took little note of these religious phenomena, but they signalled nevertheless a growing religiosity in the area. Even those churches which frowned on such exhibitions of excessive emotionalism could not be indifferent to their impact, not only on the congregations involved but also indirectly on the growth and changed outlook of their own membership.

Kentucky's First Newspapers

One of the most significant events of the first decade of Lexington's existence was the appearance of Kentucky's first newspaper, the *Kentucke Gazette* (the "y" on Kentucky was used later) in 1787. Ever since the first conventions had been held in Danville in 1784, moving Kentucky toward independence and statehood, delegates spoke of the need to inform the citizenry of what was being

Reverend James Moore, first president of Transylvania University and first rector of Christ Episcopal Church. Portrait by Matthew Jouett hangs in Old Morrison at Transylvania.

discussed and the decisions made. In 1786 a convention committee attempted to recruit a printer from the large Eastern cities with no success. At this stage, a Lexington settler, John Bradford, volunteered to undertake the task if the Danville Convention would assure him of substantial public patronage.

A native of Virginia, Bradford married into a respectable planter family, learned the surveying craft, and hearing of the vast tracts of fertile and unsurveyed land in Kentucky, explored and surveyed numerous tracts in the Fayette County area in 1779-80, enduring that bitterly cold season at Bryant's Station, Harrodsburg, and Lexington. He participated in some of Clark's Indian campaigns and also managed to survey many entries, purchasing some for himself and his brother Daniel. When the Indian threat abated, he brought his family to Kentucky and settled on land bordering the waters of Cane Run.

Though John and his younger brother, Fielding, whom he dragooned into this publishing project, were innocent of any training as printers, they went to Philadelphia to purchase a small printing press and to acquire some basic information about the printing trade. They stopped at Pittsburgh on their way back to Lexington to buy a modest supply of type from John Scull, printer of the recently established *Pittsburgh Press,* the first newspaper to be printed west of the Alleghenies.

Bradford Publishes Gazette

This heavy load they now floated down the Ohio to Limestone (Maysville) and carried by packhorse to Lexington, throwing most of the type into a chaotic mess, or what printers call pi. Though Danville may have expected Bradford to locate there, the Lexington trustees had no intention of permitting this and offered Bradford the lots where the old blockhouse had once stood to build his printing quarters. Pressed for time, however, he accepted instead the offer of the Fayette County Court to use the back room of the two-story log courthouse for an office and print shop.

Fielding being ill, John Bradford almost single-handedly set up the type for the first issue of the *Kentucke Gazette* on August 11, 1787. This proved too great a burden. Bradford scoured the countryside for anyone with printing experience, finally finding an aging, palsied ex-printer named Thomas Parvin, who had come to Kentucky in 1784 and settled near Strode's Station in Clark County. Bradford persuaded Parvin to leave his home for a few months and assist with the *Gazette.* After moving from one location to another, Bradford settled in 1795 into new and spacious quarters in the brick market house which had been built by the trustees in 1791 on Main Street between Mill and Broadway. Here the *Gazette* was published with occasional interruptions for nearly forty years.

Not until Thomas H. Stewart started his *Kentucky Herald* in 1795 was there a competing newspaper, and Bradford bought out his rival in 1802. In 1808, a more permanent competitor appeared with the establishment of *The Reporter,* which continued until 1832 when it merged with *The Observer;* this merged newspaper continued through the Civil War.

Bradford was an energetic community leader, a trustee of Transylvania University, an important figure in the town government, and a supporter of the Lexington library. Near the end of his life he assembled information gained from his own experiences and his newspaper to write "Notes on Kentucky," a notable account of those early frontier days. He encouraged the spread of literary and publishing activities in the West by sponsoring meetings of printers and booksellers at Lexington, and attempted to organize an association of interested persons in this field.

Also indicative of Lexington's growth in its first decade was the establishment of Lexington Masonic Lodge No. 25 in 1788 under a charter issued by the Grand Lodge of Virginia. The new lodge met in a log cabin on the northeast corner of Walnut and Short streets. When the Grand Lodge of Kentucky was formed in 1800, this lodge was renamed Lexington Lodge No. 1, F. & A. M.

The year 1788 also saw the formation of the Lexington Light Infantry, the first uniformed militia company west of the Alleghenies, with the ever available James Wilkinson as captain, and many of the familiar Lexington citizens as members. Engaged in every call for troops made on Lexington up to the Civil War, it split along political beliefs at that time. For years, this organization delighted the community with occasional musters and parades, handsomely dressed in blue pantaloons, blue coats with cuffs, breasts, and collars faced with red, ornamented with bell buttons, and topped with black hats, with the left side turned up and held in place by a red plume.

The Lexington Light Infantry is not to be confused with the regular militia, the state's main source of military protection which was organized by counties under Virginia law. All men between the ages of 18 and 50 were subject to call for military duty by the County Lieutenant who held the rank of Colonel. Drill and practice sessions were held every three months, but these occasions were noted more for hilarity and drinking than serious training. Some men had no arms, or their muskets or rifles were in disrepair. Yet, when serious work was afoot and men were needed for campaigns against the Indians, those who were able fighters and sufficiently equipped answered the call.

As Lexingtonians moved into the decade of the 1790's, they could look back with satisfaction at having survived the rigors of the wilderness and the Indian threat to establish a functioning and promising community. Though

Built in the late 1790's by Colonel Thomas Hart on the southwest corner of Second and Mill streets, this house was purchased in 1806 by John Bradford who lived there until his death in 1830. This historic building was razed in March 1955 to create a parking lot. Photo courtesy of the University of Kentucky.

the residents were still largely housed in log dwellings, this would soon begin to change. Lexington was a legally organized town with its own trustees, struggling to bring some semblance of order and improvement into the area by requiring the residents to remove stumps and other obstructions from the main town roads, by prohibiting easily inflammable wood and clay chimneys from being built on town dwellings, by overseeing the proper deeding of the town lots, controlling the use of the town springs, warning against polluting wells by nearby privies, building bridges across the Town Branch, and providing for the construction of a market house and a county courthouse.

The Town Branch, though confined within fairly steep banks, easily overflowed during periods of heavy rain since every freshet and drain fed into it along the stretch from what is now Midland Avenue to Jefferson Street. Thus, from Lexington's earliest days, the stream was a perpetual flood threat, pouring over its banks on to the land originally set aside by the trustees as a Commons, an area later divided into Vine and Water streets after the stream was covered. Samuel D. McCullough recalled that as a young lad attending school in a "little old brick stable . . . on Church alley" he was picked up by a friend on horseback who took him home across the swollen Town Branch which had covered the whole Commons. The

JUMP. II.]　　　T H E　　　[AUG: 178:-

KENTUCKE GAZETTE

S A T U R D A Y, AUGUST 18, 1787.

THE *PRINTER* OF THE KENTUC
KE GAZETTE TO THE *PUBLIC.*

AFTER having expended much in
procuring the materials and convey-
ing them from Philadelphia, I have ven-
tured to open a Printing Office in the
Town of Lexington in the District of Kentucke. Notwithstanding these expences
and that of procuring farther supplies of
paper for my business, and of supporting
necessary hands, I shall content myself at
present with the prospect of small gains. I
consider this country as being yet in an
infant state, harrassed by the most savage
enemies, having no profitable trade and
being drained of money by its present in-
tercourse with the Eastern parts of America. However the exertions made by a
great number of Gentlemen in favour of
the press convinces me that a Spirit pre-
vails among my countrymen superior to
their present circumstances. I am satisfied
that every possible encouragement will
be given to my present undertaking.

It is impossible to recount all the advantages that the public will recieve
from the publication of a GAZETTE in
this District. First, it will give a quick and
general formation concerning the inten-
tions and behaviour of our neighbouring
enemies and put us upon our guard a-
gainst their future violence. Secondly, it
will communicate a timely information of
the proceedings of our Legislature, and
prevent us from undergoing various evils
by being unacquainted with the laws of
our country, some of which have been in
force sometime before they reached the
district. Thirdly, it will call our attention
to the transactions of Congress, and shew
us the policy which predominates in our
great American Confederacy. It will teach
us when we are to prepare for foreign
wars; when we are to admire the successful Hero, the generous Patriot, and
the wise Statesman; or to treat with ab-
horence the betrayor of his Country.
Fourthly, it will carry our attention onto
the ancient world, and gratify our curio-
sity with respect to distant nations who
flourish in the arts of arms or peace. It

will lay open all the Republic of letters
to our view and furnish us with all necessary instructions to avoid the danger or
secure the blessings which may wait on
our rising community. Fifthly, it will
afford us an easy method of understanding one another and coming to a better a-
greement in the execution of every design which may be necessary for the common good. It will bring the latent sparks
of Genius to light, and give the world a
respectable opinion of the people who
have come so many leagues to cultivate a
deserted land. When others see what we
have done and what we are still able to
do; they will come and strengthen our
hands and be pleased to partake of our
future blessings.

Indeed it was upon a promise of patronage from the Convention in 1785.
that induced me first to attempt what I
have now accomplished. I therefore rest
satisfied, that all my Countrymen will be
sensible of my claim to their notice as the
first adventurer in a business which has
been chiefly instrumental in bringing man-
kind from a state of blindness and slavery
to their present advancement in knowledge and freedom.

JOHN BRADFORD.

To THE *PRINTER* OF THE *Kentucke*
GAZETTE

AS I expect your paper will be
employed at first in discussing political subjects, and as I
suppose that of a separation from
the state of Virginia to be the
most interesting at present; I
hope our politicisns will be pleased through your press to give us
their sentiments on both sides of
the question; and I hope they
will write, and we shall read, with
that coolness and impartiality,
which becomes men who have
the real interest of this Country
at heart, and that in the end we

may hit upon that policy which
will best secure life liberty
and property to us and our posterity.

As the most of us are farmers
and unskilled in policy (altho' we
are anxious to do for the best)
we are able to give but a random
guess at the propriety of a separa-
tion--we can see difficulties on
both sides, and would wish to a-
void the worst.

I beg leave therefore to propose
a few querries to the Gentlemen
on both sides of the question;
and will begin with asking those
who think a separation necessary

1st. By what probable means
can a new State support Government, defend itself from the savages, and pay its quota of the
foederal and state debt, without
a free trade of the river Mississippi?

Secondly. What probable prospects can a new State have of
obtaining a trade down the Missi-
sippi; and what profits can we
derive from such a trade?

Thirdly. will not a separation
lessen our importance in the opinion of the savages, and cause
them to fall on us with greater
vigour?

Fourthly. What are the great
evils we suffer for want of a new
government; and how could a
new state remedy those evils?

And I would ask those who
are against a separation

First. How shall we defend
ourselves against the savages under the present laws; and how
shall we get paid for doing it?

A copy of the second edition — the earliest known to exist — of John Bradford's pioneer newspaper, published on August 18, 1787.

man tied his young passenger to himself, and horse and rider plunged into the turbulent water. After some struggling the horse reached the High Street side.

Mail was always an important part of community life, and before the U.S. government established regular service, John Bradford devised his own. In order to distribute the *Kentucke Gazette* as widely as possible, Bradford used post riders to gather news and deliver packages and letters as well as newspapers. He maintained a letter box in his office. Not until 1794 did the Federal Government establish a post office in Lexington with Innes Brent as the first postmaster. Since he served as Fayette County jailor at the same time, Brent kept the post office in the public room of the jail on Main Street. When the rising young businessman, John Wesley Hunt, took over as postmaster, he moved the post office to Postlethwait's Tavern (later the Phoenix Hotel).

Early Education

Efforts to provide schooling continued as more and more newcomers advertised as tutors or operators of small schools. In the years following the opening of Lexington's first schoolhouse on the public square under John McKinney's direction, complete with students and the wildcat, numerous such schools appeared. Most notable was that of John Filson, early biographer of Daniel Boone and first historian of Kentucky, who advertised in the January 19, 1788, *Gazette* that he would start classes in April "and French language with all sciences and arts will be taught." The close alliance with France during the American Revolution, and the sympathies of many Americans with the French Revolution later made French one of the most popular of foreign languages.

The main enhancement to Lexington as an educational center, however, was the establishment of Transylvania Seminary. This school had been chartered by the Virginia Assembly in 1780 as a "public school" for Kentucky County to assure that learning would not be forgotten in the wilderness. It was endowed with escheated land confiscated from certain Virginia Loyalists who had substantial land claims in Kentucky. Conditions for opening

a school in the early 1780's were poor and no classes were held until the Reverend David Rice, the noted Presbyterian leader in Danville, Kentucky, and a trustee of Transylvania, arranged to hold classes in his cabin in 1785, close by Harrod's Run, between Danville and Fort Harrod. It was a short-lived endeavor, however, and the trustees — seven of whom had been killed by Indians since the establishment of the school — assessed the situation and decided in 1788 to move Transylvania to the rapidly expanding town of Lexington.

Classes were first held in this enterprising community in June 1789, in an empty cabin on the south edge of town. A number of business and professional men, desiring to encourage the growth and prosperity of a promising institution of higher learning, bought out-lot No. 6 between Second and Third streets and constructed a commodious two-story brick building near the north end of the lot facing Second Street. This lot and nearly completed building they offered to the Transylvania trustees gratis for campus and classrooms in return for a promise to locate the school permanently in Lexington. The offer was accepted in 1793, which proved to be a boon to both the school and the town. Moving to a university status in 1799, Transylvania was to provide one of the main forces in creating the cultural environment that Lexington would foster and cherish.

Kentucky's Provisional Capital

General Anthony Wayne's defeat of the Indians in Ohio in 1794, with the help of over 1,000 Kentucky volunteers, ended the Indian menace in Kentucky, although occasional incidents of attacks on lonely farms by small groups of Indians were reported in the *Gazette* late into the 1790's. This encouraged even greater migration into central Kentucky and Lexington. Virginia probably provided most of the settlers and much of the leadership in Kentucky and Lexington. The Old Dominion was the uneasy but proud parent of this vigorous, rough, adamantly independent, and prodigiously expanding adolescent. In 1792 she would release this territory from all legal ties when Kentucky assumed statehood. But Virginia political, economic, and social institutions —

including slavery — played an important part in molding the character and attitudes of Kentuckians.

Evidence of Lexington's importance was the fact that the first meeting of Kentucky's legislature was held here in 1792. Though all the conventions, including the one preparing Kentucky's first constitution, had been held in Danville, the delegates chose Lexington as the site for the inauguration of the newly-elected governor, Isaac Shelby, eleven Senators and forty Representatives. It was a logical choice, for Lexington was not only the largest town in Kentucky but the only one with adequate facilities to house the guests and provide an adequate meeting place, which was accomplished by converting the recently completed Market House into an improvised State House.

On Monday, June 4, 1792, Isaac Shelby rode into town, having been escorted from Danville by a Lexington horse troop. The Lexington Light Infantry, resplendent in their new uniforms, paraded in his honor at the corner of Main and Main Cross. John Bradford, representing the town trustees, delivered a welcoming address to which Governor Shelby appropriately replied. Shelby delivered his inaugural address to the legislature assembled in the second story of the Market House, spelling out a proposed agenda for legislative action. One of the items on that agenda was the need to appoint a commission to decide on a site for the state capital. Lexington had every reason to expect it would be chosen, though other communities were competing for the privilege, especially Frankfort, which emphasized its river location, greater centrality, and promised land grants. The five-man commission was divided between Lexington and Frankfort, leaving the deciding vote up to Robert Todd, the Lexington representative. Apparently believing that a vote for Lexington would be regarded as an inexcusable act of favoritism, he voted for Frankfort. People have been debating the wisdom of that choice ever since, and Lexington did not give up the attempt to have the capital return to Lexington until around 1900.

One other event in the 1790's indicated the dedication of Lexington's leaders to enrich the intellectual life of this frontier town. It was the establishment of a library for the benefit of the residents. In January 1795, a group of leading citizens, probably called together by John Bradford, which included Robert Barr, John Breckinridge, James Brown, Dr. Frederick Ridgely, Thomas January, and the new president of Transylvania Seminary, the Reverend Harry Toulmin, met in the Old State House (Market House) "to organize a library called Transylvania Library." This was not a public library as we know it today, established and operated under municipal authority and financed with tax funds. Such libraries were practically unknown in the new Republic. As far back as Benjamin Franklin's creation of a subscription library in Philadelphia for a limited paying membership, educated men had pooled their resources to purchase books for a common library available to its subscribers. With an initial subscription of $500, a purchasing committee of this Lexington library (the name "Transylvania Library" was dropped to avoid confusing it with the school) ordered books from the East which arrived nearly a year later. They were temporarily stored at the Transylvania Seminary until moved to the second story of a drug store occupied by Andrew McCalla who agreed to dispense books as well as prescriptions. As of 1801, the library boasted of a respectable collection of 750 books, and in 1803 it was moved to the second story of the Old State House.

During the 1790's, Lexington politically was strongly pro-Jefferson and pro-France. As the names of Fayette, Bourbon, and Versailles would indicate, the settlers felt a warm friendship for their French allies who had made possible a military victory over the British in the Revolution. Many of the tutors and small schools in town offered French as a subject.

Although admiration of George Washington transcended partisan differences to a large extent, measures of his Federalist administration and that of his successor, John Adams, caused resentment and even resistance. Such was the case with Hamilton's whiskey excise tax, which outraged Kentucky distillers as much as those in western Pennsylvania, but no such concerted and violent resistance against the revenue officers occurred in Kentucky as in Pennsylvania. The use of military force sent to quell the western Pennsylvania resistance was apparently never considered necessary in

A section of a mural by Ann Rice O'Hanlon in the foyer of Memorial Hall at the University of Kentucky. The picture shows a pioneer woman drawing water from the Bryant Station Spring just before the Indian attack on the fort in 1782.

Kentucky, but the legendary Kentucky moonshiners' hatred of revenue officers may be rooted in this experience. Kentuckians' suspicion that the federal government was indifferent to their welfare stemmed from the difficulties of the 1780's and early 1790's when it appeared little effort was being expended to persuade the Spanish to release their stranglehold on New Orleans and the Mississippi, a situation exploited by Wilkinson but not finally resolved until the Pinckney Treaty of 1795. In fact, President Washington at one time had to warn Governor Shelby to head off a proposed military expedition against the Spanish to be led by George Rogers Clark.

Sympathy with the French Revolution in Kentucky was reflected in the formation of a Democratic Society in Lexington which erected a liberty pole at Main and Cheapside and whose members jauntily wore tricolor cockades. There were a few Federalists in town, but they tended to keep a low profile except for such vigorously outspoken proponents as Humphrey Marshall, an early settler who later moved to Frankfort, served as U.S. Senator, 1795-1801, and wrote one of the earliest and most controversial histories of Kentucky.

The peak of the anti-Federalist sentiment came with the passage of the Alien and Sedition Acts by the Federalist-controlled Congress in 1798 to suppress the activities of French aliens in the country and to muzzle the anti-Federalist press and outspoken opposition to the government. George Nicholas, the distinguished Virginian who played such a significant role in the formation of Kentucky's first constitution, provided the most persuasive political rationale for the action of the Kentucky legislature in 1798, denouncing these laws as violations of the First Amendment to the U.S. Constitution and proposing state nullification of them. Though it is now known that Jefferson and Madison were active behind the scenes in drafting resolutions both in Virginia and Kentucky opposing the Alien and Sedition Acts, it was Lexington's John Breckinridge who introduced the historic Kentucky Resolution into the state legislature. Its passage was cause for great celebration in his home town on November 9, 1798, marked by a bonfire and parade, while the taverns were crowded with celebrants.

From its pioneer stockade of 1779, Lexington had emerged in the decades of the 1780's and 1790's as the predominant town in Kentucky and, indeed, as one of the fastest growing communities west of the Alleghenies. As the historian Richard Wade has stated: "Set on the Blue Grass, this frontier metropolis bestrode the arteries of overland trade and migration and served as the central depot for the surrounding country ... " Lexington's leadership would prevail well into the first two decades of the 19th century.

THE ASHLAND QUICK STEP

AS PERFORMED BEFORE THE CLAY CLUB OF LEXINGTON, KY.

On Stone by A Koellner.

P.S Duval's Lithy Phila

BY THE

AMATEUR BRASS BAND

AT THE DEDICATION OF THEIR NEW HALL

Composed and dedicated to the

HON. H. CLAY

by

W. Ratel.

Cover of composition in honor of Henry Clay written in 1838 by William Ratel, Lexington composer and musician.
Photo courtesy of Transylvania University.

1800/1837

Athens of the West

B y 1800, Lexington had been transformed from a small, crude frontier community with a fort and a scattering of cabins into a bustling urban center. That this was achieved in less than twenty years was astonishing. It demonstrated what could be accomplished when diverse and numerous human energies and talents were focused on a promising region.

W.ending his way west toward Lexington in 1806, Fortesque Cuming approached the town by way of the Russell Cave Pike and later wrote in his travel account:

> The country had insensibly assumed the appearance of an approach to a city — the roads very wide and fine, with grazing parks, meadows, and every spot in sight cultivated . . . On entering the town we were struck with the fine roomy scale on which everything appeared to be planned. Spacious streets and large houses chiefly of brick, which since the years have rapidly taken the place of the original ones, several of which yet remain . . . A rivulet which turns some mills below the town runs through middle or water street, but is covered by an arch, and levelled out over the length of the street.

Additionally, Josiah Espy, visiting Lexington about the same time, recorded in his journal:

> Lexington is the largest and most wealthy town in Kentucky, or indeed west of the Allegheny Mountains; the main street of Lexington has all the appearance of Market Street in Philadelphia on a busy day . . . I would suppose it contains about five hundred dwelling houses [it was closer to three hundred], many of them elegant and three stories high. About thirty brick buildings were then raising, and I have little doubt but that

in a few years it will rival, not only in wealth, but in population, the most populous inland town of the United States . . . The country around Lexington for many miles in every direction, is equal in beauty and fertility to anything the imagination can paint and is already in a high state of cultivation.

The diversity of enterprises was impressive: paper mills, distilleries, grist mills, tobacco factories, cabinet shops, china factories, brickyards, a reed factory, a white lead factory, saddlery shops, numerous hatters, paint shops, and — most impressive of all — the large and prosperous hemp and bagging factories. There were a large number of blacksmiths, shoemakers and tailors, according to Lexington's first city directory published by Joseph Charless in 1805. The merchants formed the largest. category, however, and their influence in the city was substantial. In addition to these groups who provided the essential services and goods for a flourishing community, there were listed craftsmen whose products reflected the growing wealth of Lexington: silversmiths, coachmakers, cabinet makers, booksellers, a clock and watchmaker, and even a portrait painter.

It has already been noted that Peter January and James Wilkinson were probably the first established merchants in town, but by the early 1800's many had followed in their footsteps. Among the more notable were Samuel Downing, J. McCoun & Tilford, William Leavy, Samuel and George Trotter, Thomas Hart & Son, James Morrison, Brooks & Crysdale, William West and John Wesley Hunt. Around 1798, Luther Stephens and

Hallett Winslow, young carpenters and joiners, came to Lexington, founded a successful hardware store and later became one of the most respected and prosperous building firms in town. They constructed the 1806 courthouse that lasted until 1883. In addition, they formed the Lexington Steam Mill Company and erected a factory to grind grains on the south end of Upper Street where it ran into Steam Mill Street, now Bolivar. They leased water from John Maxwell's plenteous springs whose overflow ran by the mill. Stephens' invention of the rotary valve on a steam engine, which was marketed by Oliver Evans of Washington, greatly improved the efficiency of their operation. Later, Benjamin Gratz from one of Philadelphia's most distinguished mercantile families and Andrew and Jonathan Holmes joined that group.

Among the most familiar names were those of William Leavy and his son, William A. Leavy, who near the end of his life wrote a remarkably detailed and accurate memoir of Lexington's early days, both as he remembered them personally, as recounted to him by his father and others who settled here in the 1780's, and from advertisements in the *Gazette.*

Leavy, Senior, had migrated in 1775 from his native Ireland to the Philadelphia region, served as a sutler in the Revolutionary Army, and was persuaded by John Duncan to come to Lexington in the late 1780's to establish a store. He bought out his partner in the early 1790's and purchased a lot from Christopher Greenup, the future governor of Kentucky and an early merchant himself. The southwest corner of Mill and Main, where once the original blockhouse had stood, was to be the location of Leavy's store and his son's for many decades. The elder Leavy died in 1831.

One of the most successful and influential of these business leaders was John Wesley Hunt. Descended from English colonists who had settled Long Island in the mid-17th century and then later moved to New Jersey where John's father concentrated on merchandising, John, born in 1773, grew up in the mercantile trade, an apt pupil of his father. Though two of his younger brothers went to Princeton for their education, John was not academically inclined. Instead, he plunged recklessly into dubious enterprises with some questionable partners in Virginia, but emerged relatively unscathed, a wiser and less impulsive man.

In 1795, he accepted a proposal from his cousin, Abijah Hunt, a merchant in Cincinnati, to enter into partnership with him in setting up a general store in Lexington to serve the local market and the constant stream of migrants moving to the West. Described by his biographer, James A. Ramage, as a sturdily built young man, "looking more like a magistrate than a merchant ... appearing older than twenty-two, with light brown hair combed back neatly from the broad forehead, with large ears, heavy eyebrows, a very prominent, straight nose and a large mouth," he exuded a degree of self-assurance that surprised both his customers and his fellow businessmen. Hunt's Cincinnati connection was valuable as it provided him with goods through Abijah's Philadelphia suppliers, and it was also a market for Kentucky products, especially needed to supply the army during its Ohio campaign.

Fayette County Courthouse erected in 1806, razed 1883. It stood on the site of the present courthouse. Photo courtesy of Transylvania University.

However, transportation between Cincinnati and Lexington of any sizable volume of trade had to wait for the railroads decades later. Hunt expanded his marketing activities to New Orleans and Natchez where he shipped Kentucky farm products and slaves. He also began to invest substantially in land.

Because of an economic slump in the late 1790's, which caused a decline in mercantile profits, John Hunt shifted his activities to horse-breeding and the manufacture of hemp products. The deeply rooted love of fine horses and racing, which the Virginians brought with them to Kentucky, led to a major effort after the American Revolution to import promising stud horses to the state to improve the quality of the breeding. It was a risky business at best, considering the difficult trip such horses had to make before the advent of horse vans, trains, and airplanes. Yet, despite these handicaps, Hunt managed to make a profit, and advanced the horse industry as well. Later he bred fine trotters and other livestock.

At the same time, Hunt invested in a profitable hemp manufacturing enterprise. An important raw material for the making of sails and ropes, its cultivation had begun in colonial days, and the ever-expanding ship industry provided a ready market. The Bluegrass region was well suited to the growing and processing of hemp, and it quickly became a main agricultural staple. Kentucky farmers produced more than any other state until the 1850's.

Then, at the turn of the century, a new use for hemp was found — bagging for cotton bales. The cotton culture, revolutionized by Eli Whitney's invention of the cotton gin in 1793, expanded prodigiously and with it came a greatly increased demand for bagging. While production of rope in the ropewalk factories in Lexington was a flourishing industry by 1800, Hunt, after first investigating the potential market for bagging, decided to enter that field and began production in April 1803. With his marketing contacts, including his cousin Abijah, Hunt made the production, sale and distribution of cotton bagging a most profitable enterprise.

Manned mostly by slaves, the ropewalks and cotton bagging factories were located all over town, and, in the days before zoning, were frequently erected immediately adjacent to private residences as in the case of January's

John Wesley Hunt, early Lexington entrepreneur and builder of the Hunt-Morgan House. Portrait hangs in Hunt-Morgan House.

ropewalk between Second and Third streets. The danger of destructive fires in these areas was formidable and the number of factories destroyed or damaged by arsonists was alarming.

The rope and bagging factories were long and narrow, sometimes four stories tall; the lower floor contained room for combing the hemp and a ropewalk; the second floor provided sleeping apartments for the laborers and a spinning room; the third story housed the machinery for weaving the bagging, and on the fourth floor was a long room where young boys spun twine.

By the time of the War of 1812, Hunt, sensing some difficulties arising in his manufacturing enterprise (although during the war itself demand for rope was high), became a commission merchant. He sold saltpetre for gunpowder production during the war and, on commission, he marketed tobacco, ginseng, flour, and whiskey in New Orleans.

In 1814, well-married, with a growing family, prosperous and respected in Lexington, Hunt purchased a lot on the northwest corner of Mill and Second streets from Thomas January and built a handsome house that he called Hopemont. At the same time he shifted his fortune into investments in banking, government stocks, and insurance. When a branch of the Second Bank of the United States was established in Lexington with Colonel James Morrison as president, John Hunt became one of the directors; later he became president of the Farmers and Mechanics Bank of Lexington, one of the few banks to remain solvent during the panic of 1819-20. He also invested in Kentucky's first railroad — the Lexington & Ohio — which laid its first stone tie in 1831. He was president of the Lexington Fire, Life, and Marine Insurance Company for several years after it was chartered in 1836. Throughout this period he continued to buy and sell land in Alabama and Kentucky. This variety of enterprises eventually increased Hunt's holdings to around a million dollars, justifying the assumption that he was the first millionaire west of the Alleghenies.

For Lexington and Fayette County, however, Hunt was far more than a successful entrepreneur; he was a concerned and influential leader in the community, contributing to its improved social and educational well-being. He served as chairman of the board of commissioners authorized to administer the Eastern Lunatic Asylum. He was a pillar of the Episcopal Church. Always a supporter of Transylvania University, he served as a trustee from 1819 to 1835 and chaired the building committee that hired Gideon Shryock to design and erect Morrison College, constructed with the funds left in a legacy by James Morrison, a successful businessman and banker similar to Hunt.

Enterprising Businessmen

John Wesley Hunt was representative of that group of enterprising businessmen, merchants, bankers, and planters, who, with a number of the lawyers, judges, and doctors, became a powerful influence in determining the economic prosperity of Lexington and also its political control and direction. A number of them were elected as town trustees, and others sponsored and financially supported those educational and cultural activities that are essential to a sophisticated society. Men like John Bradford, James Morrison, and Benjamin

Gratz contributed to this development. And as they accumulated wealth through their activities in town, many purchased estates on the edge of town, or on the borders of Fayette County, where they erected impressive houses, bought slaves, raised large quantities of corn and hemp and some tobacco, acquired fine herds of livestock and bred superior horseflesh.

However, all businessmen who started their enterprises in Lexington did not prosper and succeed. There was a considerable turnover in some shops as tradesmen would advertise their arrival and, shortly after, their departure. One of the most striking examples of initial success followed by dramatic collapse was that of James Prentiss. Coming from New England around 1805, James and Thomas Prentiss conceived the idea of building on the western edge of town an entire manufacturing center they called "Manchester," after England's industrial city. They constructed a woolen factory and paper mill and provided housing for their employees. They also bought farmland and Merino sheep to supply their woolen mill. However, James Prentiss' speculative temperament overcame his good sense. Investing heavily in the Kentucky Insurance Company, he became its president in 1817, and through fraud and deceit plunged it into ruin while he fled Lexington.

Other failures took more drastic means to terminate their business careers. William A. Leavy recalled that J. B. Borland, a Bostonian and a Yale graduate, came to Lexington in 1815 to enter the retail business. He was very near-sighted, which Leavy believed depressed the young man as he had difficulty recognizing people. In any case, a combination of uncertainty in his business prospects, and his physical handicap, apparently motivated Borland to "put a period to his existence by first cutting his own throat, and then throwing himself out of the garret window, on the pavement below in Mill Street."

Social lines developed rather quickly, as they did in Pittsburgh, St. Louis and other emerging cities, despite the western egalitarian tradition that was a reality only during the early settling and survival period. Though not as tightly drawn as in some Eastern cities, class distinctions were nonetheless meaningful. Wealth tended to be a main determinant in

Late 19th century photo of the Hunt-Morgan House showing original side entrance which has recently been reconstructed. Photo courtesy of Blue Grass Trust.

this class stratification, but professional classes also enjoyed a position among the elite. The merchants and wealthy planters headed the list, followed closely by or intertwined with lawyers, ministers, doctors, teachers and journalists. The largest group, next down the ladder, were the skilled artisans and craftsmen, clerks and shopkeepers, and a rung lower the unskilled laborers. Always on the margin were the transient and rootless individuals, and at the bottom the Negroes, slave and free.

Of those on the lower end of the scale we have few firsthand accounts with one remarkable exception, that of John Robert Shaw. This ill-fated wanderer had been impressed in Britain into the army to fight the rebellious colonists across the ocean during the Revolution. He claimed he was wounded

frequently, shipwrecked, and imprisoned at various times, joining the American army after the Revolutionary War was over to fight the Indians in Ohio. After his discharge, he came to Lexington, married, and sought work. A devoted drinker, he at turns was an inn-keeper, stone quarrier, and well-digger (his advertisements ran in the *Gazette*). He was so inept as a well-digger, which sometimes required judicious blasting, that he occasionally blew himself higher than his well was deep, nearly killing and badly maiming himself at one time. Recovering from a close call with death, he conceived the idea of writing his autobiography, a picaresque account which he had printed in Lexington in 1807 under the title *The Life and Adventures of John Robert Shaw.*

Lexington had a number of gifted inventors. Arriving as early as 1785, Edward West, a Virginian, was the first watchmaker to settle in Lexington, announcing three years later that he had opened a shop on High Street "where watchmaking and clockmaking will be done in the neatest and shortest manner." An inventive turn of mind plus acknowledged mechanical expertise led him to experiment with steam machinery, which he eventually applied to a model steamboat. Many curious townsfolk gathered one day in 1793 on the banks of the Town Branch, a section of which West had dammed up, to watch his model steamboat successfully battle the current. It was an event of some significance as far as first inventions go, but John Fitch and Robert Fulton developed their models into history-making, full-scale steamboats and West's early achievement remains little known. He was more successful with his nail-cutting machine, which he sold for $10,000 to an Eastern firm.

Nathan Burrowes is said to have introduced the manufacture of hemp in Lexington in 1796 and also invented a machine for cleaning it. His most successful venture was a special process he developed to manufacture a superior mustard, which won a premium at the World's Fair in London. It continued to be manufactured profitably for many decades.

The most notable of Lexington's antebellum inventors, however, was Thomas Harris Barlow. Settling here in 1825, he produced a number of remarkable inventions, beginning with a steam locomotive and car models in 1827. With the help of Joseph Bruen, who had established a foundry in town, Barlow constructed his locomotive and a small two-passenger car in the second story of Bruen's foundry and ran them on a specially constructed track for demonstration. Some of the town elders later recalled having ridden this pioneering model for 50 cents a ride. In addition to his locomotive, Barlow invented a self-feeding nail and tack machine which he sold to Massachusetts capitalists. He and his son also developed a percussion rifled cannon which so impressed a Congressional committee that Congress appropriated $3,000 to test it. It may well have been the model used later in versions of rifled cannon. European military men were equally interested.

Benjamin Gratz, prominent early businessman and financier for whom Gratz Park is named. Portrait painted by Thomas Sully in 1831. Photo by permission of the magazine, Antiques.

The most eye-catching and educational of Barlow's inventions was his planetarium on which he worked ten years. Demonstrating by a complicated, large mechanism the motions and orbits of the planets around a giant sun at the center, it proved to be of such educational value that Transylvania University, Sayre School, Girard College in Philadelphia, and West Point and Annapolis purchased copies. At the Paris Exposition of 1867 it received a first-class premium though its inventor had died two years earlier. The Sayre School model is now part of Transylvania's scientific apparatus museum.

Henry Clay, Lawyers and Physicians

By the 1790's and early 1800's distinguished lawyers, physicians, and professors were attracted to Lexington. Many settlers had regarded lawyers with a jaundiced eye and believed that they were piratical exploiters of the layman, whose ignorance of the law and frequent litigation made him easy prey. Legal training then was usually a casual

One of the planetariums built by Thomas H. Barlow in the 1840's and 1850's was owned by Sayre School and is now located at Transylvania University. Barlow was the city's most prominent antebellum inventor.

apprenticeship affair, and many poorly trained and unethical individuals became professed lawyers, thus fortifying the public's suspicion and distaste for them. However, the high quality of most of Lexington's lawyers helped dispel this image. The amount of litigation over land titles, as well as the usual run of civil and criminal cases, made this town a profitable center for lawyers. Among the most notable leaders of the Lexington bar at this time were George Nicholas, Buckner Thruston, John Breckinridge (grandfather of the even more famous John Cabell Breckinridge), James Brown, John Pope, William T. Barry, Humphrey Marshall, James Hughes, George M. Bibb, Jesse Bledsoe, Joseph Hamilton Daveiss, James Haggin, John Boyle, Robert Wickliffe, Daniel Mayes, Fielding Turner, A. K. Woolley, and Henry Clay. A later generation included Thomas A. Marshall, Richard H. Menefee, Madison C. Johnson, Gen. Leslie Combs, George B. Kinkead, and George Robertson, for many years Chief Justice of the Kentucky Court of Appeals (then Kentucky's highest court) and one of the most able of 19th century jurists.

Henry Clay, who was twenty when he came to Lexington in 1797, quickly became the town's most famous resident. Though his political career early overshadowed his lawyer's role, he always remained a practicing attorney. Like his senatorial colleague, Daniel Webster, he frequently restored his depleted finances (politics was a poor paymaster) by engaging in highly remunerative law cases.

He was born in 1777 into a family of comfortable circumstances (the poor mill boy of the Slashes image was strictly for public consumption) in Hanover County, Virginia, some fifteen miles north of Richmond. His father died when Henry was only four years old but his stepfather, Henry Watkins, exhibited considerable concern for his young stepson's career. In 1792 Watkins decided to move to Versailles, Kentucky, because of the glowing reports he had received from his brother who prospered there. Henry was left in Richmond to begin his study of law as a deputy court clerk, secretary to the aged but brilliant George Wythe, and as apprentice to Robert Brooke. Given a license to practice law in Virginia in November 1797, Henry decided that Lexington offered a young lawyer more opportunity to build a practice than the older Federalist Richmond with a well-established bar. He would also be nearer his family.

He was admitted to the bar in Lexington in March 1798, set up an office on North Mill Street, and married Lucretia Hart, youngest daughter of the wealthy and influential Thomas Hart. Lucretia was eminently sensible and a devoted mother to the eleven children she would bear Henry. The lanky young man with his grey eyes, large mouth and captivating voice, soon found his spontaneity, fondness for gambling, and his ambition well suited to his compatriots and to the enterprising character of the town.

Thanks to his legal gifts as a criminal lawyer and representative in civil cases, plus, excellent connections through Colonel Hart and others, Clay soon built up a flourishing practice. Though not deeply learned in the law, nor widely read, he had few superiors in his persuasive abilities in a jury trial, and his record of success in securing the acquittal or light sentencing for clients whose crimes were sometimes of an atrocious, if not murderous, character was phenomenal. One of his most controversial cases was his successful defense of Aaron Burr in 1806 in Frankfort, who was tried on suspicion of treasonable activities.

Henry Clay's wealth grew accordingly. His taxable property increased from one horse in 1799, to three slaves and two horses a year later, and by 1805 rose to 125 acres of first-class land, additional acreage of second-class or unspecified land, 8 slaves, 15 head of livestock, and town property worth $2,300. And it continued to grow. He was an

Ashland, home of Henry Clay, as it appeared before reconstruction in 1857, from an engraving published in 1853. Photo courtesy of the University of Kentucky.

28

inveterate land speculator as well, and invested in a variety of properties and businesses in the area. He joined the Lexington Lodge No. 1, F. & A. M., becoming Master of the Lodge in 1820 and later Grand Master of Kentucky. Transylvania University employed him to teach in its developing law department, and he became a trustee and devoted friend of that institution.

Beginning perhaps as early as 1805 to acquire property for his new home, Clay owned some 400 acres by 1812 and had constructed a commodious brick house on the estate which he called "Ashland," a mile east of Lexington on the Richmond Road. Though his public life kept him apart from his beloved home for long periods, he would always return to it with great anticipation, enjoying the tranquillity and refreshment he found there. He was an avid farmer, constantly expanding the acreage of the estate to accommodate his large hemp, corn, and tobacco crops, and herds of livestock — including Hereford cattle, Merino sheep, and, of course, a stable of thoroughbreds. He is also credited with planting the first ginkgo tree in Lexington.

Clay's labor force was composed mostly of slaves, despite his public statements denouncing the "peculiar institution." However, he was convinced that the best solution was to send the freedmen back to Africa.

From 1803, when he was elected from Fayette County to the lower house of Kentucky's General Assembly, to the day of his death in June 1852, Clay was to spend forty of those years in public office — as state legislator, Congressman, U. S. Senator, Secretary of State, and candidate for the Presidency. He ran unsuccessfully three times for the latter office, losing only by a hairsbreadth in 1844.

"Harry of the West" was Lexington's most famous citizen, and the residents cherished him as lawyer, orator, statesman, family man, and country gentleman.

Among the dozen physicians listed in Worsley's and Smith's city directory of 1818, the most distinguished were attached to the Transylvania University Medical Department. The first members of that department in 1799, Dr. Samuel Brown and Dr. Frederick Ridgely, were still teaching here. Dr. Brown, trained at the University of Edinburgh, is credited with

Portrait of Henry Clay by Matthew H. Jouett, which hangs in Ashland. Famous as a lawyer and politician, "Harry of the West," as Clay was known, was Lexington's most distinguished citizen for nearly a half century. Photo courtesy of Clyde. T. Burke.

introducing to Lexington Jenner's new vaccination process against smallpox, immunizing hundreds of residents against this dread and prevalent disease. He also developed the steam method of distilling alcoholic beverages, and exploited the abundant saltpetre resources in Kentucky to produce a superior gunpowder used in the War of 1812.

Daniel Drake, the nationally prominent physician, resided for a while in Lexington to teach at Transylvania, but his main base was Cincinnati. It was the surgeon, Dr. Benjamin W. Dudley, who resided the longest in Lexington and became the most noted and highly respected doctor in. the area. A skilled lithotomist, he successfully performed hundreds of operations for the removal of bladder stones without benefit of anesthesia or knowledge of asepsis.

Those who needed drugs prescribed by their physicians could find them and a wide variety of other goods at the large, well-supplied apothecary of Andrew McCalla, occupying the northeast corner of Market and Short streets. McCalla was an early settler in Lexington, active in community affairs, serving

Dr. Benjamin W. Dudley, noted Lexington surgeon for many years in the early 1800's. Photo courtesy of Transylvania University.

several times as town trustee. His son, General John McCalla, built an imposing residence on North Mill Street after the War of 1812 which was purchased by Benjamin Gratz in 1824, and has remained in the Gratz family.

A Reading Public

Lexington's promising economic future was based on flourishing mercantile and manufacturing enterprises, a growing population, and a fertile agricultural region which supplied necessary foodstuffs, raw materials for its factories and export market, and superior livestock and thoroughbreds.

But essential to an urbane society was the cultural dimension. This Lexington developed with astonishing rapidity. Not only were substantial brick and stone residences erected,

roads paved, streets lighted, fire and police protection provided, but "society is polished and polite," according to *Niles' Register*, "and their balls and assemblies are conducted with as much grace and ease as they are anywhere else . . . Strange things these in the 'backwoods.' " Timothy Flint was impressed by the fact that "Lexington has taken on the tone of a literary place, claiming to be the 'Athens of the West,' while Cincinnati was 'struggling to be its Corinth.' " Thus, we know that the well-worn designation was not the invention of a later publicist or historian, but a phrase in the mouths of early 19th century Lexingtonians who were proud and self-conscious of their achievements and status.

The diversity and number of books being brought to Lexington, mostly by merchants like William Leavy who ordered them from the East as part of his consignment of goods, was impressive as was the sale of them. The Lexington library offered more than 2,000 different titles touching on a wide range of subjects. Leavy's son wrote, "Perhaps nothing illustrates more the rise and progress of Lexington and its vicinity in its society and wealth than the rise of the Book Business here." Abraham Lincoln was most impressed by the extensive and well-chosen library of his father-in-law, Robert Todd. During his visits to Lexington, Lincoln spent hours browsing through it, memorizing passages from favorite authors.

The reading public was served by three local newspapers — *Kentucky Gazette, American Statesman, Kentucky Reporter.* Somewhat later, in 1814, after the demise of the *American Statesman*, Thomas Curry began publication of the *Western Monitor*. Other papers appeared in surprising numbers but usually endured for only a few months before folding up or moving to another town.

Printers, like John Bradford and Worsley and Smith, produced useful books for the regional market. Among these were Robert Bishop's *Outline of the History of the Church in Kentucky* (1821), *Laws of Kentucky,* David Ramsey's *The History of the American Revolution* (1815), and Robert B. McAfee's *History of the Late War in the Western Country* (1816), an account of the War of 1812, mint fresh in the minds of Kentuckians.

Transylvania's main building designed by Matthew Kennedy. It was erected in 1816 in what is now Gratz Park and burned in 1829. Photo courtesy of Transylvania University.

They also printed an amazing variety of textbooks for the western school market, mostly of an elementary level.

Less successful were the experimental literary journals. As early as 1803, Daniel Bradford published *The Medley,* the West's first literary magazine, dependent on subscribers for its existence and providing the readers with such fascinating literary fare as essays on the character of Lord Chatham, on commerce, jealousy, filial piety, intemperance, and travels in Russia. In 1821, William Gibbes Hunt brought out the *Western Review and Miscellaneous Magazine,* but even with the encouragement and contributions from Mary and Horace Holley and Constantine Rafinesque, the periodical struggled to survive for two years. *The Transylvanian,* or *Lexington Literary Journal,* appearing in 1829, was somewhat more successful, but only the medical enthusiast or professional physician would have found the substantial and scholarly *Transylvania Journal*

of Medicine and Associate Sciences interesting reading. Whatever advances Lexington may have made as a literary and cultivated center, there were not enough readers or subscribers for such periodicals.

Transylvania and Horace Holley

On the northern slope overlooking the town stood the stately main building of Transylvania University, created by Matthew Kennedy, one of Lexington's earliest talented architects, and completed in 1818. Set on its tranquil college lot near the middle of what is now Gratz Park, surrounded by an ever-growing number of handsome brick houses, this three-story structure, surmounted by an elaborate cupola and combining what Clay Lancaster, Lexington's foremost architectural historian, has called the "Classic" and "Georgian Baroque" styles, it symbolized a new and splendid period in Transylvania's history.

31

Henry Clay and the other trustees challenged Horace Holley, the foremost Unitarian minister and orator of Boston, to leave his New England roots and the Harvard-dominated collegiate tradition to create at Transylvania his vision of a great Western university. He accepted the challenge, and in the years 1818-1827 added such lustre and prestige to the university as to make it one of the nation's leading educational centers.

Drawing on the youthful elite of what was then the West and Southwest for its student body, Holley brought to the classrooms the most outstanding faculty in liberal arts, medicine, and law he could persuade to come there. This included the European-born and educated exotic naturalist, Constantine S. Rafinesque, who found in the Ohio River Valley vast numbers of new botanical and zoological species unknown to his European contemporaries, and which he proceeded to preserve poorly, but to classify and name with imaginative vigor. A strange figure, even in this town replete with European nationals of all varieties, he added a new scientific element to a curriculum still wedded to the classics. Offering classes in several European languages to Lexington residents, a device used by many newly-arrived immigrants to earn money, he also proposed an extensive botanical garden to be developed on the south side of East Main Street, not far from where Ransom Avenue is today. Unfortunately, despite his earlier friendship with the Holleys, he and the president came to a parting of the ways when Holley removed some of Rafinesque's collections from much-needed rooms in the main college building while the naturalist was on one of his extensive field trips. This enraged Rafinesque, who packed up his collections, cursed Transylvania and Holley, and left for Philadelphia in the winter of 1826.

Some of the notable physicians composing Transylvania's Medical Department have already been noted. Holley also recruited Charles Caldwell of Philadelphia who, despite his egotism and penchant for phrenology, was a learned and able man in his field, and an untiring publicist for the Transylvania Medical Department. He performed a matchless service for the school when, with $11,000 contributed by the city and the state, he went to Europe in 1821 to purchase books and apparatus which formed the core of one of the finest medical libraries in the country.

Though Joseph Buchanan had originally studied medicine at Transylvania, his intellectual creativity ranged through philosophy, mathematics, and education. He was an inventor as well. In 1812 he published *The Philosophy of Human Nature*, a pioneering study in American materialistic philosophy and psychology.

The Transylvania University Medical Department became the most distinguished component of that institution, achieving a prestige, quality, and size equal to any in the nation, and the unchallenged leader in the West in this period. Lexington was proud of the Medical Department as well as the entire university. In 1827, the Medical Department hired Matthew Kennedy to design and build the first Transylvania Medical Hall, located on the northwest corner of Market and Church streets, facing the Episcopal Church.

In addition, an ever-improving Law Department, one of a very few in the nation and the first in the West, taught scores of aspiring lawyers under such able faculty as Jesse Bledsoe, William T. Barry, John Boyle, Daniel Mayes, Aaron K. Woolley, Thomas Marshall, Madison C. Johnson, and the rigorous Judge George Robertson. Though all were able and accomplished lawyers, Robertson was the most permanent and prominent of the faculty.

Major Cultural Influence

During this period, Transylvania exerted a major influence in stimulating Lexington's intellectual and cultural life. The students were the first to engage in amateur theatrical performances, and the Lexington residents frequently came to the campus for lectures by faculty or traveling lyceum speakers. Lexingtonians like Henry Clay sent their sons to the university where they made the acquaintance of many of the nation's future leaders, such as Jefferson Davis, who roomed while a student in the house of the postmaster, Joseph Ficklin, on the southwest corner of

Limestone and High streets; Stephen Austin, who moved on to lead in the opening and settlement of Texas; and Richard M. Johnson and John C. Breckinridge, future vice-presidents of the United States.

Transylvania's progress slowed in 1825, however, when Governor Joseph Desha, a demagogic Jacksonian hostile to Henry Clay, a trustee of Transylvania, and critical of what he called the school's elitism, persuaded the legislature to stop all future appropriations for its support. This, plus the constant harassment by Holley's Presbyterian critics who regarded his Unitarianism as akin to atheism, led Holley to resign. After his departure, the main building burned down on May 9, 1829. Although the medical and law departments continued to flourish, the liberal arts department only gradually revived.

One major factor in this recovery was the construction of Morrison College (Old Morrison today). As a result of the James Morrison legacy, with Henry Clay as the executor of his estate, funds were available for both an endowed professorship and a new building. The trustees' building committee headed by John Wesley Hunt, impressed by the new state capitol at Frankfort recently designed and constructed by Gideon Shryock, employed in 1831 the twenty-nine-year-old architect to make plans for the new university building. Son of Mathias Shryock, who came to Lexington in 1800, Gideon grew up in a family of builders and carpenters. He went to Philadelphia to receive training from William Strickland, one of America's leading architects and an advocate of the Greek Revival style. Shryock returned to Kentucky to introduce that style for large public buildings in the state, starting with the capitol. In his design and construction of Morrison College, Shryock created an architectural gem whose stately columned majesty has remained a familiar and cherished landmark, not only for the university but for all Lexingtonians, who in the 1970's approved its incorporation as the centerpiece of the present city seal.

Private academies and private tutors continued to flourish in Lexington. It was traditional to have separate schools for the boys and girls, and usually the curriculum in the girls' schools did not emphasize the classics. One advertisement in 1798 stated that

> ... in order to prevent an indiscriminate intercourse of the sexes so injurious to the morals, and incompatible with the delicacy of the "Fair," an academy is starting for the purpose of conferring the degree of a classical education.

Among the earliest of the better known private schools was that operated by Mary Beck, the daughter of a French refugee. She had married the English landscape painter, George Beck, and had come with him to America in 1795 in hopes of improving his health. Arriving in Lexington around 1805, Mrs. Beck opened a school for girls. Mr. Beck had to postpone establishing one for boys upon discovering that the available advanced male students were already enrolled at Transylvania, but when his wife became ill he taught the girls.

Mary Todd, a Mentelle Student

One of the more prestigious schools was the select boarding school of Madame Victoria Charlotte Le Clere Mentelle. Both Parisians, Madame and her husband, Augustus Waldemard Mentelle, cultured and well-educated, fled the French Revolution in 1792 to the United States, settling near Gallipolis, Ohio, before moving on to Lexington. After teaching classes in French and dancing, they acquired through a donation by Mrs. James Russell, a tract of land opposite Clay's Ashland on the Richmond Road to establish a boarding school for girls, Described as "a rather large, attractive woman and an excellent dancer, a finished musician, and an accomplished scholar" in French, Madame Mentelle ran a successful school for many years, having as her most famous pupil, Mary Todd, future wife of Abraham Lincoln.

Another school that Mary attended was the academy of Dr. John Ward, former rector of Christ Church, which he directed about 1821 in the large, two-story brick building on the southeast corner of Market and Second streets, once occupied by Dr. Frederick Ridgely. Though personally kind and benevolent, Ward was a strict disciplinarian and an innovator in

St. Catherine's Academy, erected in 1847 on the site of the present Greyhound Bus Station, served as Lexington's principal Catholic school for girls until the early 1950's. The building was razed in 1959. Photo courtesy of the University of Kentucky.

permitting coeducation in his school. He was a great believer in early recitations and young Mary had to rise before dawn to walk from her Short Street residence to be at school in time for the first class at 5 a.m.

Another school favored by the elite was the Lexington Female Academy operated by Colonel Josiah Dunham in a two-story brick building on South Upper Street, at the corner of Mack's Alley, which was renamed the Lafayette Female Academy during a visit to the school by the legendary Marquis on his 1825 American tour. Also, St. Catherine's Academy, the first Catholic school in the city, was founded by the Sisters of Charity of Nazareth in 1834 on North Limestone. Two years earlier, the Reverend Benjamin O. Peers,

an innovative educator in Lexington, opened the Eclectic Institute for boys, housed in spacious quarters on West Second Street. A year later he accepted the presidency of Transylvania University.

Education for free blacks was largely non-existent, or conducted informally until Colonel Robert Patterson organized a free Sunday afternoon school for blacks, primarily to teach them trades and presumably some basic reading and writing. Education for the slaves was left entirely to the whim or interest of their masters, many of whom did provide some teaching of reading and writing and simple arithmetic until revolts like Nat Turner's in Virginia in 1831 convinced many owners that literate slaves were potentially dangerous.

Consequently, great pressure was exerted to prohibit any teaching of the slaves.

No significant movement to establish public schools in Kentucky or Lexington began until the 1830's.

Theatre and Music

The theatre had been an important part of 18th century colonial life except in New England where persistent Puritan influence made theatrical development in that region difficult. Many of the Lexington residents by the late 1790's and early 1800's enjoyed theatrical performances and entertainment of any kind. The early innkeepers tried to amuse their guests with whatever roving talent may have been available. The town trustees hoped to secure some revenue from these activities by levying a tax in 1805 whereby "theatrical performances, puppet shows, tumbling acts, rope or wire dancing, balancing of any description, or any show whatsoever, whether fictitious or real, for money shall pay from 10 to 200 dollars — permit limited to one week." They also licensed Thomas Ardon "to shew lyon at $5 per week." Whether this "lyon" was alive or stuffed, it certainly provided a bit of exoticism for this Western country.

The Transylvania students were the main source of amateur theatricals in the 1790's, frequently using the courthouse as their makeshift theatre. In March 1799, they presented *The Busy Body* by Susannah Centlivre and Macklin's popular *Love a-la-Mode.* Audiences in those days demanded a varied program which usually included a serious play or comedy followed by a farce or musical piece. Such variety placed a considerable burden on the actors' versatility, so it is not surprising that the early amateur groups confined themselves to modest programs. Some performances may have been given in Saunders' exhibition hall next to Coleman's Tavern or in Henry Clay's Traveller's Hall Hotel, located on Short Street opposite the courthouse.

It was on October 12, 1808, that a landmark in Lexington's theatrical history occurred: the opening of Luke Usher's new theatre. Usher had purchased a rather long and narrow strip of property running from Vine to Hill (High) Street along Spring Street. He built a brewery on this lot in 1807 but

apparently became infatuated with the theatre business and converted the second story into a commodious theatre, capable of seating perhaps as many as 400 to 500.

The *Gazette* reported:

> The audience was gratified on their entrance of the Theatre, with a species of accomodation not heretofore known in this country — convenient and safe seats, separated as in theatres in the Atlantic cities. They were also pleased with the plan and decorations of the theatre ... and with the scenery ... for which we are indebted to the taste of Mr. Beck.

The scenery painter, it may be assumed, was George Beck, the English landscape artist and schoolmaster.

Though the local Thespian Society and amateurs from Frankfort helped provide the casts for most of the productions in these first few years, including a production of Sheridan's *The Rivals* in their repertoire, professional actors of various levels of talent and attainment began to appear either singly or in groups by 1810. Among the earliest was John Vos from Montreal who played the lead in Shakespeare's *Macbeth* in Lexington on October 11, 1810, which is believed to be the first Shakespearean production performed in Kentucky. The opening of theatres in Frankfort and Louisville also attracted professional companies with the possibility of a more financially rewarding circuit in Kentucky. The most talented of these was the Drake company — two brothers and a sister — who played the Kentucky circuit with great success.

Lexington's preeminence as a theatrical center began to diminish as Frankfort, and especially Louisville, grew in size and theatre resources. Luke Usher suffered a setback when his tavern "The Sign of the Ship" (or "Don't Give up the Ship") burned down in 1819 and he was forced to mortgage his theatre to Robert Wickliffe, who later filed a successful suit against Usher in 1825. The theatre was sold at public auction.

Occasionally, such theatrical groups encouraged talented musicians to come to Lexington. One of the most notable was Anthony Philip Heinrich, a Bohemian musician, who, having lost his fortune in Europe, turned to music in America to make his living. After having conducted musical organizations in

Philadelphia and Pittsburgh and making the acquaintance of the Drake theatrical company and the noted actor Francis Blissit, who was employed by the Drakes, he was persuaded by them to try his luck in Lexington. This gifted and energetic individual managed to recruit sufficient amateur or semi-professional talent to present a historic grand concert on November 12, 1817, at Keen and Lamphear's Assembly Room in what later became the Phoenix Hotel. Included in the long program was music by Mozart, Viotti, Fiorillo, and Haydn. Of historic importance was the fact that the first piece performed was the *Sinfonia con Minuetto* by Beethoven, his First Symphony. Though not the first time that it had been performed in America, it was the first performance in the West and preceded its performance in either New York or Pennsylvania. Having executed this musical coup, Heinrich apparently saw little to keep him here, and he moved elsewhere to devote himself to composing.

Music in various forms had preceded Heinrich in Lexington. Hymnbooks and hymn singing appeared in the 1790's. James Moore, first rector of Christ Church and first president of Transylvania University, was a lover of music, and a flute player. When he built his home, "Vaucluse," on the west side of Georgetown Pike, he had a special room designed for musical performances.

Four musical organizations appeared before 1840, although most were short-lived: the Kentucky Musical Society, the Handel and Haydn Society, the Harmonic Society, and the Musical Amateurs. Performing concerts of varying quality, they were nevertheless enthusiastically supported by local audiences, especially as the proceeds from such events were donated frequently to charitable causes.

A visitor to Lexington in December 1817, commented on the improvements in Lexington society and was gratified "to hear a considerable part of Handel's *Messiah,* performed by a society of persons belonging to the church [Christ Episcopal] ..."

A few notable musicians such as Madame Feron, an English-born, Paris-trained singer who had performed at La Scala, included Lexington on their circuit. An amazing number of music teachers advertised their availability to budding students interested in vocal music, piano, violin,

guitar, flute, fife, flageolet, and harp. The most influential and talented teacher was probably Wilhelm Iucho, the German-born immigrant who came to Lexington from New York in the early 1830's. He taught at the Van Doren Collegiate Institute, a school for young ladies, and cultivated the public in his lyceum lectures, sold pianos, and composed music.

William Ratel, whose specialty was band music, was another active teacher, performer and composer in Lexington in the 1830's. He organized bands in Lexington and neighboring towns and composed band music for special occasions or dedicated to well-known individuals, such as "The Ashland Quick Step," which was written in honor of Henry Clay in 1838.

Numerous public concerts were thus presented to Lexington audiences during this period, adding to the cultural quality of the town. Music could be purchased at Lexington's four music stores and at other stores where merchants included music and musical instruments in their inventories.

Little known and surprising is the fact that pianos were manufactured locally as early as 1805. This demanding craft was exercised here by Josiah Green, the earliest, and later by Christian Veltenair, T. L. Evenden, J. H. Taylor, and William Thompson. A piano made by Thompson, with its Lexington hallmark, presently sits in the restored Mary Todd Lincoln house on West Main Street.

Matthew Jouett and the Portraitists

The desire of many prominent Lexingtonians to have their portraits painted in this pre-daguerreotype era created a market for portrait painters, even those of limited talent. Itinerant painters arrived as early as 1788, but not until George Beck and his wife came to Lexington in 1799 did painters of some training and accomplishment appear. Unlike his contemporaries, Beck was as much a landscape painter as portraitist, one of his landscapes finding a place on the wall of Washington's Mount Vernon.

Fathers of sons with an artistic bent usually discouraged them from pursuing such careers, viewing them as effete, financially unrewarding, and somewhat disreputable. When

Captain Jack Jouett discovered that his son Matthew was dabbling in portraiture, he exclaimed that he had educated him to be a gentleman, not "a damned sign painter." Fortunately, Matthew Harris Jouett (1788-1827) ignored his father's criticism, and after attending Transylvania University and reading law, he opened a studio in Lexington. He then went to Boston in 1816 to study under the famous Gilbert Stuart. His technique was much improved and he returned to paint portraits at a furious pace, both in his hometown and in various Mississippi River communities on his way to New Orleans, where he painted during the winter months.

By the time his short life ended in 1827, Jouett had become the pre-eminent portrait painter in Kentucky. Among the notables captured by Jouett's brush for posterity were Henry Clay, Isaac Shelby, Mrs. Benjamin Gratz, Colonel James Morrison, Dr. Benjamin Dudley, Horace Holley, Robert Todd, some of the Breckinridges, and Lafayette.

Other Lexingtonians who became noted artists, though sometimes leaving their hometown in pursuit of their artistic careers, were William Edward West, Joseph H. Bush, and Oliver Frazer. Bush studied under Sully in Philadelphia and lived most of his life in Louisville, though returning to Lexington to live out his last years. Frazer started his training in Jouett's studio, but after Jouett's death, he, like Bush, studied under Sully. Frazer was far less productive than Jouett, painting only when the mood struck him.

Sometime later, the great 19th century Swiss painter of animals, Edward Troye, came to Kentucky to settle in Scott County. He produced fine canvases of many of Kentucky's greatest thoroughbreds. Until the 1860's, however, Jouett, Bush, and Frazer dominated the portrait market in central Kentucky; but the advent of photography after 1840 spelled the decline of the portrait genre, and the patronage of the affluent which sustained these artists declined with it.

Lexington could also boast of having a sculptor of note. Joel T. Hart, born in Clark County in 1810, was trained as a stone mason before coming to Lexington to work at Patrick Doyle's (later Pruden's) marble factory at the southeast corner of Second and Upper streets.

Almost incidentally he began to experiment in carving marble busts with some help from a visiting sculptor from Cincinnati, achieving such success with his bust of Cassius M. Clay that he set up a studio at 437 West Second Street. He later was commissioned to do the busts of Henry Clay, Judge Thomas Hickey, Dr. Benjamin Dudley, the Reverend Alexander Campbell, and John J. Crittenden. His most famous work, which stood on display in the Fayette County Courthouse, was "Woman Triumphant" (sometimes called "Triumph of Chastity") consisting of a nude woman in classic Grecian style overcoming the arrows of a devilish cupid. Hart devoted over fifteen years to this work in his studio in Florence, Italy, dying there in 1877 not long after its completion. Both the sculpture and the remains of the sculptor were eventually brought back to Kentucky. Unfortunately, Hart's prized masterpiece was destroyed when the courthouse burned in 1897 and the big bell in the tower fell upon it.

Architects and Craftsmen

The physical transformation of Lexington from a frontier village to an attractive urban community, which so impressed visitors, occurred during this period. Many of the log cabins were torn down, log houses extended and clapboarded, and stone and brick structures — both business and residential — began to rise with such astonishing rapidity that visitors to the 1790 Lexington could scarcely believe their eyes when they returned a dozen or fifteen years later. The city directory listed many carpenters, house joiners, masons, bricklayers, and brickmakers who provided the labor, not to mention many unlisted black enslaved artisans, who erected these structures.

In the absence of architects, master builders used printed plans and designs for the new buildings available in a variety of publications from the Eastern cities. Occasionally, a local resident would make his own design. When the *Kentucky Gazette* in 1806 advertised for plans for the new courthouse, David Sutton, a large landowner and hemp manufacturer on the Henry's Mill Pike (now Newtown Pike), submitted the winning design. While Mathias Shryock and other master builders erected many impressive structures, usually in the prevailing Federal style of that day, sometimes substantially modified, none of them claimed to be professional architects until Matthew Kennedy so declared himself in 1824. A well-known builder who had already constructed such distinctive buildings as Transylvania's main hall and his own imposing residence on the southeast corner of North Limestone and Constitution (Second) streets, he apparently felt sufficiently trained and experienced to designate himself as an architect. He went on to erect the Grand Lodge Masonic Hall on West Main Street, 1824-26, which burned in 1836, and Transylvania's first medical hall on the northwest corner of Church and Market streets in 1827.

Gideon Shryock, the most gifted of the early architects, after designing and constructing Morrison College, which was completed in 1833, left his hometown for the busy market of Louisville.

John McMurtry, born in 1812 on a farm on the Iron Works Pike, learned his carpenter's trade in Lexington and studied architecture under Gideon Shryock for a time, assisting Shryock in the construction of Morrison College. His first major commission was St. Peter Catholic Church on North Limestone, completed in 1837. However, his most productive period was from the late 1830's to the Civil War.

The affluent Lexingtonians who built fine homes also filled them with beautifully crafted furnishings, some of which were purchased from the Eastern cities and others produced by the growing number of gifted craftsmen working in Lexington. Cabinet makers such as Porter Clay, brother of Henry Clay, advertised in 1805 that he could build "furniture of the newest and most elegant fashions as well as anywhere in the United States" and that his "regular correspondence . . . with all the principal Cabinet Makers in both Philadelphia and New York" had kept him abreast of the latest fashions. Corner cupboards, chests of drawers, sugar chests, chairs, settees, highly polished dining room tables and card tables were shaped out of Kentucky's plentiful walnut, and especially wild cherry, whose warm, rich-grained quality made it a favorite wood.

Filling those handsome cupboards and adorning the long cherry dining tables was coin silverware of every conceivable variety. Silversmiths appeared early in this frontier community. Samuel Ayres arrived in Lexington in the mid-1780's and by 1790 was advertising for a "quantity of old silver for which I give five shillings per ounce." The clients had to provide the coin silver themselves in many instances, and the Spanish dollars from New Orleans were the best source. An expanding market in Lexington provided ample business for Ayres and attracted other silversmiths. Ayres wrote around 1790 to his father in Virginia, "I have the greatest turn of business that I ever had in all my life, and have a journeyman . . . and yet we do not appear to be able to do half the business that may be had."

The dominant silversmith at this time was Asa Blanchard who worked in Lexington from 1808 to 1838. He designed and crafted a variety of exquisite silverware — julep cups, handled cups, pitchers, creamers, tongs, ladles, spoons, tea sets, candlesticks, and sugar boats.

Alexander and Robert Frazer, and their nephew Robert Frazer, Jr., eventually found their way from Ireland to Lexington, along with Charles Plimpton and a young Frenchman, Antoine Dumesneil. Later, in the 1830's and 1840's, when silver styles were changing from the Federal and Empire to Rococo, another generation of Lexington silversmiths appeared, including Eli C. Garner in partnership with David F. Winchester, George Stewart, and a clan of Poindexters.

Other silversmiths were the Woodruffs who arrived from New Jersey in 1811 with a young apprentice, David Sayre. This thrifty apprentice, who had walked barefoot all the way from Maysville to Lexington, eventually took over the silver business from the faltering Woodruffs. When the independent banking business developed in the 1820's, he abandoned manufacturing for full-time banking, becoming one of Lexington's most influential and affluent citizens.

One other craftsman who helped adorn and beautify Lexington houses and their landscaping was the ironworker. While the blacksmith had traditionally hammered out most of the iron items needed in a community — from horseshoes to hoes, plows, shovels, and hinges

Unusual silver cups made in shape of whiskey barrels by early Lexington silversmith Asa Blanchard. Photo by permission of the magazine Antiques.

— the demand for more decorative ironwork motivated some ironworkers to specialize in this area. Craftsmen, sometimes former tinsmiths, became known as whitesmiths. The market for such items as special hinges, fences, railings, arched doorways, and grills grew to such an extent that in 1818 Joseph Bruen built a foundry which continued to operate for more than half a century. It soon became traditional for the giant whistle on Bruen's foundry to "usher in with hoarse blasts the first day" of the new year.

Social Life in Lexington

Given the character and affluence of many Lexingtonians, social activities were spirited and frequently lavish. As the prosperous merchants and lawyers acquired country estates, developed flourishing farms, and built imposing houses or "villas," as they were sometimes called, a great deal of entertaining and many social events centered in them. Most lavish of these was Colonel David Meade's "Chaumiere des Prairies" in Jessamine County. Here this wealthy Virginian, dressed regally in the 18th century style, kept a crew of thirty men working constantly to extend the intricate landscaping of his large estate. Meade always dressed for dinner and nearly every evening entertained fifteen to twenty guests.

In town, dancing masters and dancing schools abounded, teaching the unskilled the intricate steps of both traditional and new dances. The town was well supplied with musicians to provide the latest waltzes and polkas, and a variety of other steps long since forgotten. Not only were modest-sized ballrooms built into the larger of the new Lexington houses, but the hotels provided the public with larger rooms. One of the most popular ballrooms was that of "Monsieur Mathurin Giron, the cordial, kindly, fastidiously-dressed little confectioner," who claimed to have been a grenadier in Napoleon's army before leaving France for America, eventually reaching Lexington in 1811. Described as "a very attractive little person of heavy build but low of stature, being scarcely over five feet in height — with a pleasant, smooth-shaven face," Monsieur Giron became the leading confectioner of Lexington, whose monumental cakes, created for weddings, dances, and banquets honoring

Drawing of the famous confectionery and ballroom of Monsieur Giron, built in 1837. Right half of building still stands on North Mill Street near Short Street.
Drawing adapted from The Transylvanian, *1907.*

such distinguished visitors as President Monroe and the Marquis de Lafayette, became legendary in the community.

This jovial figure — a veritable Dickensian Mr. Fezziwig — occupied and constructed several structures on the west side of North Mill between Short and Main streets. In 1837 he built his most ambitious one, originally seven bays long with a range of half-round Tuscan wooden columns attached to brick piers. On the second floor was "the ballroom with its great, paneled doors of polished cherry, opening to the high frescoed ceiling." Giron served delectable banquets here, ably assisted by his famous Swiss chef, Dominique Ritter. And

when the tables were cleared and the dancing began (Mary Todd, an avid dancer, loved the dances at Giron's), the dancers could rest and cool themselves on the small, graceful balcony, lean on the delicately wrought iron railing, and look down on the street below. Only a part of this storied gathering place remains today.

The inns and taverns also provided rooms for gambling, card games, and billiards, which were common activities in town despite occasional efforts by reform groups to restrain gaming. Henry Clay was an inveterate gambler, and the stakes in some of the games were extravagantly high. Fortunes might be made or lost in an evening. Tradition has it that Clay and his good friend, John Bradford, ended one such game with Bradford the loser by some $40,000. When Bradford asked Clay how the account should be settled, Clay said Bradford's note for $500 would be satisfactory, which Bradford gave him. Not long after, Clay lost $60,000 to Bradford at cards, returned the $500 note to the editor and both were satisfied. Unfortunately, gambling debts were not always settled so amicably, and brawls and duels occasionally resulted.

Barbecues and picnics were also convivial occasions, whether political in nature when campaigns were in full swing and sweating candidates would shout themselves hoarse to the large assemblage, or on holidays such as the Fourth of July when orators would expound on the glories of the Revolution. How early Kentucky's famous specialty — burgoo — appeared at these events is hard to say, but soon this amorphous conglomeration of beef, lamb, chicken, wild game, and assorted vegetables, stewed for a day or two in giant kettles, became a mainstay for such festivities, accompanied by generous libations of bourbon. One of the most popular spots for such barbecues and picnics was Fowler's Gardens. Captain John Fowler, one of the early settlers in Lexington and an active businessman and political leader, had acquired an extensive tract of land on the eastern edge of town and opened a park around 1817. The precise boundaries of this park are not known. It appears that generally it started at Scott's Pond near Walton Avenue, stretching west along both sides of Third Street to Race Street, perhaps extending north toward what today is the Blue Grass Housing Project, and south toward East Main. The park soon became the most popular site for fairs, picnics, political gatherings, and entertainments of all kinds.

Main Street was Race Course

But it was on the race track that Kentuckians' gambling spirit reached fever pitch. The Virginians' passion for fine horses came with them to Kentucky. The fertile Bluegrass region surrounding Lexington was a horseman's paradise, with its gentle slopes and rich pasturage of grass and cane, fed by the underlying limestone that built strong bones necessary for racing horses. Horses were prized possessions, an essential means of transportation, a beast of burden to carry household goods, and a lifesaving means of escape from Indian attacks. As soon as a community had a cleared area suitable for racing, then for a moment the lurking Indians and farm chores would be forgotten, the races would be arranged and the bets laid down. Lexington's Main Street was the first scene of such contests until the trustees, justly apprehensive of the dangers of flying hooves to innocent bystanders, forced the promoters of these races to move them to "the Commons."

In 1789, the *Kentucky Gazette* carried a notice of a purse race in October that was to be run in three-mile heats, "the best of 2 in 3; ¼-hour allowed between heats for rubbing ... " In later years races with two, three, or four-mile heats were advertised. Races of this length necessitated some type of race course rather than a three or four-mile stretch of uncertain roadbed, and thus race courses were established quite early. The surrounding towns likewise established race courses or race paths, some in the 1780's, mostly in the 1790's.

To set necessary rules governing racing, the more influential horsemen met in Lexington at Postlethwait's Tavern in 1797 and organized the Kentucky Jockey Club. They built the Williams Race Track, a circular one-mile grass course in Lee's Wood on a portion of what is now the Lexington Cemetery. In 1809 the Kentucky Jockey Club was reorganized into the Lexington Jockey Club and until 1825 conducted fall meetings. At first, bets were taken by Captain John Fowler at Postlethwait's.

To give the activity broader scope, the Kentucky Association for the Improvement of the Breeds of Stock was organized in 1826, replacing the Jockey Club and emphasizing quality breeding of livestock as well as horses, with rewards through racing providing incentive to the breeders. This Association supervised organized racing until 1933. The racecourse was moved from Lee's Wood in 1828 to a new course on its own property in northeast Lexington in the area of Fifth and Race streets. Here they built a fenced-in dirt track patterned after the Union Course in New York, the second such course in the nation.

Such were the major facets of this proud and flourishing town which boasted of being "the Athens of the West." Its economic predominance, however, was soon to be challenged by Louisville and Cincinnati. In 1815, the steamboat "Enterprise" docked at Louisville after a successful run against the powerful currents of the Mississippi and Ohio rivers. The rapids at the Falls of the Ohio, where the water foamed over great shelves of exposed rock, were a significant handicap except during high water; but canalization would soon circumvent this obstacle, opening the great waterway from Pittsburgh to the Gulf. Very quickly, the tide turned as the populations of Louisville and Cincinnati dramatically increased. Their docks and warehouses became piled high with merchandise brought from the South, and Kentucky produce ready to be shipped downriver.

Desperately, the Lexington merchants sought better transportation to the lifeline of the Ohio River — better roads, canals (never seriously planned), and finally the railroad, started in 1831, to Louisville. Meanwhile, as the economic upswing ended, Lexington emphasized even more its cultural distinctiveness.

The War of 1812

Throughout these decades, in which Lexington developed its economic, physical, and cultural character, it was by no means immune from the national and international events that affected all Americans. The long life-and-death struggle between the dominant maritime power, Great Britain, and the unconquerable Napoleonic landpower sweeping across Europe had placed the United States merchant shipping in a naval nutcracker as both British and French naval forces blockaded each others' ports, captured American ships, confiscated the cargoes, and impounded the seamen. To add insult to injury, Britain frequently impressed American sailors into the undermanned British navy.

Far from the Eastern ports, whose merchants, ships, and crews were most involved, the inland settlers paradoxically exhibited greater anger against these depredations than the Easterners who, despite the difficulties, were making handsome profits from the ships that successfully reached their destinations. Nor were they anxious to engage in war with Britain, whose naval power would make the Atlantic seaboard ports easy targets for their

guns and landing parties. Renewed Indian attacks around 1810 and 1811 aroused Western suspicions that they were British inspired, and the rising chorus for war against the ancient foe was led by Henry Clay himself. Elected to the U. S. House of Representatives for the first time in 1811, this dashing freshman Congressman was chosen Speaker of the House. With his warlike cohorts, known as the "War Hawks," including young John C. Calhoun from South Carolina, Felix Grundy from Tennessee, and his own ardent compatriot from Kentucky, Richard M. Johnson, he urged Congress to declare war on Britain in June 1812.

The declaration of war was received with great enthusiasm in Kentucky. "Lexington greeted the news with a brilliant illumination and great rejoicing, and as soon as it was known that a requisition had to be made upon Kentucky for troops, and even before the Governor's orders reached Lexington, a company of volunteers was formed, and its services tendered to the State." Six companies were raised in the city and the county, led by such men as Nathaniel G. S. Hart, Stewart Megowan, and George Trotter, Jr. Crowds gathered in the streets to cheer their friends, husbands, fathers and sons, as they marched off. The Revolutionary War was a dim memory. This was *their* war. Had not their own Harry of the West flamboyantly declared on the floor of Congress that Kentucky's militia alone could conquer Canada?

In late January 1813, Lexington was stunned by the news of the defeat of the Americans at Frenchtown, near the River Raisin in the Michigan Territory, and the bloody massacre of many prisoners following the surrender. The terrible news trickled back slowly. A resident in a house on the road between Cincinnati and Lexington recalled that "there was a great mourning in our neighborhood. People living back from the road would come to our house and stay all day to ask those coming up the road for news, hoping to hear of the safety of their loved ones. Women would stand for hours looking down the road with tears in their eyes." Among the dead were many Lexingtonians including Captain Nathaniel Hart, Major Benjamin Graves, Samuel Elder, David McIlvain, and the son of the Reverend James Blythe.

The following July, Isaac Shelby, serving his second term as Governor, issued a stirring call for troops to meet him at Newport on August 3, 1813, to join General William Henry Harrison in his campaign against the British and Indians. In late September, Harrison's combined forces struck the enemy on the upper Thames, forcing the British to surrender while the Kentuckians under Colonel Richard M. Johnson, yelling "Remember the River Raisin!," fell on Tecumseh's braves. Severely wounded, Johnson confronted the famed Indian chief and is credited with shooting Tecumseh, whose death so demoralized his followers that they fled.

This victory, combined with the news of Perry's naval defeat of the British on Lake Erie, bolstered Kentuckians' spirits, compensating for the humiliation of the British burning of the nation's capital. Then, in February 1815, Lexingtonians celebrated both the stunning victory of Jackson over the British at New Orleans and the Peace Treaty of Ghent, ending the war. Their own Henry Clay had been an important member of the peace delegation to Ghent.

A Visit by President Monroe

On July 2, 1819, President James Monroe, accompanied by Andrew Jackson, visited Lexington while touring the country. During his four-day stay he spoke at Transylvania, was given a large banquet at Mrs. Keen's (Postlethwait's) Tavern, and was entertained by Major William S. Dallam along with Governor Isaac Shelby, Colonel Richard M. Johnson, William T. Barry and other dignitaries at Dallam's stately house (the Pope House) on Grosvenor Avenue.

Exciting as President Monroe's visit was, it could not compare with the tumultuous welcome given the beloved Marquis de Lafayette when he arrived in Lexington on May 16, 1825, as part of his famous tour of America, celebrating the fiftieth anniversary of the beginning of the Revolutionary War, in which the French nobleman had played such a conspicuous role. Here, in the county named for him, Lafayette spent the night of May 15 at the home of Major John Keen (Keeneland) on the Versailles Pike on his way from Louisville. The next morning he was escorted into a cheering Lexington for a day crammed with activities (the aging celebrity showed amazing stamina). He was regaled with speeches at Transylvania, an open air dinner on the Frankfort Pike, exercises at Major Dunham's Female Academy, and dinner and dancing by his fellow Masons in the uncompleted Grand Lodge Hall on West Main Street before retiring at Mrs. Keen's Tavern. The next morning after breakfast, he set aside an hour to sit for Matthew Jouett who needed to complete the full-length portrait Jouett had started in Washington, and which now hangs in the Old Capitol in Frankfort.

General Andrew Jackson, now President and Henry Clay's bitterest political opponent, visited Lexington for a second time on September 29, 1832, in the midst of the hotly contested Presidential election. This was nothing less than a tour de force for Jackson's Democratic supporters in this strongly pro-Clay Whig town. Whether pro-Jackson or not, the crowds turned out in large numbers to see their President pass by. A grand barbecue in his honor was prepared at Fowler's Garden. A variety of military companies, orders, societies, bands and horsemen escorted him into the city. It was said that when the old general passed by the branch of the Second Bank of the United States which he was campaigning against, he brought down his cane with a sharp rap, muttering, "By the eternal!"

Many Lexingtonians were disappointed when Henry Clay lost his second bid for the Presidency. He came home to his beloved Ashland to recover, after arranging a compromise to avoid a violent confrontation between the United States and South Carolina in that state's wild gamble to nullify the tariff.

The Cholera Plague of 1833

Lexington seemed reasonably optimistic in the spring of 1833 as it watched the new town government function, its new railroad being extended, and the stately columns of Morrison College rising into place. Nothing prepared the residents for the deadly onslaught of cholera that summer. Kentuckians had battled epidemics of smallpox, typhoid, malaria, and yellow fever, not to mention the childhood diseases of measles, mumps, diphtheria, whooping cough, and scarlet fever that added to the terrifying infant mortality rate and the grim rows of small headstones in the family lots in the cemetery. If these had not killed one by adulthood, then tuberculosis (consumption), especially prevalent in Kentucky, might strike.

Deadly as all these were, they were familiar threats. Cholera, originating primarily in India, was something exotic and unknown. Carried by ship along the major trade routes, cholera reached the British Isles in 1831, crossing the Atlantic on immigrant ships in the spring of 1832. It was reported in New York in June 1832, spreading from there along coastal and river routes, reaching Cincinnati by the fall.

It was carried by riverboat and stage to Maysville and Louisville, which listed 22 fatalities by November. For some reason (cold weather may have destroyed or reduced the virulence of the bacillus), the winter season prevented its spread, and everyone optimistically believed the epidemic was over.

However, in May 1833, cholera struck again in Maysville and travelers or residents fleeing the city spread it along the roads to Lexington. Practically the entire citizenry of Flemingsburg fled when it appeared there, and almost the whole population of tiny Elizaville was wiped out before they could escape. Paris and Cynthiana were less severely hurt. Incredibly, Lexington deluded itself into thinking that its relatively good record of healthfulness would provide immunity against the approaching plague, and no preparations were made for its devastating assault.

Caused by a bacillus, cholera differs from other enteric diseases in its intensity, short incubation period, and high fatality rate. It was communicated by the wastes of infected individuals, but the medical profession in the antebellum period knew nothing of bacteria or viruses and how diseases were spread. All they could see were the violent symptoms of the cholera victims — the extreme diarrhea, vomiting, muscle cramps, and general prostration which dehydrated the body and usually resulted in death within a few hours to a day and a half.

In Lexington it started along Water Street behind what became the Lafayette Hotel. The town's water supply was at this time mainly dependent on springs and wells vulnerable to

Portrait of William "King" Solomon, hero of the 1833 cholera plague, painted by Samuel W. Price.

wastes from privies, especially during heavy rains. Such a storm occurred on June 3, 1833, and the Town Branch spilled out of its banks, flooding the area and the nearby wells. From Water Street the disease spread to Hill (High) Street, and thence throughout downtown. Terrified, one-third to one-half of the town's population fled to the countryside or to spas such as the Olympian Springs. The physicians, both of the Medical Department and in private practice, desperately tried all remedies without success. Baffled and frustrated in the face of this strange and relentless killer, they courageously stayed on, entering the homes of the dying and bringing as much assurance and comfort as they could muster. Some of them died from the cholera themselves.

Businesses and factories closed. The Market House was deserted although some brave farmers brought food to the distraught town. The disease struck down rich and poor, learned and illiterate, black and white. Among the victims were A. T. Skillman, General Thomas Bodley, Captain John Postlethwait, Dr. Joseph Boswell, Samuel Trotter, Mr. and Mrs.

Dumesneil, and Mrs. Andrew McCalla. The town records list 647 deaths for this fateful year, of which over 500 were from cholera — this out of a population of little over 6,000.

William A. Leavy recalled that "it came like a sudden and awful clap of thunder upon us — the whole community were stunned and paralyzed." On June 10, 1833, General John McCalla wrote to a friend, "Never in the course of life, have I spent such a week as the past, I would incomparably prefer a seven months campaign in a furious war, than to undergo another seven days such as these." Henry Clay, who had returned from Washington to Ashland in April, remained at home with his family. He wrote a friend that the town wore "a frightful gloom. All the stores and shops are closed, the presses stopt, and no one moving in the streets except those concerned with the dead or the sick."

The disposal of so many dead in a few weeks created a gruesome situation. The dead could not be buried fast enough. There were not enough coffins. The bodies were piled in heaps at the cemetery gates, most of them at the old Main Street cemetery, some at the newly opened Episcopal cemetery on Third Street and the old Maxwell burying ground near Bolivar Street. The corpses, which were uncoffined, were placed in trunks or boxes, or wrapped in the bedclothes in which they had died. Gideon Shryock had to halt work on Morrison College as the workmen disappeared. When his father Mathias died of the plague, Gideon hammered together a crude coffin and buried it himself in the Episcopal cemetery, later designing a tomb in the neo-classical mode to mark the grave. Long trenches were dug to receive the many corpses, and gravediggers were few and overworked.

Most heroic of these gravediggers was the legendary William "King" Solomon, a once reputable member of the community whom misfortune had reduced to a hard-drinking vagrant whose services just prior to the plague had been auctioned off to a free Negro woman. The crisis aroused Solomon to extraordinary efforts as he worked unceasingly to dig graves. It was said that because he rarely drank water to quench his thirst he never contracted cholera, and that if any stray bacillus had entered his bloodstream it would have died

immediately from the alcoholic content. The town was justly grateful to him and he was honored at a special ceremony at the courthouse. Samuel Woodson Price, a young, aspiring, and talented artist and one of the few students Oliver Frazer ever taught, persuaded Solomon to sit for his portrait. When Solomon died in 1854, he was buried in the new Lexington cemetery and later was immortalized in a short story by Kentucky's best-selling novelist of the late 19th century and early 20th — James Lane Allen. Thanks to the efforts of John Wilson Townsend, well known for his work on Kentucky writers, money was raised for a fine monument to mark the grave, formally dedicated in 1908.

The devastating impact of the plague on Lexington significantly modified the great optimism and sense of superiority shared by the citizens up to this time. Competing economically against Louisville, a town surrounded by swamps and long known for its unhealthiness and malarial fevers, Lexington had claimed a healthy environment as an attraction for immigrants and new enterprises. Now that image of health was shattered. Lexingtonians showed remarkable resilience in recovering from the plague, but the scars remained in areas of poverty that had not been there before, and in the creation of an institution not badly needed until then — the Lexington Orphan's Home. Over one hundred children, left parentless by the cholera, desperately needed care. As early as July 17, 1833, a special meeting of concerned citizens met at the courthouse to confront the problem. They raised $4,400 to purchase a house and provide care for these children. The first house acquired for that purpose was that of Dr. James Fishback on West Third Street, which stood at the entrance of what is now Hampton Court, with the property stretching to Fourth Street. Here the Lexington Orphan's Home operated until 1907 when it was moved to a house on West Short Street. This was, of course, for white children only. Not until 1892 was an orphans' home for black children established on Georgetown Street.

Despite this adversity, Lexingtonians could look back proudly on what they had accomplished in half a century and cherish their claim to being the "Athens of the West."

Students in front of Sayre Female Institute (now Sayre School) in 1866. Photo courtesy of Transylvania University.

Chapter III

1834/1860

Progress and Problems of Urban Growth

Traveling to Lexington from Maysville and Louisville in the late 1830's was a far more convenient and comfortable experience than in the earlier days. For the first two decades of settling and surviving in this region, transportation consisted mostly of riding a horse with pack horses bringing up the rear, laden with one's goods. Some of the time a person might walk, leading his pack horses. The roads were chiefly Indian trails and buffalo traces. Gradually, the main routes were enlarged by chopping down trees, clearing brush and removing the larger rocks. Bridges were few because they required so much labor, so one forded the streams where they were the shallowest and hoped for low water. The larger rivers had numerous ferries. As early as 1784 John Filson reported that "a large waggon-road," known for a few years as "Smith's waggon-road," had been carved out of the wilderness between Maysville and Lexington. Only the most sturdy wagons traveled this route. By 1803 so-called stage wagons were being run on irregular schedules, but the crude roads and poor shelters along the way made traveling by horseback preferable.

Greatly improved travel conditions came with the macadamized roads, better designed and constructed stagecoaches, larger and more comfortable inns and taverns, and well-run stage lines.

By 1817 Colonel James Johnson established a stagecoach line from Louisville to Lexington, and Abner Gaines a line from Lexington to Cincinnati. Edward P. Johnson, the Colonel's son, later expanded the company into one of the major stagecoach lines in the region. Crucial to the improvement of stage travel were better roads. Lacking adequate public financing, private turnpike companies raised money through stock subscriptions, laid out the routes, and macadamized the roadbeds. Named for a Scotchman — John Loudon MacAdam (1756-1836) — the process consisted of laying some nine or ten inches of broken stone of standard sizes and weights on the roadway and letting the weather and vehicles pack it down into a hard relatively weather-proof surface. The companies paid off their investment by erecting toll houses every five miles and placing a barrier (called a turnpike or toll-bar) across the road, which was lifted after the toll was paid. The improved surface of the macadamized roads almost doubled the speed at which stagecoaches could travel. Lexington became a major axis for these turnpikes in central Kentucky.

In the early 1830's, the famous Concord coach manufactured in Concord, New Hampshire, a much improved and more comfortable vehicle, began to replace the Lexington-made coaches on Bluegrass routes.

A traveler from Maysville recalled starting before dawn for Lexington, stopping at specified places to exchange horses, picking up mail, and pausing for food and refreshment at inns such as William Moreland's "where a sumptuous meal was enjoyed by the passengers who sat at a long table with the popular driver at the head." The coach driver, as a captain of a

Tollgate house on the Harrodsburg Pike near the Mason Headley Road was torn down about 1902.
Photo courtesy of the University of Kentucky.

ship, gave orders to passengers and assistants as he saw fit. A master of the whip, the driver prized it highly, and used it not only to keep his horses in line but also to display his extraordinary dexterity.

Unfortunately, the egotistical drivers engaged occasionally in hair-raising and dangerous races with their rivals, sometimes overturning the coaches, injuring the passengers, and tumbling the baggage across the countryside. Admonished by their employers and sued in the courts, the drivers nevertheless remained adamant in their determination not to be passed en route.

Next to their whip, the drivers — or "jehus" as they were commonly called — cherished their horns or bugles. When approaching a town or hamlet, they would stoutly blow a piercing blast to let everyone in earshot know the stage was coming and to make preparations accordingly. It was standard practice to blow two blasts to start, three to clear the road, and one long blast when the destination had been reached. Fancy variations were made by the drivers, however, and the country air might be pierced by these horn calls, and the sleeping townsfolk roused by the blasts of an early-departing stage.

Ebenezer Stedman, an early Bluegrass papermaker from New England, recalled that

while fishing near the Georgetown and Frankfort turnpike he

> heard the Stage from Frankfort Comming. I tell you the Stage Coach was looked upon at that time with more interest Than the Rail Road Car is at present. Evry Few Miles, he, the Driver woold Blow his Bugle & Some of the Drivers Could Blow them Fine ... He played Washington's March & when he stopt in Front of a store Kept thare he told of the news that General Lafayette arival in Frankfort.

With whip cracking and bugle blowing, the swaying, yellow Concord coach would thunder into Lexington with a flourish, pulling up in front of the stage office at Brennan's Hotel (Postlethwait's Tavern, later the Phoenix Hotel). One of the passengers described the scene:

> There was a large crowd milling around waiting to get the latest information and news from Washington and the East. The out-of-town newspapers were sold and read in front of the stage office and there was always a crowd to question the driver of what messages he had received at the other end of the line and along the way. The stage office was the hub of the town and the center of news distribution.

Fayette County abounded with inns and taverns of all sizes and varying quality of accommodations. Some of the smaller ones were actually private homes with a few extra rooms and a tiny taproom in the corner of the dining room.

Most famous of all taverns in Lexington was Postlethwait's on the southeast corner of Main and Limestone streets. Started first by Adam Steele in 1796, it was taken over in 1800 by Captain John Postlethwait, a native of Carlisle, Pennsylvania, who furnished this rambling structure with cherry and walnut pieces made by local cabinet makers. Good whiskey and wine, a bountiful table, and attentive service became hallmarks of this popular hostelry. Postlethwait operated the inn at various periods until his death from cholera in 1833. At other times Joshua Wilson, Sanford Keen and Mrs. Keen managed it. Wilson added a two-story addition in 1804, but in 1820 fire destroyed the thirty-eight room hotel. A local paper expressed the hope that, like the mythological Phoenix bird rising from the ashes, a new hotel would be erected. A new hotel was built, adopting the name Phoenix, replacing the old Postlethwait identification, and the Phoenix it remained until it was razed in 1982.

Following Postlethwait's death, John Brennan became the proprietor and the hotel was occasionally called Brennan's. He sold it to John G. Chiles in 1846, who added to the building and managed a stagecoach line until the 1850's.

Lexington's distinguished visitors usually lodged there if they were not accommodated at such private residences as Clay's Ashland. Among the earliest of the famous guests was the notorious Aaron Burr in 1805, and later President Monroe, General Andrew Jackson, and Lafayette.

In the absence of hospitals, sick travelers were treated at the hotels. James Atherton, visiting from New Hampshire, spent several weeks at the Phoenix suffering from ague, fever, and delirium. He recalled that an unidentified doctor gave him an "emetic & calomel and also a pound of blood." Professor Hedge of Harvard College, visiting his sister, the wife of Colonel Dunham, fell ill while staying at the Phoenix, and when he inquired of his doctor the nature of his illness was told that it was a "bilious fever with sundry accompanyments." He appreciated the warm

Lexington-Versailles stagecoach in 1881 at stage office on Short Street near Mill Street.

This view, looking east on Main Street before the Civil War, shows the old Phoenix Hotel on the southeast corner of Main and Limestone. Photo courtesy of Transylvania University.

hospitality of the Kentuckians, however, as thoughtful visitors dropped in to see how he was recuperating. Professor Hedge was quite surprised to find how well educated the Lexington women were, and thought the female schools in Lexington better than those in Boston.

Kentucky's First Railroad

Travelers arriving by stagecoach in the mid-1830's would have been fascinated in their walks around town to see the beginnings of a form of transportation that eventually would render the stagecoach obsolete — the railroad. In the desperate search for an efficient form of overland transportation to meet the competition from cheap riverboat traffic, Lexington found its options limited. Though this was a period of great canal building throughout the nation, Lexington's topographical location made this choice unworkable. An excellent road system in

1830 looked to be decades away, especially as President Jackson's veto of the Maysville Road bill sealed off the flow of federal funds for highway construction. But the nascent railroad movement in America, already materializing along the Atlantic seaboard at Charleston and Baltimore, excited the Lexington merchants. Here, perhaps, was the lifeline to the Ohio River they needed.

The project caused heated controversy. Communities which might be bypassed by the new railroad clamored that it was unwise, premature, too costly, and open to monopolistic control, but the proponents moved ahead. The Lexington and Ohio Railroad Company — Kentucky's first railroad — was incorporated in January 1830 with authority to construct a railroad from Lexington to one or more points on the Ohio River. Louisville was eventually chosen as the Ohio River outlet. The majority of the directors were from Lexington, and

50

within five days after the books were opened for stock subscriptions in March, $932,900 of stock was bought by individuals in and near Lexington. The remaining $400,000 was subscribed by Elisha I. Winter and his wealthy associates. Elected as directors in addition to Winter were Elisha Warfield, John W. Hunt, John Brand, Henry C. Payne, James Bruen, Richard Higgins, Walter Dunn, Benjamin Dudley, Henry Clay, Benjamin Gratz, and George Boswell. Winter was the first president, succeeded by Gratz. Professor Thomas J. Mathews of Transylvania was employed to make the preliminary survey of the topography between Lexington and Louisville via Frankfort, but teaching duties interrupted his survey and two engineers were hired to complete the study. The report was encouraging, indicating that few major obstacles confronted construction of the road.

On October 22, 1831, a grand parade was formed at Transylvania. General Leslie Combs was marshal, followed by Governor Metcalfe and representatives of practically every organization in the city. They marched down Mill Street to Water Street accompanied by the sounds of tolling bells and gun salutes. Here Mr. Winter handed a hammer to Governor Metcalfe who drove the first spike, after which Professor Caldwell of the Transylvania Medical Department delivered an address. The great project was underway, and with it the hopes of Lexington's economic resurgence.

It was an odd-looking railroad. Instead of the familiar wooden ties laid crosswise on which T-shaped molded steel rails are laid and spiked, this road was made of long, narrow blocks of limestone laid end to end, parallel to the route. Holes were drilled in the sills and thin strips of iron were spiked to them. The first cars were horse-drawn. On August 15, 1832, Governor Metcalfe returned to ride the first stretch of a mile and a half, and everyone marveled that one horse could pull forty passengers as easily as one carriage.

By the following March the first six miles had been completed. A right of way in Woodford County was purchased through the 216-acre farm of Colonel John Francisco, who became so outraged when the company built a fill in front of his house, obstructing his view,

that he sold his entire farm to the railroad company. Since this farm was halfway between Lexington and Frankfort, the company built there a small town called Midway, and named the streets for its directors.

On January 31, 1834, the railroad reached Frankfort and a grand ball was held at the Phoenix Hotel. The steam engine used on the road in 1833 was designed and built by Barlow and Bruen in Lexington and was a strange-looking contraption which broke down frequently and was incapable of carrying heavy loads. Horses were used again until replaced by engines bought in the East. The first one was called *Nottaway,* and a later one christened *Logan.* These successfully increased the speed to Frankfort, reducing the traveling time from four to two hours. The sharp descent into Frankfort was a hair-raising experience for the

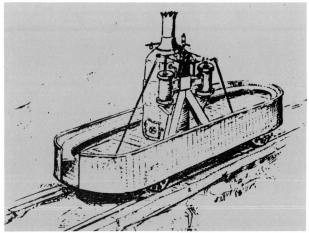

Rough sketches of first locomotive and early passenger car on the Lexington and Ohio Railroad, ca. 1835, from The Register *of the Kentucky State Historical Society. This was Kentucky's first railroad.*

Lexington and Ohio Railroad Depot built in 1835 at Water and Mill streets. The third story was added in the 1850's. The first railroad depot built west of the Allegheny Mountains, the building was razed in 1959. Photo courtesy of University of Kentucky.

weak-hearted, so for an extra fee one could take a carriage at the top of the hill and ride more leisurely and safely into town.

The railroad — soon to be known as the Lexington & Frankfort Railroad as construction from Louisville was delayed — began to encounter severe technical problems. The stone sills cracked under the weight of the engines and cars, and from weather changes. This weakened the spikes holding the rail strips which then pulled loose and disconcertingly curled up to form "snakeheads." These wrapped themselves around the wheels or smashed through the flooring of the cars. Derailments and injuries resulted. Added to these difficulties were the poor management and financial indebtedness that resulted in the company being sold at public auction to the state. Under new management and additional financing in the 1840's and 1850's, the road was entirely rebuilt with red cedar strings and T-shaped rails from England. A new route to circumvent the Frankfort descent was laid out, using a gentler approach and a tunnel to reach the capital.

Meanwhile, the Louisville to Frankfort section was completed in 1852 and the dream of a railroad connection with Louisville became a reality. In Lexington a need to shelter passengers and freight led to the building of a depot by John McMurtry in 1835 at Mill and Water streets. Unique for its time, the structure was a long, narrow "two-story brick building with a series of French doors below, permitting easy access to and from the trains. This feature made the structure one of the most advanced designs of its period . . . " Later, a third story was added and this depot served the public until the Union Station replaced it in 1908.

Lexington's City Government

Tensions between town and county governments were rife throughout Kentucky, especially in the larger towns like Lexington, which felt themselves hamstrung and ruled by a county government indifferent to urban needs and often dominated by members of a different political party. To resolve this conflict,

Lexingtonians, tired of seeking piecemeal solutions through scores of special legislative acts, successfully persuaded the General Assembly to pass on December 7, 1831, "An Act to Incorporate the City of Lexington." This not only replaced the trustees with a mayor and twelve councilmen, provided city taxpayers immunity from county taxes, and gave city officials almost complete independence in running their own affairs, but established a city court with the mayor as the chief judicial officer.

The combining of an executive office with a judicial office raised serious constitutional problems, and county residents, especially farmers doing business in the city, chafing under new city regulations, challenged the charter in the courts. The provision establishing the City Court of Lexington was found unconstitutional in 1835. Lexingtonians then secured a constitutional amendment validating the court, after which the county residents attempted to have the entire city charter repealed. Compromise between the contenders finally resulted in preserving the charter. Amendments were passed, creating a separate judge for the City Court and returning the responsibilities of chief executive to the mayor, removing civil matters from the City Court's jurisdiction, and restoring the ward system of representation to the city council.

Confined to an area one mile in radius from the courthouse, the government had been wrestling with a variety of problems common to all towns. The greatest difficulty was getting enough money to meet community needs because the authority and taxing powers of these young city governments were specified by state statutes. This restricted local officials who were constantly petitioning the General Assembly for expanded powers.

In addition to the problems of clearing and paving streets, building storm drains, sinking wells, erecting pumps, and constructing market houses, the trustees had to deal with fire and police protection.

Fire was an ever-present danger to every town from early colonial days. The tendency to place wooden structures with rickety, inflammable chimneys close together created ideal conditions for destructive fires. Early ordinances attempted to prevent such dangers,

banning all wooden chimneys, and requiring them to be built of brick or stone, but effective enforcement took years. Meanwhile, the threat of fire hovered over all. A Lexington city ordinance of 1806 required Lexington householders to buy and have easily available fire buckets, the number dependent on the value of the property. All free male inhabitants were required to help fight fires.

Formal fire-fighting organization began in 1790 with the creation of Lexington's first fire company, the "Union Company," at the instigation of John Bradford, who became secretary of the company. He worked zealously to expand membership and equipment of what was doubtless one of the earliest organizations of its kind in the Ohio River valley. Later, other fire-fighting organizations were established and a healthy rivalry developed among them in the promptness with which they responded to fires. Headquarters of the Union Company was first on Main Street near Mill, later moving to Water Street near the old police station. But these were private companies, not owned, operated, and financed by the town. Equipment was primitive, consisting of buckets, ladders, and hooks with which to pull down burning structures to prevent the fire from spreading.

In 1818 the town trustees purchased two small newly invented engines. These may have been water storage carts supplied with water by a bucket brigade, with a cylinder and pistons that were manually pumped. These wagons were either horse drawn or pulled by volunteers called "vamps." Later crude leather hose was used, heavily oiled to assure pliability and to prevent water absorption — guaranteed to ruin the clothes of anyone coming in contact with it!

Two Fire Companies

The Kentucky legislature in 1830 authorized creation of two Lexington fire companies of not over seventy-five members. The city began to organize a municipal fire department, but still primarily depended on the Union Fire Company and the later Independent Fire Company. Shortly thereafter, the operators of the Union Fire Company's engine — the "Lyon" — organized an additional company called the Lyon Fire Company. (This company had an engine house at 149 South Limestone Street.) By 1842 the city had three companies under the general supervision of a city supervisor. These three companies appeared prominently at public celebrations and in parades, their engines elaborately decorated and the firemen decked out in uniforms of red shirts, white pants, and red firemen's hats.

State laws of 1798 against arson were severe, providing prison sentences of five to twelve years of hard labor for burning private structures, and seven to twelve years for public buildings. Slaves committing arson were executed.

One of the more significant fires affecting all of Fayette County did not occur in downtown Lexington but on the farm of Levi Todd, the county clerk, on January 31, 1803, destroying priceless early records including land claims. Some of the partially burnt records were saved and carefully copied.

Three major fires endangered Lexington in 1812. Two of them, of conflagration proportions, were incendiary in origin. All the arsonists were black. The one who set fire to Tibbatt's Soap & Candle Factory was hanged. The two who confessed to torching John Wesley Hunt's bagging factory were reprieved by the governor as they stood on the gallows.

Losses from fires motivated the General Assembly in 1811 to charter the Kentucky Mutual Assistance Society to insure buildings and property against fire damage. This fire insurance company was organized in Lexington in March 1812, and appointed agents throughout central Kentucky.

The antebellum period saw a dramatic fire on Short Street in 1819 that spread from Murphy's stable to adjacent buildings including Luke Usher's tavern and the county jail. Other notable fires of this time destroyed Postlethwait's tavern in 1820; Transylvania's main building in 1829; the Grand Masonic Hall on West Main in 1836; and Transylvania's Medical Hall on the northwest corner of Second and Broadway in 1863. The post-Civil War period would see even larger and more devastating fires.

Crime and violence were common to most communities and Lexington was no exception. The town government was given certain police powers by an Act of the General Assembly of Virginia when the town was established. The earliest police force consisted of a night watchman, then enlarged to include a city marshal and watchmen in 1832. The marshal's salary was $300 a year and his four night watchmen received a total of $1,300. An assistant was employed on Sundays for $1 a day to assist in dispersing loafers on street corners.

Of all the western urban centers, Louisville and Lexington were in the forefront in the use of public funds for police organization and in the maintenance of regular watchmen on the streets. This was due, in part, to the fact that Kentucky was a slave state. The need to control .the slaves and free blacks in a town where, as in the case of Lexington, they composed a sizable portion of the population, accounted for the use of night watchmen. In 1800, the trustees passed a resolution:

> Whereas, there is an assemblage of negroes in Lexington on the Sabbath day, and they have become troublesome to the citizens, a committee composed of John Hull and Robert Campbell, appointed to secure a watchman.

George and Jacob Sowerbright were "allowed thirteen pounds, for serving sixteen days as watchman and patrolman . . . " Peter Carter and George Sowerbright were later appointed watchmen for $26 a month. "They to parade at least three nights in the week from 9 o'clock to six in the morning." The watchmen were authorized by an 1810 ordinance to call upon any citizen to assist them in apprehending criminals, any person refusing such assistance to be fined from $3 to $10.

Not long after, the town was divided into five districts for purposes of police supervision and the personnel was doubled. A watch-house was built on the northwest end of the engine house on the public square. Since it contained an underground story of stone, it obviously was to serve as a temporary detention center as well. Police activity in the county was minimal until the antislavery agitation of the 1830's, when the increase of runaway slaves, and slave unrest and rebellion, resulted in county patrols being established and heavily repressive measures instituted.

Unruly blacks, however, were not the only targets of police activity. Horse thieves were regarded as dastardly criminals as were arsonists and counterfeiters. In 1795 the *Gazette* reported that one such man "was

The Lexington police station was located on Water Street during a major part of the 19th century. This group of policemen was photographed in front of the station in the latter part of the century. Photo courtesy of Transylvania University.

executed in this town for horse stealing, agreeable to sentence of late court of Oyer and Terminer." He had been pardoned for a similar crime a year before but apparently would not mend his ways.

Nor is it surprising to find the world's oldest profession operating in Lexington. On December 23, 1797, "a complaint was lodged by Nathaniel Barker that the house occupied by Free Nancy, being the property of Jacob Kizer, is a disorderly house and that on that account may thusly be deemed a nuisance." Mr. Kizer was ordered to remove said nuisance, and Free Nancy had to find other quarters to ply her trade.

Lexington led the way in trying to combat crime through better street lighting. In 1812 the trustees decided to erect twenty street lamps in town, five of them on Main Street. Samuel Trotter was sent to Philadelphia to study their street lamps, long known to be some of the nation's best, thanks to the improved design made decades earlier by Benjamin Franklin. Free oil was offered to any citizen providing his own street lamp.

Jails were erected almost as soon as Lexington began. On March 20, 1780, the trustees provided funds not only to build a courthouse but a jail as well. It was a log hut located west of Broadway on the north side of Main Street. A large, strong jail was not believed necessary at this time since sentences were mostly public and physical rather than consisting of long terms of confinement, which were costly. A whipping-post, stocks, pillory, and gallows were the most common devices. A locust whipping-post, one foot in diameter, became a familiar landmark. It was first located near the log jail and later moved to the rear of the courthouse. Public floggings were common, and the cries of the victims could easily be heard for some distance. Other quick punishments included branding. In 1798, Fayette Circuit Court records show that a preacher was found guilty of stealing another man's saddle. Under the Acts of the General Assembly, he claimed his right to choose the punishment, to be burned in the hand, and this was done before the jury.

A second jail, made of stone, 32 feet long and 25 feet wide, was constructed in 1790 on the west side of Limestone above Short Street.

It was obviously not very secure as many prisoners escaped, so another was erected on the same location in 1797. When fire destroyed this one in 1819, a much larger, stronger, two-story jail of stone and brick was constructed. This formidable-looking structure on the northwest corner of Limestone and Short streets, named after Thomas B. Megowan, the jailer for many years, was used until 1891.

A carry-over from British practices was seen in the establishment of a workhouse near Megowan's jail. In 1835 a poorhouse was combined with the workhouse and the joint establishment was housed in buildings on Bolivar Street, where it remained for thirty-five years until the poorhouse was moved to the county.

The Dark Strain of Violence

Violence, though by no means an American monopoly, was woven into the warp and woof

Cover of a published edition (1858) of the so-called "Code Duello." Photo from Famous Kentucky Duels *by J. Winston Coleman, Jr.*

of the American experience. The obvious crimes of murder, robbery, rape, and arson were the main targets of state and local statutes, which provided for arrests, court trials, sentences, and punishments. But the vicious brawls that occurred in frontier communities seemed particularly frequent in Kentucky, and new forms of brutality learned from the Indians were quickly adopted by the white man. Countless brawls marked the march westward between men whose perpetual encounter with an untamed wilderness and Indians may well have kept violence close to the surface. At camps, at taverns, at barbecues and dances, as the raw whiskey began to flow, anger was easily fueled by a few words, a look, or an unintended action viewed as an insult, and the knives would be quickly bared. Or, frequently, there was hand-to-hand wrestling as the sweating, cursing contestants rolled on the ground, battering one another with their fists, chewing off parts of ears and noses, and viciously gouging out eyes. How many such brawls occurred in Lexington taverns, or on court days, urged on — even wagered on — by enthusiastic spectators, we will never know. How many such combats were broken up by the town watch is uncertain. Many were allowed to take their course. In 1820, Adlard Welby, an English visitor, was shocked to find a cultured center such as Lexington with so many dirks for sale.

The elite had for a long time structured their violent encounters in the formal ritual of dueling. The 18th century use of the rapier was gradually replaced by the dueling pistol as the quality of craftsmanship of these firearms improved. Moreover, the use of dueling pistols required far less skill and training, and individuals whose lack of swordsmanship might have disqualified them from engaging in a duel, were more inclined to resort to the pistol.

Books on codes of honor and proper rules for sending challenges, responding to challenges, and arranging for a duel were available to the uninitiated. One such brief manual printed as late as 1858, when dueling was outlawed in most states, was entitled *The Code of Honor; or Rules for the Government of Principals and Seconds in Dueling* by John L. Wilson and was reprinted in J. Winston Coleman's *Famous Kentucky Duels* (1969). This mode of resolving

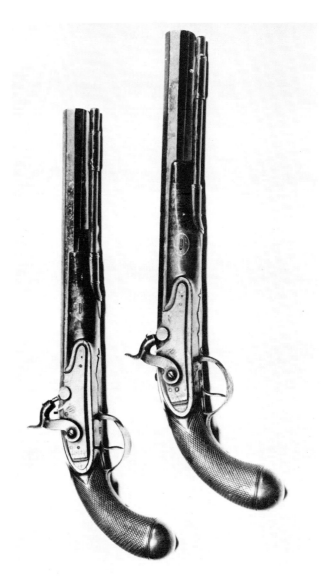

Pair of dueling pistols of the type used in the early 1800's. Photo courtesy of Transylvania University.

conflicts was especially popular in the Western and Southern states.

If Lexingtonians had any qualms as to the morality or acceptability of dueling, they received some justification from the fact that their most famous citizen, Henry Clay, engaged in the activity. His first duel was with Humphrey Marshall in January 1809. These two political opponents, sharply divided over the Jeffersonian embargo, actually came to ungentlemanly blows in the Kentucky House during a heated debate, until separated by General Riffe, a powerfully-built representative from Lincoln County. Clay sent Marshall a written challenge which was accepted and the designated seconds made the necessary arrangements. To avoid breaking the Kentucky law against dueling, they met in Indiana across the Ohio River from Louisville. Neither man was a crack shot! It took three rounds at ten paces (thirty feet) before Marshall wounded Clay in the thigh, though not seriously, and he was back in the House within three weeks.

Some years later, Clay wrote a friend that he feared that "in spite of all efforts of Legislation, we shall go on to fight in single combat, and go on to condemn the practice." Like many of his contemporaries, he did not have the courage to abandon the code of "the duello," though he might condemn it. In 1826, while Secretary of State under President John Quincy Adams, he was so infuriated by the virulent verbal attacks of the eccentric John Randolph, U. S. Senator from Virginia, that he challenged him to meet on the field of honor. Fortunately, neither was injured after two exchanges, and reconciliation was achieved.

Dr. Benjamin Dudley and Dr. Daniel Drake became involved in a controversy over an autopsy performed by Dudley on an Irishman killed in a quarrel. Drake made remarks reflecting unfavorably on Dudley's professional abilities and a heated controversy resulted. Dudley, who must have been unusually provoked, challenged Drake to a duel, an act quite contrary to Dudley's usually calm behavior. Drake refused the challenge but a young colleague and friend of Drake's, Dr. William Richardson, also of the Transylvania Medical Department, apparently felt compelled to pick up the gauntlet and act as Drake's substitute. On an August morning in 1818, the two confronted one another on a field not far from Lexington. Neither was a skilled marksman, and Richardson missed Dudley completely while the surgeon's bullet, somewhat off target, wounded Richardson in the groin, severing the inguinal artery. The young man would have rapidly bled to death had Dudley not rushed over and, after asking Richardson's permission, placed his thumb over the ilium and thus gave time for a ligature to be applied. The two were lifelong friends from that moment.

Dueling continued in the central Kentucky area until after the Civil War. The Danville *Central Kentucky Gazette* reported on July 31, 1867, that two young men fought a duel over a girl and shot each other to death.

Cassius Marcellus Clay, scion of a distinguished Madison County family and a distant cousin of Henry's, aroused considerable hostility because of his antislavery views and frequently found himself in contentious circumstances which he preferred to resolve by hand-to-hand combat, wielding his favorite weapon, the bowie knife, with great dexterity and devastating effect. In this respect he was a maverick in the dueling class.

Physical encounters were not the only manifestation of violence in the antebellum period. It was also a period of intense verbal violence. Political campaigning released torrents of vituperation that would not be tolerated today. Speakers on the campaign trail and editors crusading for their candidates invoked scorching epithets to denounce or characterize their opponents. This, in turn, provoked physical violence. Depending on whether an aggrieved party regarded a newspaper editor as a gentleman or not, he might descend on the editor with a cane, or challenge him to a duel.

Clay Defends Wickliffe

One of the most sensational incidents involving newspaper editors in Lexington occurred in 1829. Robert Wickliffe was running for the legislature against John McCalla. A defamatory article about Wickliffe appeared under a pseudonym (McCalla was probably the author) in the *Kentucky Gazette* of which Thomas Benning was the editor. Though "Duke" Wickliffe took it in stride, his son Charles, just turned twenty-one, took offense at the article, and armed with a pistol, stormed into the *Gazette* office demanding of Benning the name of the author. Benning refused, and the infuriated Wickliffe advanced upon the editor, who raised his cane to defend himself, and shot and killed him.

The trial of Charles Wickliffe took place in the courthouse, a three-story brick building with a cupola and spire, built in 1806 by Lexington's most talented builders, Hallet Winslow and Luther Stephens with plans by David Sutton. Pictures of the old structure show a pleasing exterior, but the interior apparently was less attractive and Clay himself said that "the miserable building [was] ... the disgrace of the town and the derision of

Glendower, home of the prominent Wickliffe and Preston families, erected about 1820, was located on Second Street, west of Jefferson. Photo courtesy of Transylvania University.

everybody." Within its gloomy interior the masterful defense attorney gave some of his greatest performances. This case was no exception. John J. Crittenden and Clay defended Charles Wickliffe and Clay's oratory so bewitched the jury with its theme of the natural right of self-defense that the jury returned within five minutes with a verdict of acquittal.

In October 1829, Charles Wickliffe again took umbrage at something George Trotter, Benning's successor, had printed and challenged Trotter to a duel. The editor wounded Wickliffe who was carried to Glendower, his father's residence on West Second Street, where he died within a few hours.

Though cloaked in the garb of honor and chivalry, such violence hardly enhanced Lexington's image as a cultured and civilized society.

The Eastern Lunatic Asylum

Despite a massive indifference to public education, there was a rising social consciousness both in the state and Lexington. The General Assembly abolished imprisonment for debt in 1821, ten years before New York. Kentucky was also one of the most progressive

states in the reduction of the number of crimes for which capital punishment could be imposed. It was somewhat slower in providing adequate prison accommodations as the first penitentiary built in Frankfort in 1799 soon became heavily overcrowded.

Lexington was the location, however, of the second hospital for the insane in the United States, the first being established in Williamsburg, Virginia, in 1773. It was founded in 1816 under the name of the "Fayette Hospital" for the purpose of accommodating "lunatics and other distempered and sick poor of Fayette." Andrew McCalla was the main leader in its organization with support from almost every major figure in town. Property for this purpose was purchased on West Fourth Street near Newtown Pike known as the "Sinking Spring" property, on which, as the name implied, a huge spring existed. The cornerstone of the building was laid on June 30, 1817, with a ceremony which included an oration by Henry Clay. Unfortunately, the financial crisis of 1819 struck just about the time the building was nearly completed, and there not being adequate funds to operate it, the directors offered the structure to the state, which purchased it, naming the institution the

Eastern Lunatic Asylum. The asylum was formally opened May 1, 1824, and a special commission of ten men screened all applicants, making sure they were of unsound mind. A Negro woman, named Charity, was the first patient to be admitted. Patients were classified according to their mental conditions and provided with adequate food, clothing, and recreation. An English visitor in 1835 toured the asylum and commented that it was "conducted with regularity and cleanliness, as well as with a praiseworthy attention to all the comforts of which the unfortunate inmates are capable." Of special interest were the applications for admission of individuals who presumably became overwrought at religious revivals and needed some type of confinement or therapy.

The institution had its problems as occasional fires destroyed some of the facilities and killed a few patients. Epidemics such as the cholera of 1833, and especially that of 1849, caused many deaths, and the custodial concept of treatment led to widespread use of chains and other restraints.

In 1844, a more enlightened policy and administration were introduced under the superintendence of Dr. John R. Allen, a member of the Transylvania Medical Department, and his successor, Dr. W. S. Chipley, who remained until 1869. This period was sometimes referred to as the "golden age" of the institution in the 19th century.

The so-called "moral treatment" was introduced at this time, based on the philosophy that the insane should be treated with as much dignity and gentleness and as little force as possible. The use of physical restraints such as chains and straitjackets was reduced, and, whenever possible, patients were given work assignments, recreational activities, and religious services. Restoration was the aim, and by the end of Chipley's term, one out of every three had been released. Chaplains were used sporadically from 1842 on, until the Reverend William Pratt, one of Lexington's outstanding Baptist preachers and the writer of an invaluable diary, began to visit on a regular basis in the 1850's. He recalled the visit in 1847 of Dorothea Dix, the remarkable Massachusetts woman who almost single-handedly brought about major reforms in the care of the insane in her home state. Even though he noted that most of the patients, while orderly and attentive, had vacant looks, indicating their inability to follow his discourse, he nevertheless faithfully visited the asylum and preached. On one memorable Fourth of July celebration at the institution during which "one of the crazy folks read the Declaration of Independence," Pratt recorded a toast one of the patients made at dinner: "General Jackson, the Hero of New Orleans, when he died he kicked the devil out of the way and walked straight up to heaven."

Eastern State Hospital, founded 1846, then known as Eastern Lunatic Asylum, the second oldest mental institution in the United States. The hospital still operates at its original location at Fourth Street and Newtown Pike. Photo courtesy of Clyde T. Burke.

Morton School, named for William "Lord" Morton, who was an early financial supporter of public education in Lexington. Located at the southeast corner of Walnut and Short streets, it was erected in 1849 and demolished in 1908. Photo courtesy of Transylvania University.

Public and Private Education

Unwilling to levy a tax for public schools, the Kentucky legislature had salved its conscience by first donating public lands to the counties in the late 1790's and early 1800's for the establishment of county academies, many of which either never materialized or existed only briefly, and hardly served as true public schools. In 1821, the legislature provided that the profits derived from the Bank of Kentucky should constitute a "literary fund" as a basis for a general school system, which likewise failed. Despite this, some counties, such as Bourbon, had made substantial progress in providing schooling of various kinds. In 1829, the legislature appointed President Alva Woods of Transylvania and the Reverend Benjamin O. Peers, an educator and founder of the Peers' Eclectic Institute on West Second Street, to prepare a report. This report so accurately delineated Kentucky's pitiful educational situation that an education convention was held in Lexington in November 1833, which drafted plans for a statewide common school system. A state "common school society" was founded in February 1834, with Governor John Breathitt as its first president, but the state looked to the federal government for funds.

Beginning in the 1830's in Lexington, slow progress toward a much-needed public educational system was made. Mayor Hunt appointed a committee to study "some plan for the education of the poor children of the city." Before results were forthcoming, the cholera plague had left so many children destitute that an Orphan Asylum was established through private means. The city also felt some responsibility for these children, thus giving impetus to the opening of a "common" or public school. The city trustees were offered the old Rankin Church building on the southeast corner of Walnut and Short streets, and on March 1, 1834, this first city school was opened with 107 pupils, housed in the solid log structure (probably clapboarded by then) under the watchful eye of its principal, Joseph Gayle, assisted by his daughter. The trustees appointed a school committee consisting of James O. Harrison, William A. Leavy, and Thomas Hart.

In 1836, William Morton, or "Lord" Morton as he was sometimes called, died and left a legacy of over $12,000, about one-third of his estate, for the school which was named Morton School, or City School No. 1. A new building replaced the old log structure in 1849. That same year, City School No. 2, named after James Harrison, head of the school committee, was erected on Main Street, west of Jefferson, and still stands. In 1851, No. 3 school, named for Dr. Benjamin Dudley, was started in a former residence at the northeast corner of Mill and Maxwell streets. Overcrowding in this school two years later necessitated the use of a small cottage adjacent to the old Maxwell cemetery on Bolivar Street as an annex, later called Davidson School. This was closed when a large, imposing structure replaced the old Dudley School in 1881.

Meanwhile in Fayette County, several districts were operating schools, including those on Georgetown Road, Bryan Station Pike, Tates Creek Pike, Richmond Road, and Spurr Road near Greendale. There were doubtless others as some 41 county school districts existed in 1871, but the districts were as small as the schools, and records fragmentary.

By 1853, some 1,378 pupils were enrolled in public schools. A greater degree of egalitarianism existed in the educational climate, and families from all walks of life could meet to share the schools' festivities, processions, and closing exercises.

Meanwhile, the state, feeling financially flush from receiving funds from the one and only federal surplus distribution in 1837, appropriated some $850,000 to school use, and by setting guidelines for its distribution sketched out the foundation of the state's school system, headed by a superintendent of education. One of the most prominent superintendents was the Reverend Robert J. Breckinridge, at one time pastor of the First Presbyterian Church, who persuaded the constitutional convention of 1849 to include provisions for public schools in the new constitution. By the time of the Civil War, schools had been established in every county, with the state obligated to pay each district a fixed amount and the local districts authorized to impose a school tax.

Unlike some other states, Kentucky never passed legislation forbidding the instruction of slaves to read and write. Religious instruction provided by the churches was favored by slaveowners who believed it to be beneficial in keeping slaves moral and happy. Transylvania University permitted the use of one of its rooms in 1816 to allow a women's group to instruct black females. In 1830 a white man from Tennessee enrolled 30 black children in a Lexington school but apparently this did not last long. No attempt was made to include them in the public school system.

Private schools did not disappear in Lexington, however. St. Catherine's Academy flourished, as did the additional Catholic schools of St. John's and St. Paul's. Samuel D. McCullough was principal of a female academy on Market Street. The Misses Jackson opened a boarding and day school for young ladies in 1848 under the auspices of the Episcopal Church.

The private school that proved to be one of the most successful and permanent was that founded by David A. Sayre, November 1, 1854, in a large house on the northeast corner of Mill and Church streets, first called the Transylvania Female Seminary. A year later, the school, renamed the Sayre Female Institute, was moved to the Edward P. Johnson mansion on North Limestone, north of Pleasant Stone.

In its gleaming white Morrison Hall, Transylvania University continued to struggle with the depressed enrollment in its liberal arts department. A succession of presidents, including Holley's arch critic, the dedicated Presbyterian divine, Robert Davidson, failed to resuscitate the school, so the trustees made an arrangement with the Methodist Episcopal Church of Kentucky in 1842 to operate the school, though the Medical and Law departments were to continue to function independently. The energetic and forceful Reverend Henry Bidleman Bascom was recruited from the faltering Methodist Augusta College in Kentucky to serve as president. Within a year, the enrollment soared tenfold, exceeding even that of the Holley years. Unfortunately, this resurgence was short-lived as Bascom became involved in the fierce struggle within the Methodist Church over the slavery issue, and was one of the leaders in the formation of the Methodist Episcopal Church, South, formally established in Louisville in

1845. His failing health, tensions within his marriage, and involvement in church affairs reduced Bascom's effectiveness as president. Meanwhile, the Methodists became disenchanted with their educational experiment at Transylvania, especially since they had no legal control of the university. Funds began to dwindle, and formal ties with the school terminated in 1850. Various attempts to strengthen the school, such as making it the first normal school in the state to train teachers for the public schools, lasted only a year or two and its future appeared dim as the Civil War began.

The Medical and Law departments seemed immune from the adversities confronting the liberal arts department, but trouble was brewing. A number of the Medical faculty, increasingly frustrated by the lack of a significant hospital in town and the difficulty of securing enough cadavers for anatomical dissection (grave-robbing being the main source), looked longingly at the booming river town of Louisville with its rapidly expanding population, hospitals, and a sufficient number of dead drifters and paupers to meet the cadaver need. When Louisville launched its Medical Institute in 1837 and invited any interested Transylvania faculty to join its ranks, the controversy already boiling within the Medical Department erupted into public view. Lexington, alarmed at seeing doctors Caldwell, Yandell, Cooke, and Short leave for Louisville, rallied around their prestigious medical school. A group of 100 private individuals formed the Transylvania Institute in 1838, pledging $100 a year each for five years. The city followed suit by appropriating $70,000 to Transylvania, with $45,000 to go to the Medical Department. Of this, $30,000 was used to erect a splendid building, designed and built by John McMurtry on the northwest corner of North Broadway and Second. Drs. Peter and Bush used the remaining $15,000 to purchase books and apparatus in Philadelphia, England, and France to supplement, update, and enrich their already excellent resources.

These efforts stemmed the decline of the Medical Department for over a decade, but eventually the competition from both Louisville and Cincinnati medical schools proved insurmountable. The remarkable Transylvania medical school closed its doors in 1859 after having taught 6,456 students and graduated 1,881 doctors to minister to the medical needs of the nation, especially in the South and the Southwest.

The Law Department also began to decline in the 1850's until only Judge George Robertson remained, and this department ceased to function in 1858. Unlike the Medical Department, law instruction was resumed on the Lexington campus after the Civil War.

Growth of the Churches

The impact of revivalism in the areas surrounding Lexington around the turn of the century, previously noted, began to affect the urban churches as the influence of the 18th century rationalism and liberalism began to fade. Indeed, Horace Holley's resignation in 1826 from Transylvania, while primarily caused by legislative and gubernatorial hostility, reflected the growing religious orthodoxy of that day. The First Presbyterian Church on North Broadway prospered under such forceful ministers as the Reverend Nathan Hall, whose powerful revival in 1828 aided in the churches' assault on infidelity. In 1857, a new building was erected on the same site, and the congregation worshipped there until 1870 when they sold it to the Christian Church and moved into the present structure, which was designed by Cincinnatus Shryock in 1872 at 174 North Mill Street.

Another Presbyterian Church was organized in 1815 by remnants of Rankin's old congregation and others attracted by the preaching of the Reverend James McChord. A church was built on Market Street, just a few doors north of Christ Church. Here McChord created such a following that after his premature death in 1820 at age 35, they named the church after him and interred his remains beneath the pulpit. In 1828, the name of the church was changed to Second Presbyterian, and the Reverend Robert Davidson preached here for eight years before assuming the presidency of Transylvania. A new edifice designed by Major Thomas Lewinski and built by John McMurtry on the same site was dedicated in 1847, McChord's remains still being preserved beneath the pulpit.

Just down the street, the Episcopal Church built in 1814 was being replaced by a new structure designed by the busy Major Lewinski,

Christ Church, Episcopal, at Market and Church streets, designed by Thomas Lewinski and built by John McMurtry in 1846-48. Drawing from The Church Record, New York, 1897.

who was introducing the neo-Gothic style more frequently into his work.

In October 1830, Benjamin Bosworth Smith, a graduate of Brown University, who was to become one of the most influential Episcopalians in antebellum Kentucky, arrived in Lexington with his wife and four small children, having somewhat reluctantly left his native Rhode Island and Philadelphia to assume a missionary role as rector of Christ Church. In 1832, he was elected the first bishop for the Diocese of Kentucky, and shortly thereafter established a much-needed seminary in Lexington, which was formally chartered in 1834. The property formerly used by the

Reverend Benjamin Peers for his Eclectic Institute on West Second Street was purchased to house the new seminary.

Smith became a storm center of controversy when certain dissenters in the church found fault with him on various counts, including what they thought to be improper handling of finances. This led to a so-called trial in September 1837 in Lexington that aroused considerable local interest and passions. Smith was acquitted of all charges, however, and he continued his work in the Diocese.

Around the corner from Christ Church on the north side of Church Street, between Limestone and Upper streets, was the large, two-story brick Methodist Church, built in 1822 and dedicated by Bishop Enoch George. The congregation moved to a new church on High Street in 1841. Independent Methodists met in St. John's Chapel, built in 1821 on the north side of West Main east of Spring Street, led by the eccentric and independent Dr. Caleb Cloud, but this group eventually disbanded.

After early dissension over the emancipationist issue had split the original congregation, the Baptists re-formed in 1817, meeting in the chapel of Transylvania University until their own church, built on North Mill facing the college campus, was completed in 1819 with Dr. James Fishback as pastor. Fishback became attracted to the newly developing Christian Church and he and a few of his adherents left. Later, the Baptists erected a Gothic Revival building a block south on the east side of North Mill Street, two doors north of Church Street. The Reverend William Pratt was pastor of the congregation when it first occupied the new church in 1855, which, tragically, went up in flames in 1859 in a fire caused by sparks from a nearby burning livery stable.

The decision was made to return to their historic first site, the old burying ground on West Main, and John McMurtry was hired to construct the new church. It was dedicated January 1, 1860, but the incredible streak of bad luck had not yet run out. Fire destroyed the new structure in 1863, and its replacement burned down in 1867. It would not have been surprising if the Book of Job had become the regular topic for Sunday sermons. However, the 1868 structure survived until 1913.

The Catholics, having worshiped in their Gothic chapel on Third Street since 1812, moved to more spacious quarters in 1837. This was St. Peter Church, designed and built by John McMurtry in an interesting hybrid of Gothic and Greek Revival styles, located on North Limestone Street, north of Constitution. An even larger edifice, St. Paul Church, was designed by Cincinnati architects on West Short Street, and this church, with its towering spire, was dedicated with impressive services in 1868.

Probably the most unusual religious development at this time was the emergence of the Christian Church in Lexington and surrounding areas. The Reverend Barton Stone, a former Presbyterian minister who had become

Main Street Christian Church, located west of the Harrison Avenue Viaduct, was completed in 1842. The congregation moved in 1894 and became the Central Christian Church, which is now located at Short and Walnut streets. The old building used for shows and other events, was torn down in 1903. Drawing from George W. Ranck's Review of Lexington, Kentucky, *1887.*

the main figure in the 1801 Cane Ridge revival that blotted out denominational attachments and led to his separation from the Presbyterian fold, had been preaching in Lexington and throughout the central Bluegrass area. Stone settled in Lexington in 1815 and organized a group of adherents. At the same time, Alexander Campbell of western Virginia, preaching the same message but calling his adherents Disciples of Christ, visited Lexington. Services were held in the houses of the members. As these two groups began to move closer together, they were joined by the group Dr. Fishback led out of the Mill Street Baptist Church, and they acquired a former cotton factory on Hill (High) Street to which they built an addition and dedicated it in 1831. Here a year later the Stone movement and the Campbell movement united to form the Christian Church (Disciples of Christ).

As the Hill Street Church prospered under the dynamic leadership of Dr. L. L. Pinkerton, the congregation outgrew its facility, and built

Former building of Pleasant Green Baptist Church at West High and Patterson streets. The church adopted the name Pleasant Green in 1829. Photo courtesy of Pleasant Green Baptist Church.

the Main Street Christian Church in 1842 on the south side of the street just west of the present Harrison Avenue viaduct. This impressive structure with its recessed portico and two Doric columns was a familiar landmark on Main Street until it was razed in 1903. The congregation had moved in 1893 to its present building at the northeast corner of Walnut and Short streets, where once the Masonic Grand Lodge Hall had stood.

In November 1843, at the Main Street Christian Church, Henry Clay presided over a debate between the Reverend Nathan Rice, a Presbyterian minister from Paris, and Alexander Campbell, which lasted for several weeks and centered on the issues of baptism, the spirit of God, and human creeds. Arousing a great deal of community interest, the debate engendered more heat and division than light and reconciliation.

Numerous independent Negro churches also appeared at this time which were important religious and social centers for the urban blacks, whether free or slave, and were the only organizations they felt they could actually control. The oldest of these, as mentioned earlier, was the congregation whose preacher was Peter Duerett, known as the "Old Captain," a slave of John Maxwell's, who gave him the use of a small cabin. By 1810, there being about fifty converts, the African Baptist Church was organized, using a building on Winslow Street (Euclid Avenue) in which to worship.

In 1820 the church split into two congregations. One, the Pleasant Green Baptist Church, with Duerett remaining as its pastor until his death in 1823, bought a lot from Dr. Frederick Ridgely in 1822 on Maxwell Street, and assumed the name Pleasant Green in 1829. The other group was led by one of the most remarkable black preachers in Lexington's history — London Ferrill. Born a slave in Virginia in 1789, he became a deeply devout individual after a close escape from death. He and his wife, both of whom had been freed, came to Lexington about 1814 where the proof of his emancipation was recorded. His name was listed in the 1818 city directory as a waiter, and he began preaching in the weaving room of Thomas Hart's hemp factory. The town trustees engaged him to minister to the entire black congregation of Lexington which was, apparently, the African Baptist Church, and the split resulted. Ferrill's followers became associated with the Elkhorn Baptist Association as an adjunct to the white First Baptist Church. In 1833, they bought the former white Methodist Church building on the southwest corner of Dewees and Short streets, and replaced it with a new building in 1856. Ferrill remained in town during the cholera epidemic of 1833, ministering to hundreds of blacks and whites.

The inter-relation between black and white Baptist churches was reflected in the frequency with which Pratt of the white first Baptist Church preached at both the Pleasant Green and the black First Baptist churches, sometimes to mixed congregations. In May 1846, while Ferrill was on tour, Pratt substituted for him and recounted in his diary that he took

> much enjoyment preaching for them, they seemed to enjoy the truth so much. I believe they enjoy more of the power of Religion than any other church in town.

On the occasion of the Pleasant Green congregation moving into a new building in 1848, Pratt presided as moderator and later attended the ordination of their new pastor, George Brent. On January 1, 1856, Pratt wrote

that he "bid off by direction of our church Geo. Duprey [sic], a colored Baptist preacher about 32 years old and pastor of the Pleasant Green Baptist Church. As a slave, he was about to be sold as part of the settlement of an estate, and the Pleasant Green congregation importuned us to buy him stating they could raise the money & reimburse us." The energetic George Dupee did not stay very long at Pleasant Green but became a great organizer of churches in Kentucky and pioneered in religious publications. He organized the first association of Negro Baptists in the state in 1867.

When London Ferrill died in 1854, his congregation of over 1,800 members was the largest in Lexington. Newspaper accounts of his funeral indicate that thousands, both black and white, turned out, making it the biggest funeral since Henry Clay's. He was buried in the white Episcopal cemetery on East Third Street, though graveyards then were generally segregated. Ferrill left his property to the Orphan Asylum, First Baptist Church (black), and Morton School.

Another group of blacks organized the Main Street Baptist Church in 1862.

However, the Baptists were not the only black churches being organized. The white Methodist Church, in which a small group of blacks had been worshipping, assisted the blacks in purchasing an old stable on North Upper Street. This was replaced by a small brick building in 1826, and more land was purchased. Formally designated the African Methodist Episcopal Church, the building was enlarged in 1850 and 1877, and extensively remodeled to its present form in 1906. Asbury Methodist Episcopal Church was organized in 1847, and the first black Christian Church about 1851.

Fayette County's Agricultural Riches

As each decade passed, the productivity of the central Bluegrass region increased. In the surrounding areas in Fayette County — eventually designated into the six major election districts of Athens, Brier Hill, Dog Fennel, Sandersville, South Elkhorn, and East Hickman — hemp, corn, rye, wheat and some tobacco were raised successfully. Fruit orchards produced apples, peaches, and pears although the raising of grapes was a more difficult task as they proved vulnerable to insects and a number of fungi. Wines were made on a modest scale compared to the booming distillery business. Some, like the Ashland Distillery, were within the city limits, others including the Henry Clay Distillery were scattered throughout the county. These distilleries consumed large quantities of corn, wheat, and rye produced by the neighboring farms.

Grazing on the fertile pastures were large herds of cattle and sheep, constantly being improved through selective breeding as fine bulls and rams were imported into the region early in the county's history.

In the antebellum period, the Thoroughbred and trotting horse, or Standardbred, industries did not dominate the area as they would later. Horses were a part of the total livestock industry that included the raising of quality jacks as well as horses, and the breeding of good mules for the large market in Kentucky and the expanding one to the south. Indeed, it was Henry Clay who imported the first Catalonian jack into Kentucky in 1832. Wealthier planters sent special agents to England to purchase outstanding stock for

mate, price eighty cents each, delivered in Lexington.
Apply to   MASLIN SMITH.
Lexington, Jan. 29, 1839 47-3t.

THE BIG JACK, BLACK HAWK,

WILL make his present season at my stable, in this county, on the Ridge Road leading from Richmond to Boonsborough, eight miles from the former place, and four from the latter, at *Thirty Dollars* the season. Any Jennett failing to prove in foal will have the privilege of being put the next season free of additional charge. Good blue grass pasturage will be furnished for Jennetts, gratis, and corn fed at a reasonable charge if required. Care taken to prevent accidents and escapes, but no liabilities should any happen. The season will commence on the first of March next.
                                        N. G. TEVIS.
Jan. 26, 1839 47-3t

I have several times seen the Jack-Ass BLACK HAWK, recently purchased by the Hon. John White, of Madison county, from Mr. Gilmer of Maryland. He was got by old Warrior, and was raised by Loyd Roggers, Esq. I consider BLACK HAWK the finest Jack I have ever seen. I cannot speak of his get, not having seen enough of them to form an opinion. I will add that his dam is one of the two finest Jennetts I have ever seen.
                                        H. CLAY.

Henry Clay's interest in the breeding of fine livestock is shown by his endorsement of the noted jack, Black Hawk. This advertisement appeared in the Lexington Intelligencer, *February 1, 1839.*

Kentucky. Clay is said to have been the first planter in the state to import Hereford stock directly from England, and possibly some of the earliest Merino sheep.

There was also a large hog industry in the Bluegrass. The principal markets for beef cattle in these decades were Louisville, Cincinnati, New Orleans, Baltimore, New York, and Charleston. Livestock provided one of the most important Kentucky exports and a steady stream of horses, mules, cattle, sheep, and hogs were transported to the South Atlantic states via the Cumberland Gap, and to the central Southern states by rail and roads.

While the Lexington town dweller was conscious of this rich and productive environment as he visited the Market House to buy his meat and produce, County Court days were even more colorful reminders as farmers brought cattle and horses to sell or trade in the teeming crowd milling around Cheapside.

The first cattle show and fair, probably the first in Kentucky, was planned and sponsored on July 25, 1815, by Lewis Sanders on his farm on the Georgetown Road about two and a half miles from Lexington. Fine cattle from all over the state went on display here, prominent citizens acted as judges, and specially crafted silver cups (perhaps the first julep cups) were awarded for prize livestock, and a cup was even presented for the best piece of woven hemp or flax.

In 1816, the Kentucky Society for Promoting Agriculture was organized and shortly thereafter held fairs at Fowler's Garden, making them easily accessible to all Lexingtonians. Each year saw larger fairs with more horses, livestock, produce and manufactured goods such as whiskey, cheese, woven cloth, and industrial products.

The Kentucky Association, organized in 1826 primarily as a racing association, became involved in sponsoring these fairs in Fayette County during the 1830's when racing began to predominate. On September 9, 1851, Pratt recorded in his diary that he had been attending the fair four days, but that since there had been no rain for a month "the dust was suffocating" in a crowd he estimated at 15,000. The dry weather had diminished the quality of the produce, he said, but the cattle and horse shows were very good.

Ingelside, a Gothic Revival mansion designed by John McMurtry for Henry Boone Ingels, was erected in 1852 on the Harrodsburg Pike, where it stood until it was demolished in 1964. Photo courtesy of the University of Kentucky.

In 1850, the Kentucky Agricultural and Mechanical Society was established in Lexington which purchased land adjacent to the Maxwell Spring Company in the area bounded by Winslow (Euclid), Limestone, and Rose (Van Pelt) streets, stretching southward. Here the society established a fairgrounds for animal fairs, complete with running and trotting races. In 1853 it was permitted use of the Maxwell Spring Company grounds where the society built a large two-story amphitheatre capable of seating 800 persons, a floral hall, and race courses. This, in total, became the Fair Grounds until the property became a city park and in the late 1870's was donated to the Agricultural and Mechanical College of Kentucky for its new campus after separation from Kentucky University (Transylvania).

As of 1860, Lexington had a population of 9,521 out of a total county population of 22,599. Of the city's population, 3,080 were black. This ratio would change dramatically by 1870.

In the decades prior to the Civil War, Lexington and Fayette County's population growth was modest. Indeed, between 1830-1840 there was an actual loss of about 2,000 in total county residents. From 1840 to 1860, the city's population increased by over 2,000, but the total county population remained almost static. Yet the balance of the town's manufacturing, retail, and wholesale enterprises with the abundant productivity of the rich agricultural hinterland resulted in a notable stability. How important the construction of the Louisville & Frankfort Railroad was in contributing to Lexington's prosperity is difficult to assess. It obviously did not promote the growth its builders had hoped for.

On this base had Lexington's educational and religious institutions and its cultural achievements been built. Some of these were in jeopardy as the decline of Transylvania University on the eve of the Civil War signified.

This imposing 120-foot tall monument to Henry Clay (below which is the sarcophagus of the illustrious 19th century statesman) towers over the Lexington Cemetery. The monument was dedicated on July 4, 1861, nine years after his death.

Chapter IV

1792/1865

Slavery and the Civil War

It was in the early 1830's that a young Frenchman named Alexis de Tocqueville and his companion toured the United States, initially to study prison reform but ultimately to investigate this expanding, experimenting, and diverse American republic spreading across the vast North American continent. It was a spectacle that fascinated thousands of European travelers who publicized their experiences and viewpoints in their travel accounts.

What struck de Tocqueville, whose *Democracy in America* has remained the classic of such accounts, as he crossed the Ohio River from Cincinnati into Kentucky, was a fundamental change in the tempo and style of life which he attributed to the existence of slavery in Kentucky. He wrote that

> the traveler who floats down the current of the Ohio ... may be said to sail between liberty and servitude ... Upon the left bank [Kentucky] ... the population is sparse; from time to time one decries a troop of slaves loitering in the half-desert fields; ... society seems to be asleep, man to be idle, and nature alone offers a scene of activity and life.
>
> From the right bank, on the contrary, a confused hum is heard, which proclaims afar the presence of industry ...
>
> Upon the left bank of the Ohio labor is confounded with the idea of slavery, while upon the right bank it is identified with that of prosperity and improvement ...

Blacks, both slave and free, were included in the first groups of pioneers that slashed their way through Cumberland Gap. In 1775, when the Shawnee Indians attacked Daniel Boone's party headed for the Kentucky River, two of the three persons killed were slaves. Inevitably, settlers who were slaveowners brought their property with them. Since many of them came from Virginia and North Carolina, slaves quickly became a significant portion of the population of Kentucky, including the Bluegrass. The Virginia Assembly had no inclination to stop such migration, and the issue became acutely visible when, at Kentucky's constitutional convention of 1792, delegates like the Reverend David Rice, a Virginia Presbyterian, spoke out vigorously against permitting the institutionalization of slavery in this new Edenic state. It was a critical juncture. Given the strong opposition to the introduction of the "peculiar institution" evidenced by a number of church leaders and others hoping to keep this trans-Allegheny paradise an all-white Utopia, the state might have prohibited slavery. However, the pro-slavery faction led by George Nicholas, who was not enthusiastic about slavery but saw no solution to the problem created by emancipation, won out. Kentucky thus became a slave state, and by the time of the Civil War counted over 225,000 slaves as part of its population. In Lexington and Fayette County slaves composed about half of the population.

Any traveler wending his way from Cincinnati or Maysville to Lexington saw the relatively modest size of the farms compared to the vast expanse of the Virginia Tidewater plantations. Many owners of these farms owned a few slaves, but the gangs of slaves characteristic of the cotton plantation were rare, and most often were used on the large hemp-producing farms.

Life for the rural slave was remarkably different from that of the urban slave. On the relatively isolated farm, the slaves, whether field hands or domestic servants, were under the constant surveillance of their master, mistress, or overseer. Only infrequently did any of them have occasion to leave the farm. Their living quarters usually consisted of a cluster of simple masonry or log cabins at the rear of the main house. Larger plantations, such as "Waveland," built slave quarters of brick adjacent to the stables, carriage house, hemp house, smoke house, ice house, and other facilities essential to the functioning of the farm.

The feeding, clothing, sheltering, work schedules, general health and welfare of the slaves were all the responsibility of the owners. So, too, was the dispensing of justice — rewards and punishments. Out of sight of neighbors and municipal authorities, the power of the owner, whether white or freed black, was almost absolute. There were laws against wanton abuse and brutality, but these were often violated without any serious fear of retribution. The use of the whip was the most common mode of punishment, but cropping ears and branding were not unheard of. And should a slave run away, it was the legal responsibility of the owner to advertise the fact and to use all available means, including bloodhounds, to capture him.

Formal marriages between slaves did not exist. Each individual slave was property to be bought, sold, or otherwise disposed of as the owner saw fit — whether man, woman, or child. Under such circumstances, an assured, permanent family life was impossible. Husbands and fathers could be sold separately from wives and mothers, and children separately from both. The more concerned owners usually attempted to keep the informal family together, and, indeed, for many of them the selling of slaves was an abhorrent though occasionally necessary task. The hostility toward the slave traders, whose business was essential to the existence of the institution, was as intense as it was illogical.

The traveler, having observed the pattern of slave life in the countryside, was undoubtedly struck by the differences in that pattern when he visited Lexington. There were blacks everywhere, engaged in a great variety of tasks. In the morning, many could be seen going to the Market House where, at the various stalls, other blacks were butchering meat or selling vegetables, fruit, and flowers. Early in the morning, many of the male blacks headed for the factories, or to their tasks as bricklayers and masons, blacksmiths and carpenters, or perhaps to work on the building of the Lexington and Ohio Railroad. Others would be driving wagons or carriages, repairing streets, digging sewers, tending to horses and equipment at the livery stables. Others performed the thousand and one menial tasks at the Phoenix Hotel and many other inns and taverns. Domestic servants in hundreds of

December 6, 1838.—34-a5d—Cin. Whig.

RAN AWAY

FROM th· mouth of the Wabash, on the 2nd October, a negro man, named

LAWSON,

About 22 years of age, about 5 feet 8 inches high, weighs about 150 lbs, remarkably well made; lack; has a small foot and ankle, no marks recollected except those on his back, is cunning and artful. He was purchased of the estate of John Bruce, Esq. of Lexington, and when last heard from was on his way to Lexington. A liberal reward will be given for his apprehension and delivery to the Jailor in Lexington.

A. WICKLIFFE.

Nov, 13, 1838.-26 tf.
Observer and Gazette insert tf.

An advertisement for a run-away slave, which appeared in the Lexington Intelligencer, *January 15, 1839.*

residences performed innumerable tasks to keep the daily routine operating successfully.

Like their rural counterparts, the urban slaves were housed in quarters adjacent to the master's house, but in a much more restricted space. Some lived in the main house. Certain of the hemp factories provided sleeping quarters for their hired slaves. The urban slaves were generally better clothed and fed than the rural slaves.

Slaves not needed for household duties were hired out to the hundreds of employers who employed them as workmen, sometimes under yearly formal contracts, but more often under an informal agreement. When such a slave went to work he had to have some certificate of permission from his owner or a written pass to satisfy the municipal authorities, keeping a watchful eye on this mobile black population. In contrast to the rural slaves, however, the urban slaves who were hired out were out of sight and supervision of their owners during the day which inevitably created a sense of some freedom and independence, a fact commented on by Southern newspaper editors, who feared that the blacks would become increasingly disrespectful and disorderly. It was this fear that led the town trustees to establish some form of policing, even though the number and quality of the poorly paid watchmen in Lexington was limited.

Fear of insurrection was a perpetual nightmare for the Southern slaveholders, and any dramatic outbreak, infrequent though it was, sparked nervous vibrations throughout the whole area. White fears were intensified by Denmark Vesey's abortive rebellion in 1822 in South Carolina, and Nat Turner's bloody revolt in 1831 in Southampton, Virginia, in which sixty whites, many of them women and children, were killed before the militia and U. S. troops crushed the desperate band.

Many Kentucky communities tightened their security forces considerably after hearing of the Nat Turner affair. The Lexington newspapers, which reported the Nat Turner insurrection in scattered news items in the weeks that followed, did not react as intensely as might have been expected. The Fayette County Court did appoint reputable citizens to divide the county into districts to be patroled by mounted bands of "discreet and sober men" to disperse suspicious-looking assemblages of slaves or to arrest slaves lurking about other plantations or traveling without a proper pass.

The number of runaway slaves in the Bluegrass area, while not a significant percentage of the total slave population, was a persistent aggravation to the slaveholders. The fact that the Ohio River — the River Jordan of freedom — was only about eighty miles away, encouraged far more slaves in this region

Negroes Wanted.

THE undersigned wish to purchased a large number of **NEGROES**, of both sexes, for which they will

Pay the Highest Prices in Cash.

Office on Main-street, opposite the Phœnix Hotel, and 2d door above the Statesman Office, Lexington.

SILAS MARSHALL & BRO.

March 15, 1859–50–tf

Dealers in slaves frequently advertised in Lexington newspapers prior to the Civil War. Photo courtesy of the Lexington Public Library.

to attempt to escape than slaves in the Deep South. This only intensified the patrols' activities.

Fayette County's greatest scare came on August 5, 1848, when some seventy-five escaping slaves, thought to be armed and dangerous, and led by a white Centre College student named Patrick Doyle, were heading for the Ohio River. Intense excitement spread throughout the whole region as men with horses and rifles joined in the hunt to round up the runaways. A $5,000 reward was offered to encourage even greater efforts. The fugitives were sighted near Cynthiana and the posse converged on them, forcing them to surrender. Doyle was brought back to Lexington in chains. He and the ringleaders were tried and found guilty. Three of the Negroes were hanged and Doyle sentenced to twenty years at hard labor in the state penitentiary.

No incident could have more dramatically brought home to every pro-slavery Kentuckian that, while they might pride themselves on Kentucky's reputation for operating as mild and well-run a slave system as any slave state in the Union, not all bondsmen were content with their condition of servitude. Some were so desperate to secure freedom that they would take an enormously risky gamble such as this.

Meanwhile, in the heart of Lexington itself, punishment of blacks was painfully and publicly exhibited in the frequent floggings at the

massive locust whipping-post on the northeast corner of the courthouse yard, and in the increased number of hangings.

Another benefit the urban slave enjoyed over his rural counterpart was the greater freedom for informal, and frequently illegal, meetings, usually at night or on Sundays, with other slaves and free blacks at numerous inconspicuous and shabby-looking dwellings.

The black churches also gave the urban blacks a center for independent organization, religious expression, and socialization apart from the surveillance of the whites, although as Pratt's experience indicates, there existed an important dependence on the white ministers to assist them in a variety of ways. Pratt not only preached in the black Baptist churches, baptized children and adults occasionally, ordained new pastors, and assisted in solving financial problems, he also on request went to slave auctions to act as the representative of these churches to buy certain individuals, either to secure their freedom or to prevent their being sold downriver.

Though in Southern cities like Charleston, many whites believed the black churches were potential centers of rebellious organization or insurrection, Lexington did not share this fear, and the black congregations were generally left free of interference.

Added to the white community's problems in maintaining control over the blacks was the presence of numerous free Negroes. Some migrated here already free, some earned their freedom and others were freed by their owners. It is estimated that about 250 slaves were freed in Fayette County between 1825 and 1861. On the eve of the Civil War, 685 of the 10,015 blacks in Fayette County were free. Many lived in the county, but the City Assessor's book in 1832 shows 287 living in the city, of whom the large majority were women and children. Because a black was presumed to be a slave unless proven otherwise, free Negroes had to keep their "free papers," or certificate of freedom, with them at all times to prove to any white authority the validity of their status. The free Negro created an ambivalent attitude on the part of the white community, most of whom would have preferred they not be permitted to come here, or stay here. They feared the insidious influence a free Negro might have on the enslaved Negro. A few white members of the community sought to improve the status of the Negro through teaching them a craft, providing employment and education, and they supported the development of the black churches as means of inculcating the virtues of morality and industry.

In Lexington many of the free Negroes found employment as craftsmen — coopers, carpenters, shoemakers, bricklayers, tailors, etc., — while some worked in the factories or other manual labor. Most lived on Mulberry Street (Limestone), and the others were scattered on Broadway, Upper, High, Water, Short, and Main streets,. Some acquired enough property to leave wills. Among these were Baron Steuben, a barber, Rolla Blue, a blacksmith, William Tucker, a prosperous merchant, and London Ferrill.

Police records did not indicate that free Negroes committed many offenses. Occasionally they were arrested for unlawful assembly, vagrancy, uttering lewd and obscene language, drunkenness, disorderly conduct, and stealing. "Free Celia" was repeatedly fined for selling liquor to slaves, and she was finally committed to the workhouse. The free Negro was more apt to be fined or sent to the workhouse than whipped.

The most vicious aspects of slavery were the incidents of unpunished atrocities perpetrated on slaves, and the slave trade itself.

A bizarre and melodramatic incident of brutality and the consequent reaction occurred in the Caroline Turner case. A wealthy Lexington lawyer had married a Boston lady, reared in an antislavery environment, and brought her back to Lexington. Her latent sadism now found release in her vicious flogging of her servants, male and female. She had once hurled a small Negro boy out of a second-story window, breaking his back and crippling him for life, because the innocent child had whimpered while she was lashing a servant. Judge Turner had his wife committed to the Eastern Lunatic Asylum to protect her from legal retribution, but she was eventually released. He also requested in his will before he died in 1843 that his slaves go to his children as it would be hell to give them to his wife. Despite this, Caroline Turner managed to keep a few slaves, including a young coachman named Richard, whom one day she chained and flogged mercilessly. The enraged victim tore himself loose and strangled his tormentor. Had Richard been a white man the crime would have been called justifiable homicide, and, indeed, many in the community sympathized with Richard, but the system permitted no slave this recourse and Richard was hanged.

Slave Auctions on Cheapside

Public auction of slaves, usually held adjacent to the courthouse on Cheapside, was a familiar sight to Lexingtonians, yet many detested the practice and the slave traders involved in it. Though the number so auctioned off was relatively small in the early decades of the community's history, it expanded considerably after the cholera epidemic of 1833 and the later epidemic of 1849 which killed off many slaveowners who had made no wills, and in the settlement of the estates their slaves were frequently put up for auction. Though the 1833 Non-Importation Act prohibited the importing of slaves into Kentucky for the purpose of selling them, there were many slaveowners in the state who provided a sales market from those slaves already here. As the demand for slaves in the lower Mississippi Valley grew along with the expansion of the large cotton and sugar plantations, the temptation to sell slaves at high prices was strong. All sales were not made on the Cheapside auction block. Slave traders bought many at plantations, or in the confines of their own slave pens.

Yet, public auctions continued to be held. Most abhorrent to public taste was the auctioning of young slave girls, especially octoroons with light, tawny skin, for their dramatic sexual qualities. A famous sale occurred in May 1843, when a beautiful, graceful, and cultivated female servant named Eliza was put on the block. A New Orleans Frenchman and a young Methodist minister named Calvin Fairbank became the top bidders. In order to incite the men to bid higher, the callous auctioneer stripped Eliza to the waist and lifted her skirt waist high to expose her charms. Fairbank finally outbid the Frenchman at $1,485. When asked what he intended doing with his new purchase, Fairbank retorted: "Free her!" The crowd roared its approval.

Even Robert Wickliffe, known as the "Old Duke" and through marriage the largest slaveowner in the Bluegrass, told the 1840 Kentucky General Assembly that he hoped that "for the honor, as well as the security of our state . . . [they] will put a stop to the abominable traffic." But the legislature showed little inclination to do so. The human commerce continued, growing in the 1840's and booming after the Non-Importation Act of 1833 was repealed in 1849. More and more slave traders chose Lexington as the preferred center for their traffic since the distance from the Ohio River reduced the number of attempted escapes compared to Louisville.

William Pullum, one of the better known slave traders, operated a sizable slave mart in a two-story brick structure facing North Broadway, just a few doors north of Short. "In the yard at the rear of the building were rows of slave pens, eight feet square, seven feet high, constructed on damp brick floors covered with vermin-infested straw, with tiny barred windows near the roof and heavy, rivet-studded, iron-grated doors." These pens backed up to the property of Mrs. Parker, grandmother of Mary Todd, and Lincoln, on one of his visits to his wife's hometown, might well have stood on the porch of "Grandma" Parker's home and looked into those slave pens. Or he might have gazed across the street at the establishment of the notorious Lewis C. Robards who by 1849 had acquired the reputation of being the leading slave trader of Lexington. His large volume of sales included many diseased, infirm, and aging slaves whose defects he skillfully concealed until he sold them, and though he was sued frequently he won most of his cases.

Robards had leased not only Pullum's property but also acquired the former Lexington Theater on West Short Street with an adjoining commodious two-story brick house. Here on the ground floor he established his offices, complete with bar, tables and chairs to provide for the comfort of his customers. Overhead in well-furnished apartments he kept his "choice stock" of attractive mulatto girls, available for $1,600 or more.

Despite his booming business, Robards apparently overextended himself, and in order to satisfy his creditors he sold his jail and stock in 1855 to the firm of Bolton, Dickens and Company, more prosperous Lexington slave dealers.

The Anti-Slavery Controversy

The antislavery forces were by no means quiescent in Kentucky. Practically all the major religious denominations favored the antislavery crusade in the early decades of the 19th century, especially the Baptists, Methodists, and Presbyterians. In some instances slaveholders were made so uncomfortable in their congregations they withdrew entirely, or formed their own churches.

In 1808, the emancipating Baptists organized the Kentucky Abolition Society, the first of its kind in the state. The society prospered for almost twenty years. Gradually, the proslavery factions gained strength as a tremendously expanding cotton economy based on slave labor overrode earlier doubts concerning the economic viability of a slave-based economy. So great did these pressures become that toleration of antislavery activity began to disappear entirely, and violent attacks upon antislavery proponents became commonplace. The churches gradually abandoned their antislavery stance, so that by 1830 an almost complete reversal had taken place. A few courageous pastors continued to speak out against the "peculiar institution" but only at the risk of dividing their congregation or inviting attacks upon their persons and

Cassius Marcellus Clay (1810-1903), pictured in 1846, the "Lion" of Madison County's White Hall, located just a few miles south of Lexington, which today is a State Shrine. Clay was an ardent and colorful anti-slavery proponent. Photo courtesy of Transylvania University.

property. The Reverend William Pratt experienced such attacks.

What should be remembered, however, is that many critics of slavery were not necessarily abolitionists. Henry Clay had spoken out frequently on the injustice and defects of slavery, but this did not motivate him to free his slaves. The sticking point was the problem of disposing of large numbers of freed blacks. Clay found the answer in the appealingly simplistic solution of returning freed blacks to Africa. This led him to assist in the organization of the American Colonization Society in 1816 (he served as its president many years) which secured funds to purchase land on the west coast of Africa and establish Liberia whose capital, Monrovia, was named for the popular President of the United States. It soon became apparent that the scheme was unworkable, although several thousand blacks were sent to found this unique African nation.

An antislavery advocate like Pratt also spoke out against slavery while criticizing the radical abolitionists. This stance was so

unpopular in the 1850's that his church and personal property were targets of arsonists, although there is no proof that proslavery agents lit the torch.

The antislavery forces won a small victory in 1833 when the General Assembly passed the Non-Importation Act, but this hardly laid the axe to the root of slavery. More disturbing to the proslavery forces were men like the Reverend Robert J. Breckinridge, son of John Breckinridge, Attorney General in Jefferson's cabinet, who spoke out for gradual emancipation in 1830. Their arguments swayed some 48 rather prominent slaveholders to meet in Lexington on September 6, 1831, to form a society whose members pledged to free the future offspring of their slaves at age twenty-one. Coming on the heels of the Nat Turner insurrection, this action greatly excited other slaveholders and apparently this organization and plan never materialized.

Meanwhile, the town authorities began a crackdown on the blacks. Arrests greatly increased, filling the jails, and though none had been executed in Fayette County in the fifteen years prior to 1831, four were publicly hanged on August 13, 1831, in Megowan's jail. The expanding antislavery sentiment in the North and extremist views of such men as the Bostonian William Lloyd Garrison, whose newspaper *The Liberator* became an anathema to both proslavery and moderate factions, muzzled antislavery talk in the South even more.

The storm center of antislavery turbulence in Lexington was Cassius Marcellus Clay. Born in 1810 in Madison County, son of Green Clay, a large landowner and slaveowner, Cassius became a Lexington resident, first as a student at Transylvania (he later said it was his servant who had inadvertently started the fire that destroyed the main college building in 1829), and after he had attended Yale College and heard the antislavery views of Garrison. He had seen how an industrious free white population could prosper even on thin and rocky soil. He returned to Lexington to promulgate his ideas. Kentucky would flourish only as slavery was abolished and white labor replaced it, he argued. He wrote his brother Brutus prophetically that "the slave question is now [1832] an importance in the opinions of the enlightened and the humane, which prejudice and interest cannot long withstand." He predicted that slavery must be abolished soon or a dissolution of the nation within fifty years was inevitable. He began to study law at Transylvania, and married Mary Jane Warfield after a tempestuous courtship. Living at the plantation at White Hall in Madison County in the 1830's, he became an ardent Whig and was twice elected to the Kentucky House. His political career ended because of his increasingly strong antislavery sentiments.

In the 1840's he continued his antislavery crusade, though making clear his belief that blacks were an inferior and non-self-reliant class. Freeing the slaves, he argued (and he freed most of his own) was not only a just act but liberated the white man's dependence on black labor. Though not a candidate for office, he vigorously campaigned for the Whig candidates. Violence erupted at some of the political gatherings. The most dramatic incident took place at Russell Cave Spring. Robert Wickliffe, Jr., with whom Clay had already fought a duel in which no one was injured, was the Democratic candidate for the legislature in 1843 against Garret Davis, whom Clay supported. During Wickliffe's address, Clay interrupted the speaker to brand as a lie certain allegations. Nearby stood an ex-Kentuckian, one Samuel Brown, renowned for his quick temper and fighting ability, who had returned to his native state from New Orleans. Brown called Clay a liar whereupon Clay began to beat Brown with his whip before he was held back by bystanders. Clay shook himself free, drew his bowie knife which he preferred to firearms, and advanced on Brown who aimed a pistol at Clay's heart, firing it when Clay was but an arm's length away. The bullet hit the scabbard of Clay's bowie knife, thus saving his life. Clay then leaped upon Brown, and after cutting off an ear, gouging out an eye, splitting his nose and skull, threw the senseless adversary over a bluff into the waters of Russell Cave. Clay was tried for mayhem, but, ably defended by his cousin Henry, was acquitted.

Cassius decided to publish a newspaper in Lexington as the mouthpiece for his opinions. To be closer to his press, he purchased what he regarded as the most elegant house in the city. It was the house on North Limestone at

No. 6 North Mill Street, where Cassius Clay's True American, an abolitionist newspaper, was published in 1845. The building was demolished about the turn of the century. Photo courtesy of the Lexington Public Library.

the northeast corner of Fifth Street, built by William "Lord" Morton in 1810 in a modified Federal style. The one-story house was set impressively on a spacious lot rising gently from the street.

Clay leased a sturdy brick building for his press at No. 6 North Mill Street between Short and Main streets. Anticipating trouble, he asked Major Thomas Lewinski, an architect and military engineer, to assist him in fortifying the building with small cannon, firearms, iron pikes, and even a keg of powder to blow up the place as a last resort. The True American appeared in June 1845, advocating constitutional emancipation supported by Clay's old arguments. His columns bristled with typical journalistic bombast of that day, especially as he dealt with individuals. The reaction was predictable. His opponents, who called him "meaner than the autocrats of hell" and told him "the hemp is ready for your neck," waited only for an opportune moment. It came sooner than expected. In mid-July 1845, Clay contracted typhoid fever, and while bedridden, the opposition, threatening mob action against Clay's press, secured a court injunction, and Clay, served with a writ of seizure, reluctantly handed over the keys to his plant. A crowd converged on the building, secured the keys from the city marshal guarding the door, dismantled the press and shipped it to Ohio.

Though Clay continued to speak out for his cause, involving himself in other violent encounters, he never again tried to publish a paper, nor was it possible to establish another abolitionist newspaper in Lexington. J. Brady, a New England schoolmaster, tried his luck in December 1855, but he was immediately "surrounded by a mob of poor whites," reported the *Louisville Times,* "who were anxious to 'taste the blood of an Abolitionist.'" The city officials made no attempt to protect him, saying "it would cost them lives if they did," and Brady courageously faced the crowd who "wreaked their cowardly vengeance upon him," and forced him to leave town.

The most intense hatred centered on those who incited slaves to escape or join in an insurrection, as Patrick Doyle had done, or those who aided and abetted slaves to secretly escape to the Ohio River and the sanctuary of the underground railroad system that might eventually enable them to reach Canada. The most famous local ringleaders in this latter type of venture were the Reverend Calvin Fairbank, the purchaser of Eliza's freedom, and Delia Webster, a native of Vermont and principal of the Lexington Female Academy. In the fall of 1844 they secretly drove Lewis, a waiter at the Phoenix Hotel, his wife and son, to Maysville, ferried them over the river, and took them to the Reverend John Rankin of Ripley, Ohio, conductor of a station on the underground railroad.

Miss Webster and Fairbank were arrested at Paris on their way back to Lexington and thrown into Megowan's jail. Found guilty at a trial in Judge Richard Buckner's court, Miss Webster was sentenced to two years' confinement at the Frankfort State Penitentiary while Fairbank received a fifteen-year sentence. Despite the vigorous protests of slaveholders, Governor Owsley pardoned Miss Webster after she had served only six weeks of her sentence, and Governor Crittenden pardoned Fairbank four years later. Miss Webster returned to her native Vermont for a while, but within two years Fairbank was arrested again in 1851 for helping slaves to escape near Louisville, and

Cassius Clay purchased this residence in 1838 and lived there until 1850. The house, located on the northeast corner of North Limestone and Fifth streets in what is now Duncan Park, was constructed for William "Lord" Morton in 1810.

again sentenced to fifteen years in the penitentiary, where he remained until 1862. Miss Webster eventually returned to Kentucky in 1854, and with funds provided by Northern abolitionists purchased a 600-acre farm in Trimble County which soon became a sanctuary for fugitive slaves.

The last major effort by the antislavery forces to initiate some form of gradual legal emancipation came in 1849 when they persuaded the state legislature to call a constitutional convention in which they hoped to incorporate an antislavery provision. After a bitterly fought campaign for delegates, not a single emancipationist candidate had been elected and the new constitution supported slavery more stringently while the legislature proceeded to repeal the 1833 Non-Importation Act.

Building and Business

Despite the ever-present tensions created by the controversy over slavery, a levelling of economic expansion, and slow growth of population, Lexington gradually recovered from the impact of the cholera plague of 1833 and resumed the mode of its community life, which not only suited the residents but still impressed visitors. One such visitor at this time commented that

> the tone of society is fashionable and pleasant. Strangers, in general, are much pleased with a temporary sojourn in this city, which conveys high ideals of the refinement and taste of the country. There are now much larger towns in the West, but none presenting more beauty and intelligence.

Lexington's main economic competitors — Cincinnati and Louisville — whose great commercial and manufacturing expansion in the 1820's and later decades left Lexington far behind, continued to evidence a begrudging admiration and jealousy of Lexington's cultural superiority. One Cincinnati newspaper editor said that "Cincinnati may be the Tyre, but Lexington is unquestionably the Athens of the West." Another Cincinnati resident commented that if his townsfolk could pause for a moment in their pursuit of commercial success, they might "admire the varied sweets of those literary and scientific effusions, which have stamped Lexington as the headquarters of *Science* and *Letters* in the Western country."

Louisville, expanding and confident of its economic superiority, envied Lexington's educational and cultural institutions, and sought vigorously to lure the Transylvania Medical Department faculty to the Falls City in 1837. The bitter controversy between the two cities was occasionally forgotten as they both levelled their attacks on Cincinnati which, even after the canal at Louisville overcame the obstacle of the rapids, promised to outstrip its Ohio River competitor. In addition, the towns of Newport and Covington, though rightly regarded as economic components of Cincinnati's expanding economic complex, passed Lexington in size, leaving the once dominant Bluegrass city behind as far as population was concerned.

Lexington continued as a viable economic center and as the central mart for the abundant agricultural produce and livestock of this fertile region. Hunt's Row, named after Lexington's first mayor, was built along the railroad on Water Street to expand facilities for more businesses. In 1840, Lexington had a population of nearly 7,000, an increase of only 1,000 within a decade, but in real numbers a larger gain if the more than 500 persons lost in the 1833 cholera plague are taken into account. The Lexington & Frankfort Railroad was in operation. A variety of associations of skilled mechanics, including typographers, saddlers, and cabinetmakers, operated successfully in Lexington. Some 18 rope and bagging factories capitalized at $1,300,000 and employing nearly 1,000 men continued to fill the needs of the shipbuilding industry and the burgeoning cotton market in the Deep South. Craftsmen of every kind prospered. Six brickyards produced about 5,000,000 bricks annually for the fine brick homes and businesses being erected in the town and country. It was estimated that the capital investment in all Lexington establishments totalled about $14,000,000.

To handle the large amounts of cash generated by such activity, banks were established with increasing frequency. Since rural legislators in the General Assembly were at first suspicious of banks, Lexington's earliest bank operated as one of the functions of the Kentucky Insurance Company, chartered in 1802 with William Morton as president. This company erected a handsome building, said to be designed by Latrobe, on Main Street

This building, on the northeast corner of Short and Mill streets, was used as a bank by David Sayre from the 1820's until his death in 1870, and later by his nephew Ephraim D. Sayre. It is now the site of the Security Trust Building. Photo courtesy of the Lexington Public Library.

between Upper and Limestone. It operated successfully as a bank until James Prentiss bought controlling interest after the War of 1812 and so atrociously mismanaged it as to force its collapse by the time its original charter expired in 1818.

One of the most stable of the early banks was a branch of the First, and later, the Second Bank of the United States. The latter opened in January 1817, under the presidency of Colonel James Morrison with such directors as John Wesley Hunt and William T. Barry. Indeed, the boards of directors of all these banks included the top business and professional men in Fayette County. The Second Bank of the United States was located in an impressive structure on the west corner of Market and Short streets, later occupied by the Northern Bank of Kentucky after President Andrew Jackson sealed the fate of the Second Bank of the United States. The Northern Bank of Kentucky was chartered in 1835 with John Tilford as its first president and B. W. Dudley, William A. Leavy, and Benjamin Gratz among its directors.

As mentioned earlier, David Sayre founded his own banking house in 1823. A branch of the Bank of Kentucky was established in 1834 with Benjamin Gratz and Joseph Bruen among its directors. It continued operating until 1865. In 1863, the banking firm of Grinstead & Bradley began operations on Jordan's Row, later moving to the old James Morrison residence on the northwest corner of Short and Upper streets. The First National Bank of Lexington was organized in the spring of 1865 as was the City National Bank, both located in the area around the courthouse, to form a concentration of banking institutions in that area.

The early 1840's were apparently economically stringent years for Lexington as bankruptcies multiplied, improvements were postponed, law suits increased, and many had to sell their property at substantial losses. By the late 1840's an economic recovery developed. The town became greatly excited over the arrival of the telegraph in Lexington in 1848, the first line stretching to Louisville. In 1853 a coal gas works was established and the city was lighted with gas for the first time in July. The lard oil lamps became obsolete.

In the 1840's, Lexingtonians could have their images captured for posterity by a medium other than the oils of the portrait painter. The Frenchman Daguerre had introduced his revolutionary photographic technique in the late 1830's and the Englishman Fox-Talbot had made similar advances. Cameras of various types began to make their appearance in Lexington. T. W. Cridland, a former glass manufacturer, was probably the first professional photographer in Lexington in the early 1840's. His shop at 85 West Main and others like his, were called Daguerrian galleries. Early daguerreotypes cost $6 to $10, later dropping to $1. Exposure time for the earliest photographs around 1840 was almost twenty minutes, necessitating the use of a neck clamp, if not hypnosis, to keep the subject's body quiet for that period. But within a year, improved techniques reduced this time to 10 to 90 seconds, and by 1853, to one second.

As the Democratic party began to gain strength in central Kentucky, a newspaper to support its viewpoint was established in Lexington. *The Kentucky Statesman,* organized in October 1849, with B. B. Taylor as its first

Loudoun, Gothic Revival mansion erected in the 1850's for Francis Key Hunt, is now part of Castlewood Park. The architect was A. J. Davis of New York and the builder was John McMurtry. Photo courtesy of Burton Milward.

editor, remained active until suppressed by Union Army officials in September 1861. After the war it reappeared in January 1867, with William Cassius Goodloe and W. Owsley Goodloe as editors and proprietors.

This was also a period of active building of both public and private structures. John McMurtry, Major Thomas Lewinski, and Cincinnatus Shryock, Gideon's younger brother, were the major architects in Lexington during this time, Gideon having moved to Louisville. By the late 1830's the Greek revival style began to prevail and McMurtry executed a number of projects reflecting this style, sometimes in combination with the previous Federal style before the neo-Gothic influence began to predominate.

The James Weir house on the northeast corner of North Limestone and Third streets, now the Whitehall Funeral Chapel, reflected the Greek revival style, as did the refurbishing of the Joel Higgins home on Lexington Avenue. Other examples were Giron's Confectionery, Transylvania's Medical Hall (1839), the Masonic Grand Lodge Hall built in 1840 on the northeast corner of Walnut and Short streets, and Lewinski's addition of an imposing Greek portico to the old Thomas January house

on West Second Street, then known as the Tobias Gibson house.

Thomas Lewinski, soldier of fortune and Polish emigre, became a popular architect in the city in the 1850's. He used the Gothic and later the Italianate styles in his designs, reflecting the influence of the Romantic Age in literature, the popularity of the Waverly novels by Sir Walter Scott, and the flood of so-called Gothic romances in the wide-selling popular periodicals of that day. The new Christ Church, completed in 1848, was an excellent example of the neo-Gothic style. McMurtry's plans for the Second Presbyterian Church likewise manifested elements of the neo-Gothic.

Most grandiose of the private residences constructed in the neo-Gothic style was that of Francis Key Hunt. A veritable manor house, which he called Loudoun, this castle-like structure, located on a wide expanse of land, now Castlewood Park, was designed by one of the finest architects in America, Alexander Jackson Davis of New York, and built by McMurtry in 1849-50. At the time it was doubtless one of the most impressive houses in Kentucky.

Downtown, the Renaissance style was reflected in the remodeling of a three-story brick building on the southwest corner of Main and Upper streets with the addition of an attractive cast-iron facade. The second and third stories were converted into a concert gallery known as Melodeon Hall with an auditorium seating 300 to 400 people, a balcony running around the third story, and a well-equipped stage. Here operas and concerts were given from the 1850's to 1887.

Cincinnatus Shryock designed another large hall downtown for the Odd Fellows, built on the southeast corner of Main and Broadway in 1856. This contained a large auditorium on the second story capable of seating 1,200 persons. While designated primarily as an opera house, it was the site of theatricals of all types, and a number of memorable public gatherings.

The Death of Henry Clay

Politics was always an important topic in Kentucky. The Lexington newspapers were heavily laden with political news and the complete speeches of Congressmen and Senators, printed in type so small as to test the eyesight of the keenest reader. Yet both news items and speeches were read, discussed, and argued over. Despite the occasional differences with his constituency in the Bluegrass, Henry Clay remained the indisputable political favorite of the region, and though a Democratic resurgence for Andrew Jackson challenged Whig supremacy, this was never a dominant factor while Clay was alive. The Whig victory which elected General William Henry Harrison in 1840 was encouraging, though Clay had hoped to be the candidate at a time when a Whig victory seemed assured. He bided his time, and having fought President Tyler tooth-and-nail for control of the Whig party after Harrison's death, viewed the 1844 election with great expectations. He was 67 years old and could hardly hope to be a viable candidate after this, but the fates were against him. The Texas annexation issue and the activities of the Liberty party in the Northeast lost him New York and the election by a handful of votes. The embittered, aging statesman returned to the solace of his beloved Ashland.

In January 1846, his unchallenged legal talents were once more summoned in a difficult case. Lafayette Shelby, grandson of Kentucky's first governor, shot down in cold blood a young

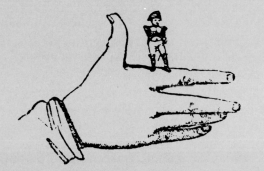

Positively fcr 3 Days Only!

THE ORIGINAL
GEN. TOM THUMB!

THIS world renowned MAN IN MINIATURE, and justly celebrated MYSTERY IN NATURE, 18 years of age, 28 inches high, and weighing but 15 pounds, who has been received with the highest marks of distinction by all the crowned heads of Europe, and whose levees in this country and Europe, during the past seven years; have been attended by upwards of *seven millions of persons*, will have the honor of appearing before the citizens of Lexington, for THREE DAYS ONLY,

AT THE MELODEON,

On Monday, Tuesday and Wednesday, January 28th, 29th and 30th,

Afternoon and Evening of each day.

The LITTLE GENERAL will appear in all his performances, consisting of SONGS, DANCES, GRECIAN STATUES, &c., &c.

The Miniature Carriage and Ponies presented by Queen Victoria will promenade the streets daily, and may be been in front of the Hall, at the close of each day's levee.

Hours of exhibition—Afternoon, from 3 to half-past 4: Evening, from 7 to half-past 8 o'clock. Doors open half an hour in advance of performance.

☞ ADMITTANCE 25 Cents—*No half price.*
J. G. BURNETT, Agent.

jan 23   78

Advertisement publicizing the appearance of the famous General Tom Thumb at Lexington's Melodeon Hall, from the Lexington Observer & Reporter, *January 23, 1850.*

acquaintance of his, Henry Horine, in front of the Phoenix Hotel after a drinking party. This senseless act of brutality aroused the community, which turned out in large numbers for the trial, forcing its removal to more spacious quarters in the chapel of Morrison Hall at Transylvania. Clay took the unpopular job of defense attorney only because of the pleas of the family. In his still masterful fashion he managed to divide the jury and brought about a mistrial. The Reverend William Pratt, who attended the trial, was angry. "The community have been outrageously treated and the laws trampled under feet [sic] . . . Old men say that for 30 years a white man has not been hung in Fayette Co. although numbers of murders have been committed." The community was so incited that they hung and burned effigies of the judge and jurors on the courthouse lawn. Shelby, out on $10,000 bail, fearing for his life, fled to Texas and was never heard of again.

In May 1846, came the news that the United States had declared war on Mexico following reports of Mexican troops attacking American forces under General Taylor along the Rio Grande. Pratt recalled that "troops were summoned to meet in Lexington. I should think there were 1500 or upwards in rank and file. After forming a parallelogram on [the] College lawn they were addressed by R. Combs & C. M. Clay & Maj. McKee." Three weeks later three companies of cavalry left for the war. The war was popular in Kentucky. Ever since the days of Stephen Austin's connection with the opening up of Texas, Kentuckians had been enthusiastic about its development, and many had migrated there to seek their fortunes. Cassius Clay had denounced Polk's war message and the war itself as a means to extend slavery. But his patriotic fervor overcame his political sentiments, and, despite ridicule by abolitionists for his inconsistency, he flung himself into the saddle and headed for Mexico, where he promptly was captured by the Mexicans while on patrol and spent the rest of the war as a prisoner in Mexico City. Henry Clay's son did not fare so well. On March 30, 1847, word was received that in the victory at Buena Vista young Lieutenant Colonel Henry Clay, Jr. had lost his life as had Colonel William R. McKee, Adjutant Edward Vaughan, and Captain William Willis.

The old man at Ashland had one more burden to bear.

Out of this war came a new hero, General Zachary Taylor, who would carry the Whigs successfully into the White House in the 1848 elections. Henry Clay returned to Washington for one last time as Senator from Kentucky.

Meanwhile, the year 1849 descended on Kentucky and Lexington like a curse. First, there was the desperate and bitter struggle over the slavery issue during the campaign for delegates to the constitutional convention. Cassius Clay, though acclaimed as a hero on his return from the war, was once again the hated foe of the proslavery forces as he campaigned for the antislavery cause. He nearly lost his life in a murderously bloody brawl with the Turner clan at Foxtown in Madison County.

To the horror of the people of Lexington and Fayette County the dread cholera returned. In June 1849, an autopsy of the body of Tom O'Haver, an old Irish quarrier, was diagnosed as cholera. The disease spread quickly through the town. Pratt estimated that as many as 1,500 whites fled the city. Cholera was particularly virulent at the Lunatic Asylum, which Pratt visited frequently. The city poorhouse was turned into a hospital. In desperation one of the faculty at the Transylvania Medical Department suggested that batteries of artillery be stationed at various sections of the town and fire off salvos at regular intervals on the rather far-fetched theory that rending the air might reduce infection in the atmosphere. It is doubtful that an already jittery citizenry appreciated this tactic.

While the cholera lasted longer than the 1833 plague, it was for some reason less deadly. About 345 persons died, 69 in the asylum alone.

The elections, which were held on the heels of the cholera's departure, resulted in an overwhelming victory for the proslavery forces in the state.

Meanwhile, in Washington, Henry Clay made one last effort as a master of political compromise to resolve the issues dividing Congress and the nation after the Mexican War. Congress was paralyzed. Dissolution of the Union was predicted. Clay brought forth his Compromise of 1850 which received the

The elaborately decorated hearse bearing the body of Henry Clay to the Lexington Cemetery on July 10, 1852. Photo courtesy of E. I. Thompson.

accolades of the Lexington press though denounced by Calhoun of South Carolina with his dying breath. The crisis was averted, and the declining Harry of the West could rest quietly on this accomplishment. On June 29, 1852, Clay died at the nation's capital.

When the news of Clay's death reached Lexington, bells began to toll and businesses closed. The mayor called a public meeting at the courthouse to allow expression of grief and to make plans for the funeral. A special committee of Lexington's leading citizens was sent to Washington to accompany the body home. They returned on July 9 and placed the body at Ashland. Very early the next morning crowds began to gather for the funeral. A special escort formed at the courthouse and proceeded to Ashland where the Reverend E. F. Berkley of Christ Church delivered the funeral oration, standing by the bier resting on the porch. Then, placing the coffin in a handsomely decorated hearse, the funeral escort accompanied it down Main Street past buildings festooned with black, to the Lexington Cemetery. The Episcopal burial service was read, and the Masonic fraternity deposited the body in the public vault to the sound of tolling bells and gun salutes in the distance.

Clay's body was interred by his mother's grave, where it remained until the death of his dovoted wife Lucretia on April 7, 1864. Both bodies were then placed in the massive chamber of the towering monument which had been erected to his memory.

The death of Henry Clay symbolized the demise of the Whig party in Kentucky, and, indeed, throughout the nation. In Kentucky, the Whigs had increasingly become identified with the elite, had opposed calling the 1849 convention, but later supported it after its ratification. The Whig domination of Fayette County was broken with the election of the charismatic John C. Breckinridge to the legislature and that of a Democratic governor in 1851. Though Kentucky voted for the Whig candidate for President in 1852, it was the swan song for the party as the Democrat Franklin Pierce won, and Kentucky sent as many Democrats as Whigs to Congress.

The ex-Whigs, attempting to avoid committing themselves to the increasingly Southern dominated proslavery Democratic party or the emerging Republican party with its principle of slavery containment, entered into the ranks of that aberrant political movement, the American or Know-Nothing party. Old

Kentucky Whigs eventually slipped into the Democratic party, but continued to play an influential role in state politics, successfully supporting the Constitutional Union party in 1860, and then Union parties of whatever variety during the Civil War.

The Whigs attended the laying of the cornerstone of the Henry Clay monument on July 4, 1857, saddened by the loss of this leader of compromise and reconciliation. Four years later, when the monument was dedicated with the 14-foot statue of Clay atop the 120-foot column, the nation he had devoted his career to keep united was torn apart by civil war.

It was a sign of the times that more military groups began to form in the city: the Lexington Rifles were organized in 1857 with John Hunt Morgan as captain and Major Lewinski as commandant; the Ashland Rifles were organized in 1859 with Robert J. Breckinridge, Jr., as captain; and the Lexington Chasseurs in 1860 with Sanders D. Bruce as captain.

These various military groups engaged in both social and military activities prior to the Civil War, holding musters and military drills on some occasions, and dances and banquets at other times. In January 1861, just prior to the beginning of the Civil War, the historic Lexington Light Infantry was honored at the Odd Fellows Hall. Veterans of the War of 1812 were seated in places of prominence, a roll call of its captains read out, and a fine flag presented to the company. Soon the grim events of actual war would either split or energetically activate these groups into real fighting, tragically on opposite sides of the conflict.

The Civil War

The crucial Presidential election of 1860 placed most Kentuckians in a very peculiar and ambivalent position. A four-way race gave them sufficient options, it might appear, but this was an illusion. Though Lincoln could claim Kentucky as his birthplace, this was the only asset he had in his native state, for the Republican party was most unpopular in Kentucky, being regarded, though inaccurately, as a party of abolitionists. Stephen Douglas, the candidate of the Northern wing of the cloven Democratic party, had sold his soul to popular

John C. Breckinridge, member of one of Lexington's most prominent families, served as Vice President of the United States under President Buchanan. This painting hangs in the National Portrait Gallery at the Smithsonian Institution in Washington, D.C. Photo courtesy of the Filson Club.

sovereignty, and the proslavery sentiments of Kentuckians, though most did not own a single slave, rejected Douglas as an undependable opportunist. What, then, about their own John C. Breckinridge? Grandson of the distinguished Bluegrass leader, Breckinridge was a popular, gifted, and energetic political leader who had rocketed into prominence from being a Democratic representative in the General Assembly to being Vice-President in the Buchanan administration and U. S. Senator. Representing a moderate, pro-Union, proslavery border state, he appeared the ideal nominee for the Southern wing of the Democratic party. He was Lexington's favorite son, now that Clay was dead, and on September 5, 1860, he returned home after campaigning in the Southern states. Thousands gathered for a huge barbecue in the Ashland woods, stuffing themselves with beef, mutton, and burgoo and quenching their thirst with Kentucky's favorite beverage. Then they listened to Breckinridge effectively demolish Douglas, ignore Lincoln, and counter the appeal of the Constitutional

Union party with his own pro-Union stance. Realizing how intensely many Kentuckians had reacted to the John Brown escapade at Harper's Ferry the year before, he denied having in any way supported leniency for Brown.

The final option for Kentucky voters was the ticket of John Bell of Tennessee and Edward Everett of Massachusetts, whose platform ignored all the divisive issues and eulogized George Washington and the patriotic experience that tied the Union together.

On election day Lexington voted for Breckinridge, but Kentuckians, correctly perceiving the strong secessionist element in the Breckinridge faction, voted their hearts and hopes for the Constitutional Union party of Bell and Everett. Only Virginia and Tennessee joined them. Lincoln's wife's hometown gave him two votes, and only five in the county. His victory was therefore regarded with great dismay. The *Kentucky Statesman* reacted by saying that "no intelligent man of the South ... will fail to deprecate the election of Lincoln and therein the success of the Republican party as the most serious and lamentable calamity which could have befallen our Republic."

Lexingtonians read with alarm the news of South Carolina's secession in December, followed shortly thereafter in the first two months of 1861 by the secession of six other states and the formation of the Confederate government at Montgomery, Alabama, with Jefferson Davis, another native son, as president. President Buchanan fumed and did nothing to prevent federal forts and property from being taken over by the seceding states. Lincoln appealed to the patriotic sentiments of Southerners in his inaugural address to keep the Union, but he would not relinquish Fort Sumter.

Pratt wrote in his diary on April 13, 1861:

> News reached us that the war has commenced between federal & Confederate troops at Fort Sumpter [sic] in the harbor of South Carolina. Our hearts are filled with sadness and great gloom in the community. There are many secessionists that I have no doubt rejoice in it, for its effect [is] to array the Whig South to a united Confederacy against the North, but a majority of people in Ky. are union & it is distressing to us to see sections of our nation thus arrayed in warlike hostility & that blood has commenced to flow.

This was the reaction of most Kentuckians. While proslavery they were adamantly pro-Union, and this ambivalence forced them to assume a stance of militant neutrality. They would not be secessionist, yet neither would they lift up swords against their proslavery Southern brethren.

This sentiment was manifested in the issuance by Governor Beriah Magoffin on May 20, 1861, of a proclamation of neutrality. On that very date the First Regiment of the State Guard, composed of the Lexington Rifles, Chasseurs, Old Infantry, Governor's Guard, Bourbon Rangers, and Flat Rock Grays encamped at Camp Buckner at the Lexington Trotting Track. Yet within these pro-Kentuckian ranks, pro-secessionist and pro-Union sentiments were expressed and divisiveness appeared. Both Lincoln and Jefferson Davis treated Kentucky gingerly for the Bluegrass border state was of crucial strategic importance to both of them.

The Union element of Lexington used a giant celebration on July Fourth to express its views and also used the occasion to formally dedicate the completed Henry Clay monument. Four weeks later Lexingtonians elected Judge R. A. Buckner, an avowed Unionist, over James B. Clay, son of Henry Clay and a secessionist, to the state legislature. On a statewide level, all but one Congressmen elected were Union candidates. This event, plus the invasion of western Kentucky at Columbus by the Confederates, turned the scales in favor of Union intervention. On September 19, 1861, the first Union troops arrived in Lexington and camped at the Fair Grounds. It was during this occupation by the troops that a fire destroyed the large two-story amphitheatre, floral hall, and other buildings. Before the end of the war, the area was also largely denuded of its large trees for firewood.

Shortly after the arrival of the Union troops, Captain John Hunt Morgan and his Lexington Rifles, by a clever ruse, slipped out of Lexington with their equipment and headed south to fight for the Confederacy, but he would pay a number of visits to his hometown before the war was over.

Outspoken secessionist leaders were rounded up and arrested, among whom was James Clay. Pratt recalled seeing him pass through town under guard along with 16 other prisoners, headed for a Louisville jail. "I felt sad," he wrote, "at the spectacle to see the son of the

Morrison College on the Transylvania University campus was used as a military hospital during the Civil War. This charming photo, taken at the beginning of the present century, was provided by the Lexington Public Library.

distinguished statesman ... brought through his native city, not permitted to meet his family or to speak to anyone."

Lexington was a deeply divided town. Not only were neighbors on opposite sides, but many families as well. The Reverend Robert J. Breckinridge, one of the most powerful spokesmen for the Union and uncle to John C. Breckinridge, saw two of his sons join the Confederate army. Benjamin Gratz's stepson, Joseph Shelby, became one of the ablest Confederate cavalry leaders, while his own son, Cary, served as a captain in the Union army.

The Union forces commandeered a number of large buildings to use as hospitals, including Morrison Hall at Transylvania, the Medical Department building, and the Masonic Grand Lodge Hall. Dr. Robert Peter served as a medical supervisor in a number of them. At least three Union commanders occupied the Bodley house in Gratz Park.

Throughout the winter of 1861-62, the town appeared relatively untouched by the war. Social life for the pro-Union families may have been somewhat gayer as young Yankee officers appeared at dances and other festivities, including balls in the Bodley house itself. Some Lexington theatre-goers attended performances

at the Opera House (Odd Fellows Hall) on the southeast corner of Main and Broadway or at Melodeon Hall, including a memorable rendition of Shakespeare's *Richard III* starring a promising, darkly handsome young actor by the name of John Wilkes Booth.

By the spring and summer of 1862, that tranquillity was disrupted. The invasion of Kentucky in the west by General Braxton Bragg, and the forces of General Kirby Smith from the southeast heading for Lexington and Cincinnati created apprehension among the residents. In a remarkably uncoordinated campaign, Bragg and Smith operated almost independently of each other. General Smith moved effectively toward Richmond and Lexington, defeating the Union forces under General Nelson at Richmond and then moving on to Lexington as Union troops evacuated the city and Union residents feared the worst. Looking from her window onto Gratz Park (the Old College Lot), Frances Dallam Peter, a staunch Unionist, kept a diary of what she heard and saw, until her premature death in 1864. She was the teen-age daughter of Dr. Robert Peter, distinguished physician, chemist, and geologist who received his M. D. degree from Transylvania and joined its faculty in

1838. The Peter house on the south corner of Mechanic and Market streets, once occupied by Gideon Shryock while building Morrison College, was an attractive Federal style building. The Peters were Unionist. Just across the park was the imposing home of his pro-Union neighbor, Benjamin Gratz, while adjoining Gratz's place on the south was the home of Mrs. Henrietta Morgan, mother of John Hunt Morgan.

The Confederates entered the city September 2, but "very little demonstration was made over them," according to Miss Peter. Other accounts describe an enthusiastic welcome, with Confederate flags suddenly appearing at many windows while Union flags disappeared. When John Hunt Morgan and his men arrived, there was a more enthusiastic greeting as "the secesh ladies paraded about with the stars and bars in their hands & streamers of white and red on their dresses and bonnets." Compared to the well supplied and uniformed Union troops, the Confederates "wore no uniforms but were dressed in grey & butternut jeans ... and looked like the tag, rag, & bobtail of the earth & as if they hadn't been near water since Fort Sumter fell," said the critical Miss Peter. But she did think some of the officers a bit more impressive and they had "very fine" horses.

Bodley House, circa 1815, still stands on the corner of Market and Second streets. During much of the Civil War it was used as a Union headquarters.

General Smith made the Phoenix Hotel his headquarters and issued what George M. Ranck, the Lexington historian, terms "a conciliatory proclamation very reassuring to the Union men, and gave the strictest orders for the protection of all citizens and their property." The Confederates had been fortunate to capture a huge store of Union army equipment and food, valued at $1,000,000. Certain items were not included in this windfall, however, and General Smith intended that the Lexington storekeepers provide those needs, indicating in an order that all citizens should accept Confederate scrip without question. Those storekeepers who had not fled town reluctantly obeyed the order, realizing that the dubious value of Confederate money made all purchases, in reality, confiscation of their goods.

Dr. Peter, outspoken in support of the Union, was arrested three times, but seems to have suffered no more hardship than confinement to his home. The hospitals in town over which he had supervision were now taken over by the Confederates.

The *Observer & Reporter* closed down after the battle of Richmond, and the *Statesman* made a short recovery.

Though as far north as Covington feverish military preparations were being made in anticipation of a strong Confederate push to Cincinnati, Smith seemed quite content to remain at Lexington while waiting for some word from Bragg. Meanwhile, General Don Carlos Buell had moved from Bowling Green to Louisville and was preparing a major thrust against the Confederate forces. In early October he moved out against Bragg, colliding with him first at Frankfort where the Confederate general was in the process of installing a Confederate government. Bragg and the newly inaugurated Confederate governor departed quickly. Bragg withdrew his forces southeast toward Harrodsburg.

Almost by accident, the Union and Confederate forces, desperately searching for water in the drought of a bone-dry Kentucky fall, stumbled on each other at Perryville, and on October 8 fought a bloody and inconclusive battle, after which Bragg continued to withdraw southward. General Smith had no choice now but to evacuate Lexington and rejoin Bragg as

Dr. Robert Peter, prominent local physician and historian, and his family lived in this house on Market Street during the Civil War. Built circa 1813, it was the home of Horace Holley, president of Transylvania University in the 1820's and was lived in by architect Gideon Shryock when he was supervising construction of Morrison College.

soon as possible. Departing October 8, he was too late to participate in the Perryville conflict.

Colonel John Morgan, wishing to make one final raid through the Bluegrass to damage Buell's supply lines and, perhaps, to salvage a small victory from this depressing retreat, returned to Lexington October 18, successfully surprising a contingent of 300 to 500 Union troops encamped at Ashland and taking them prisoner. He then galloped into town to disperse a small Union force at the courthouse before disappearing within a few hours toward Versailles and Lawrenceburg. Out of this brief escapade came an heroic incident.

Some of Morgan's men had captured a large American flag that had been made by a Lexington woman for the Union troops here. They dragged the flag through the city streets. When Ella Bishop, the 17-year-old daughter of a hardware dealer and an ardent Unionist, saw this desecration, she seized the flag from Morgan's men, and wrapping it around her body declared she would surrender it only at the cost of her life. Morgan's men were gentlemanly enough not to attempt to retrieve the flag and indeed may have applauded her courage. In any case, when Brigadier General

G. Clay Smith heard of the incident, he issued an order naming the Union encampment Camp Ella Bishop. Today that flag hangs on the wall of the State Shrine at Waveland.

With the departure of the Confederate forces, life in Lexington returned to a reasonably normal pattern. The *Observer & Reporter* resumed publication. Pratt recorded a quiet and peaceful Christmas Day. Yet the presence of the Union troops was an everyday reminder that life was really not normal. Some of those troops were not averse to interfering with slave property or hiding escaped slaves. On January 1, 1863, Lincoln's Emancipation Proclamation went into effect. Though this act did not free a single slave in Kentucky (only those states still in rebellion on that date were subject to emancipation), nevertheless many Kentucky Unionists spoke out against it and expressed their fears about the future of slavery in Kentucky.

Fortunately, Lexington's nerves were soothed somewhat when the Forty-Eighth Pennsylvania Regiment was detached from the Army of the Potomac and sent here in March 1863, for provost guard duty. These seasoned veterans apparently behaved with greater poise and civility than the raw Wisconsin and Indiana troops who had preceded them. Most of them were housed in an old hemp factory on North Limestone. One soldier wrote to his sister back in Pennsylvania that Lexington "is a very fine place. It is about as large as Reading and has splendid houses ... We are treated better than we could expect among strangers ... " General Orlando Wilcox, commander of the Central Kentucky Military District, moved his headquarters to Lexington and used the Bodley house, on the northeast corner of Market and Second streets, for dances, even bringing an orchestra from Cincinnati for the occasion.

A disaster in the spring of 1863 was the burning on May 23 of the handsome Transylvania Medical Hall at Second and Broadway, which was being used as a hospital for the troops. The sick and wounded were all safely evacuated, but the building and some teaching apparatus were destroyed. Fortunately, most of the library and apparatus had been removed earlier to various places of safekeeping when the building was converted into a hospital.

Ella Bishop, a seventeen-year-old Lexington girl, rescued an American flag from invading Confederate troops in September, 1862. Photo courtesy of Transylvania University.

With the departure of the Forty-Eighth Pennsylvania in the fall of 1863 to rejoin the Army of the Potomac on that last massive campaign to end the war in Virginia, friendly relations between the Bluegrass and Union officials began to deteriorate. General Stephen Burbridge became the symbol of Union repressive and dictatorial measures in Kentucky as he attempted to control the expanding activities of numerous guerrilla bands active throughout the state, and especially in eastern Kentucky. Innocent citizens were frequently made accountable for guerrilla atrocities on the assumption that they might either have prevented them from happening in the first place or that they were sheltering the offenders. General Burbridge issued an order in 1864 that four guerrillas be killed for every loyal Unionist murdered. Lacking enough verified guerrillas to fill the quotas, innocent Confederate prisoners were sometimes made to pay the price. On one occasion, two Confederate soldiers were hanged in Lexington despite public protest.

Kentuckians had also been truculent in their response to draft measures initiated by the Federal government in 1863. Compulsion of this kind irritated them. Lincoln moved slowly in attempting to enforce the draft in Kentucky as long as volunteers from that state filled a

portion of the quotas assigned them. Even worse, from the Kentuckians' viewpoint, was the recruitment of Negro soldiers. This nearly brought an outright rebellion on the part of the Kentucky government.

Indicative of the strong feelings about this policy was a startling incident in Lexington on March 10, 1864. At a ceremony in Melodeon Hall honoring Colonel Frank Wolford of the First Kentucky Cavalry for his heroic service against the rebels, Wolford launched into a tirade against Lincoln and his administration for their unconstitutional measures and repressive methods. Negro recruitment was the worst example of this, he said, and he urged resistance to its implementation. This outburst led General Burbridge to arrest Wolford but Lincoln later ordered his release.

Shortly after the Wolford incident, Governor Bramlette prepared a proclamation of actual opposition to the recruitment of blacks. Only a night-long session with General Burbridge and the Reverend Robert Breckinridge led to the Governor's cooling off and the issuance of a proclamation that advised calm and acquiescence toward the policy. Eventually 23,703 Kentucky Negroes wore the Union uniform, second in numbers only to Louisiana.

To add to General Burbridge's problems, General John Hunt Morgan made one last desperation raid through his home state in June 1864. He struck successfully at Mt. Sterling, routing the Union forces there, and then headed for Lexington. Pratt hid his horse in the smokehouse about 2 a.m. on June 10 "fearful the rascals" would steal it, and indeed Morgan failed to control his men who, in desperate need for supplies and horses, took what they wanted in bandit fashion, robbing the banks and setting fire to various structures, including the Covington depot and Wolf's brewery. Pratt so feared the town would be engulfed in flames that he had his servants fill every available container with water. Adding to the chaos of that early morning raid, the Union troops, which had retreated to Fort Clay, began to open fire on the rebels with artillery. "It was frightful to see these vessels of death flying, whizzing over our houses," Pratt wrote. Having garnered what they could, Morgan's men left Lexington for Georgetown and Cynthiana, burning a good part of the latter

John Hunt Morgan rose to the rank of brigadier general for his daring exploits as a Confederate cavalry leader. He was killed in 1864 at Greeneville, Tennessee. This likeness, which is the property of the Hunt-Morgan House, has deteriorated with time.

town before Burbridge's troops caught up with them and dealt Morgan's troops a smashing defeat that dispersed his forces across the countryside and left many dead and wounded behind. Morgan escaped to Virginia where his superior officers suspended him from command and ordered a court of inquiry for September 10, but Union troops finally trapped and killed the "Thunderbolt of the Confederacy" at Greeneville, Tennessee, a few days before the court was to meet.

In November 1864, the Presidential election was held, and despite strong pressure by Union forces to keep Kentucky dissidents from voting, Kentucky was one of two states to cast its vote for General McClellan and not for Lincoln, though the Republican party polled a significant number of votes, thus indicating political battle lines for the future.

Finally, in April 1865, the long, bitter war was over. Many in Lexington fired off guns, rang bells, gave or listened to speeches, or watched the fireworks. Yet the sounds of cheering had barely died away when the terrible news of Lincoln's assassination reached the town. "I went downtown," Pratt wrote,

"and every countenance was sad — even Secessionists (the more considerate ones) lamented the event. But, still I feel, that Mr. Lincoln could not have died at a more propitious time for his own glory." The Lexington *Observer & Reporter* stated that though it had differed with the deceased President, he was a remarkable individual and that "the nation has seldom seen a sadder day . . . " The City Council proclaimed April 19 as a day of mourning and prayer. Special exercises were held in the chapel at Morrison Hall and at various churches throughout the city. Most businesses were closed or draped in black but a few indicated their true feelings by staying open and evidencing no expression of sorrow.

Kentucky, the only border state not to ratify the Thirteenth Amendment to the U. S. Constitution formally ending human slavery, faced the difficult period of Reconstruction with more contradictory opinions and ambivalent feelings and pent-up resentments than many of the defeated Confederate states to the south. Lexington, as one of the significant cities in Kentucky, shared those problems.

Transylvania Medical Hall (depicted in this drawing on a student ticket) was completed in 1839 on the northwest corner of Broadway and Second streets. It burned on May 3, 1863, while being used as a Union Army hospital. Photo courtesy of Transylvania University.

Lexington Opera House on North Broadway soon after its completion in 1886. The building was restored in 1975-76. Photo courtesy of Transylvania University.

Chapter V

1866/1890

Readjustment and Development

I n James Lane Allen's short story, "Two Gentlemen of Kentucky," published in *Flute and Violin and Other Kentucky Tales* in 1891, the best-selling Lexington author described an old Confederate colonel and his black servant Peter as they tried unsuccessfully to adjust to a post-Civil War society. The colonel had sold his farm and come to town to live where he "haunted Cheapside and the courthouse square," seeking out anyone who would sit with him and talk over old times. Occasionally, he would encounter one of his poverty-stricken former servants who warmed the aging man's heart "by contrasting the hardship of a life of freedom with the ease of their shackled years." This retreat into nostalgia was doubtless shared by many others who found their antebellum social structure in fragments about them. Even the colonel's disastrous venture into the hardware business only enhanced the image of the impractical planter trying his hand at a more hard-headed enterprise, for he used the store mainly as a social center. Yet, he could see

> the town was reshaping itself slowly, and painfully, but with resolute energy. The colossal structure of slavery had fallen, scattering its ruins far and wide over the state; but out of the very debris was being taken the material to lay deeper foundations of the new social edifice. Men and women as old as he were beginning life over, and trying to fit themselves for it by changing the whole attitude and habit of their minds — by taking on a new heart and spirit.

Unfortunately, the colonel and Peter would never become part of the rebuilding element in society. They would live out their lives only in the familiar shadows of a lost world.

Lexingtonians, both black and white, did indeed have major readjustments to make as they confronted the problems of race relations, a changing economy, and a complex political picture on both a state and national scale. Unlike the Confederate states, which had suffered a terrible loss of manpower and property, and were to experience the tension-filled period of military Reconstruction under the Radical Republican policies, Kentucky could face the future with some optimism as it sought to expand its economic production and transportation system. The development of burley tobacco would soon grow into a very important part of the state's economy at a time when the market for hemp was declining.

Though Lexington had suffered some property damage from Union military occupation, and the occasional forays of Morgan's men, it came through the Civil War relatively unscathed. The wounds from the war were more psychological, social, and political. The challenge to Lexington was one of undertaking the necessary municipal improvements, expanding railroad facilities, and promoting energetic and inventive economic enterprise to stimulate the growth and prosperity of the city. Both local and national economic conditions hampered a really significant expansion until the decade of the 1880's when major changes did occur within the city, and a promising watershed of metropolitan development seemed to be forming.

The most important social and economic challenge was the ending of slavery and the need to establish a new framework of race relations. The major political change was the shift from a strong pro-Union sentiment, fostered for so many years by Henry Clay, and which kept Kentucky in the Union ranks during the Civil War, to an increasingly hostile anti-federal feeling, created in large part by the abolition of slavery and by the treatment Kentucky had received under Union military occupation, both during and after the war. It has been said, with some justification, that Kentucky waited until after the Civil War to secede.

Nothing signified this change more dramatically than the hospitality given by Lexingtonians to returning Confederate veterans. The pro-Southern, or states' rights, viewpoint became increasingly popular. The hammer blows of the 13th, 14th, and 15th amendments to the U.S. Constitution only strengthened the anti-federal hostility.

Indicative of the growing sympathy with the Confederate cause was the warm reception given to Basil Duke's historical account of General John Hunt Morgan and his men. When Morgan's body was returned in April 1868, to Lexington and reinterred in the Lexington Cemetery, there was a large funeral ceremony. John C. Breckinridge, Confederate general and a member of Jefferson Davis' cabinet, returned to his hometown on March 13, 1869, after years of exile. In October 1870, there was a sizable crowd at the courthouse to mourn reverently the death of Robert E. Lee. When Breckinridge died in 1875, the town was draped in black and an elaborate funeral was conducted. In that same year, a special Confederate monument was erected in the cemetery. The fact that the two monuments now dominating the courthouse lawn are the statues of John C. Breckinridge and John Hunt Morgan clearly reveals the post-war Confederate feeling.

The Democratic party remained predominant in Kentucky politics, but it was split between the ex-Confederate Bourbon agrarian wing and the Union Democrats who, though hostile to the Radical Republicans, had nevertheless condemned secession and supported the Union military effort. The Republicans, despite the support of federal troops, officials, and Radical Republican laws and policies, made little headway in Kentucky and were soundly beaten in both state and local elections.

Henry Watterson, dynamic editor of the Louisville *Courier-Journal,* forged a new coalition of New Departure Democrats, whether ex-Confederate or Unionist, dedicated to promoting Kentucky's economic and political progress. He advocated accepting the 13th, 14th and 15th Amendments, advancing the welfare and education of the Negroes, and generally promoting Kentucky's industrial and transportation expansion.

Lexington reflected this diversity of political positions, though the Bourbon agrarians predominated. Union Democrats were disgruntled at the rapidity with which ex-Confederates assumed influential roles in local and state affairs. Though both Bourbon and Union Democrats had no problem uniting against the Republicans, they did not agree necessarily on local officials and policies.

Political Stagnation

This was best seen in the neutral, non-controversial character of the Lexington mayors elected between 1865-1880. Dr. Joseph Chinn, a respected physician, was seventy-one years old when he was elected for one year. Though he was a Union sympathizer, all his sons had joined John Hunt Morgan's regiment. Thus, his qualifications as a compromise candidate were excellent.

His successor, Jerry T. Frazer, a tailor and dry goods merchant, had been elected mayor by the City Council first in 1867. The Council chose him as mayor again in 1869 — he was sixty-four years old at the time — and reelected him annually until 1880, when at the age of 75 he had served longer than any other mayor to date.

The City Council reflected the same stagnation as the mayors. Their indifference to unhealthy sanitary conditions in the city and the severe water supply problem prompted Henry T. Duncan, editor of the *Press,* to complain that "it is true that our corporate existence is only a living monument to the disgraceful stupidity and shameful Rip Van Winkleism of our community." The county

96

Treacy and Wilson's livery stable (Horseman's Headquarters) located on East Main near the Phoenix Hotel. Drawing courtesy of Transylvania University.

courthouse was badly deteriorated, and other cities had installed street railways years earlier.

This state of affairs did not bother Dennis Mulligan, the prosperous grocer and city councilman who had built a strong Democratic bloc which controlled much of the city government's activities and patronage. Leader of what was called "Mulligan's Ring," the strong-headed Irishman supported a policy of parsimony in government expenditures, low taxation, and limited indebtedness, regardless of the impact of such policies on the welfare of Lexington. This passive attitude of the city government did not change until the reform movement of the 1880's.

It was during this same 1865-1880 period that Lexington was struggling to adjust to fundamental changes in race relations, brought on by the influx of the freedmen into the community and the campaign for black legal rights, which created new housing patterns and tense social and political problems.

The Crisis of Race Relations

Race relations became the most immediate and constant problem for both blacks and whites. The whole antebellum slave framework was now destroyed by the 13th amendment, and the 14th amendment ratified in 1867 made the freedman a U.S. citizen. In 1870 the ratification of the 15th amendment gave him the right to vote. Kentucky adamantly refused to ratify any of them.

What intensified the problem in Lexington, as in many other towns, was the dramatic increase in the size of the black urban population. Between 1840 and 1860 the number had remained relatively static, but between 1860 and 1870 it jumped from 3,080 to 7,171, an increase of 133 percent, while the white population increased by only about 2,000, an increase of nearly 27 percent. The data from the 1870 U.S. census are unreliable, and the increase for both whites and blacks was probably higher than printed, perhaps by as much as 12 percent. The ratio of whites to blacks was almost one to one, however, regardless of overall numbers.

Most of Lexington's new black residents were from rural areas. Fayette County's rural black population dropped about 29 percent in the 1860-1870 period. Some blacks wished to escape persecution by hostile rural whites, others sought aid from the Freedmen's Bureau or searched out the army recruiting stations for jobs. Some came to the city because they were destitute and hoped to find employment for themselves and schooling for their children.

The end of slavery and the influx of rural blacks changed the housing patterns of Lexington. The tremendous demand for new low-cost housing after the war led to several types of solutions and projects. One was the so-called street-front settlement, seen mostly in the county, where landowners set aside a part of their property along an existing highway, and divided it into small lots to be sold to house-seekers, or to an enterprising builder who might construct cheap rental housing. However, most Negroes found housing in the urban clusters located in the interiors of city blocks, to which access was gained by alleys or narrow streets. This new housing was usually located in the less desirable areas of Lexington, near railroads and bridges, or close by stockyards or cemeteries. Usually they were named either for the developer or the owner of the estate on which they were located, who might be the same.

The largest of these was Goodloetown (named after William Cassius Goodloe, nephew of Cassius Marcellus Clay), located north of East Main Street between Dewees Street and what is now Midland Avenue, and reaching all the way to Third Street. Adjoining this to the north was Kinkeadtown, subdivided by George B. Kinkead in 1870. To the west, between Fourth and Fifth, Broadway and Upper streets, was Taylortown. North of this was Brucetown, named after W. W. Bruce, noted hemp manufacturer, who subdivided land adjacent to

his hemp factory. In the southern part of Lexington, John A. Prall, a lawyer, created Pralltown, stretching from South Limestone to the railroad tracks. Lee's Row and Davis Bottom were both located in deep valleys alongside railroad tracks.

Houses in these clusters were usually single-family, "shotgun-style" structures built on extremely narrow lots. This design was one room wide and three to five rooms deep, built quickly and cheaply. The clusters were close enough to town to allow the black workers to walk to their jobs.

Though largely due to the great demand for cheap housing, the concentration of blacks into certain housing areas also reflected a change in social attitudes. Whereas in the antebellum slavery period dispersion of black housing was a means of control, the whites now sought to maintain superiority through segregation, the physical and social separation of the races.

Blacks in the 1870-1880 period found employment in 80 different types of work, including craft skills. The most common were domestic service, laundress, cook, laborer, farm hand, and factory worker. Most of them did not earn enough money to own property, only 11 percent possessing either real or personal property worth $100 or more in 1870. Yet, despite these handicaps, a number of Negroes achieved remarkable distinction and financial success over the next few decades. The number of black-operated businesses increased significantly, and included a bakery, two saloons, restaurants, grocery stores, barber shops, blacksmith shops, and a jewelry store.

Successful Businessman

Moses Spencer epitomized the successful black businessman at the time of his death in 1877. As a free Negro before the war, he owned and operated a second-hand furniture store on Main Street and even owned a slave. Shortly after the war he bought a business on the corner of Short and Market streets, selling his store on Main Street. His furniture business prospered and in 1870 his real property was valued at $17,500 and his personal property an additional $2,000. By the end of the century there would be a number of blacks equally prosperous.

One of the important issues at this time concerned the right of Negro testimony in the courts. In the antebellum period neither slave nor free black was permitted to testify in court against a white person. While other legal restrictions on blacks were lifted by the 1866 General Assembly, the prohibition against Negro testimony was preserved. In that same year, the federal Civil Rights Bill was enacted over the President's veto. That legislation guaranteed to the Negro the right to take his case to a federal court if he were prevented from giving testimony in a state court. There were many such cases on record.

The Kentucky newspapers remained quiet for some time on this issue and the Democratic party dodged the question in 1866. Meanwhile, the federal courts were active in convicting whites found guilty of attacking blacks, and some opponents to black testimony began to change their minds, believing that the state courts might be more lenient in such cases. Leading legal figures in the state petitioned the General Assembly to enact a law admitting Negro testimony. Watterson and the *Courier-Journal* supported this cause but Howard Gratz and the *Gazette* opposed it. When the Negro was given the right to vote in 1870 by the 15th amendment, some Democrats had a change of heart, and in 1871 Preston Leslie, the Democratic candidate for governor, spoke out for Negro testimony. This weakened the conservative Democratic opposition, and in January 1872, the General Assembly adopted a new law on evidence permitting black testimony.

Suffrage Volatile Issue

The suffrage issue was highly volatile since it impinged on the political power structure. Black leaders campaigned for the vote shortly after the war ended, and even more enthusiastically with the ratification of the 14th amendment, which the General Assembly predictably voted down. At a barbecue in Lexington on July 4, 1867, attended largely by Negroes, the speakers included Brigadier-General James Brisbin, chief of staff to General Burbridge; John Fee, founder of Berea College, Kentucky's pioneer institution in integrated higher education; and William Cassius Goodloe, editor of the *Statesman* and staunch supporter of the Radical Republican cause, who was apparently imbued with the same courage as his great-uncle, Cassius Marcellus Clay. All spoke in favor of Negro suffrage though Goodloe was rather pessimistic about seeing it accomplished in his lifetime.

The Republican politicians found the issue especially embarrassing because they knew it would cost them votes, yet they included black delegates in the Fayette County nominating convention and even placed some blacks on the ticket. Black leaders, however, urged blacks to refrain from running for office because it would certainly defeat Republicans. After the ratification of the 15th amendment, some blacks drifted into the Democratic party to spite Republicans, who may have believed they could monopolize the black vote.

It is probable that many white Kentuckians shared the opinion of the editor of the Lexington *Observer & Reporter*, who called the 15th amendment "a monstrosity in legislation, the crowning infamy of an unscrupulous and despotic majority." Thus was the Radical Republican regime in Washington regarded by many Bluegrass citizens.

This attitude was reinforced in the *Gazette's* pleas in the fall of 1869 for a change in the city charter, which expressed fear that if Negroes were enfranchised "they will get control of the city government." The editor said he felt kindly toward the blacks but would "deprecate the attempt to transform them into citizens." The charter was amended in 1871 and the City Council was delegated power not only to elect the mayor but other city officials as well. It also provided for a "capitation" (poll) tax as a prerequisite for voting, thus substantially reducing the number of voters.

Racial harmony was severely strained by outbreaks of violence. On February 2, 1870, the Ku Klux Klan claimed credit for hanging a Negro on the Tates Creek Pike, nine miles from town, because they were angry that he had been acquitted of the charge of hog stealing. Then, in August of that year, a bloody riot was barely averted. Following a mass meeting of blacks at the First Baptist Church at Dewees and Short streets, a number of them, ignoring the advice of their leaders to disperse and go home quietly, marched down Main Street, singing "John Brown's Body."

When they arrived in front of the Phoenix Hotel, some of them began firing pistols into the air. As they proceeded to Mill Street, they were confronted by the police who attempted to arrest them. In the ensuing fracas a policeman was killed. As the demonstrators started up North Broadway, the fire bells sounded the alarm, calling out the state guard. In ten minutes the crowd had dispersed. Guards patrolled the streets for the next thirty-six hours. The murderer was caught, large-scale bloodshed was avoided, and the possibility of an attack on the Negro enclaves prevented. It was a close call, but indicative that most Lexingtonians were committed to preserving order. The *Gazette,* hardly a pro-Negro paper, later stated that the Negroes, who composed more than half of the residents of Lexington, were "one of the most law-abiding populations in America."

Civic and Social Activities

Life in Lexington and Fayette County was not totally absorbed in the race question, however. New houses were built, new businesses established, and more banks chartered. People complained about the condition of the city streets. They bought their meat and produce at the Market House. This facility was still under the control of the city, which supervised the proper weighing of goods, set the hours, and prohibited the sale of fish during the summer months. The city set the rates for the omnibuses, and in April 1867, officially named Dewees Street, which had recently been completed from East Main opposite Montmollin's lumberyard to Third Street. Railroad trains were prohibited from traveling faster than four miles an hour within the city limits. A city physician was hired to care for the indigent at the City Small-Pox Hospital, and a health officer employed to supervise the collection of waste and to "prevent the Drivers from idling away their time during working hours." He may also have kept an eye on householders to see that they obeyed ordinances requiring that privies be five feet deep "unless hitting rock, then 4 feet," and to be regularly drained and limed. In 1868, a Sunday closing ordinance went into effect, only drug stores being exempted. This was later liberalized. In 1872, the city insisted on mass vaccination for smallpox and established a $15 fine for violators.

Circuses came to town, and crowds gathered at the station to watch them unload from the train and then march grandly down the city streets with the band playing, and children gawking at the strange animals and the gaudy attire of the circus performers. Later, people would go out to the Fair Grounds, or some other empty field near town to see the performance under the big tent.

During the summer months, Lexingtonians could relax and listen to concerts given by Saxton's band on the courthouse lawn or in the pleasant surroundings of Gratz Park. Henry Saxton, Jr., organized his cornet, quadrille, and orchestral bands in the fall of 1866, which became familiar features at barbecues, dances, and fairs.

Saxton was later joined by the talented Herman Trost who, with his brother Charles, had immigrated from Prussia to Kentucky a year before the Civil War started. Both enlisted in the Union army where Herman, because of his musical talent, was assigned the duty of conducting the regimental band. After the war he was engaged to teach music at the new Agricultural and Mechanical College. He, like Saxton, organized musical groups in Lexington, and almost inevitably they joined forces to form the Saxton & Trost band and orchestra, which soon won the reputation of being central Kentucky's finest musical group in the late 19th and early 20th centuries.

In the 1880's and well into the next century, the most popular place for events of many kinds was Woodland Park. The park was only a portion of Woodlands, the estate of James Erwin, son-in-law of Henry Clay. The Woodland Park Association bought 110 acres of the estate in 1882, sold off 480 lots and used the remaining 15 acres for a park. Here an impressive frame auditorium was erected. Nearby, where the baseball diamond is today, was a small pond called Lake Chenosa where people could go swimming or boating in the summer and skating in the winter.

The park, which was completely fenced in with an entrance at Park Avenue, was opened to the public in May 1885, and made accessible by a special line built by the street railway company. Two years later a Chautauqua Association was chartered here. The universally popular Chautauqua programs had originated at Lake Chautauqua in western New York,

A Women's Christian Temperance Union (W.C.T.U.) convention at Woodland Park about the turn of the century. The park, used as a Chautauqua and assembly ground for many years, was purchased by the city in 1902. Photo courtesy of Transylvania University.

combining a summer-camp-like vacation experience with a variety of cultural and educational programs. In July 1887, about 1,000 persons participated in the Chautauqua activities of Woodland Park, some coming from considerable distances to camp within the fenced-in park area, creating a tented village. Family reunions were held. For the several weeks that the Chautauqua program lasted, a full schedule of lectures and musical performances filled the auditorium.

Under the masterly direction of the stocky, genial Gus Jaubert, operator of the Magnolia Saloon on Mill Street, giant barbecues were frequently held.

The summer season saw the organization of teams to play the new American sport of baseball. These teams played one another on whatever grassy lot was available. As early as 1867, the Fayette Baseball Club was playing the Frankfort club frequently, and occasionally matching their talents against a team from Maysville. In May 1870, "the celebrated Red Stocking Baseball Club of Cincinnati," which had already achieved a national reputation, came down to meet the Lexington Orion Club.

For musical and theatrical entertainment, Lexingtonians and residents of Fayette County could attend performances at Melodeon Hall, Jackson Hall, or the Opera House. The latter,

not to be confused with the present Opera House on North Broadway, was the roomy Odd Fellows Hall built in 1856 on the southeast corner of Main and Broadway, with shops on the first level and a large auditorium on the second.

Another smaller park and beer garden on the north end of town was Gross's Garden, established in 1875 on East Sixth Street, a few hundred yards from Limestone. Advertised as a "Pleasure Resort & Beer Garden," it catered to a variety of groups including the Jolly Young Bachelors.

Shortly after the war the minstrel groups began to appear, sometimes for worthwhile charities such as the Orphans Home. The Undine Opera Troupe performed in 1868. Miss Helen Western, a native Lexingtonian, starred in "the celebrated play, *Under the Gaslight,* with scenery gorgeous beyond description from the National Theatre" in Cincinnati. There were variety shows featuring such celebrities as General Tom Thumb and his wife, groups of bell ringers, and humorists like Alf Burrett. Heavier drama featured such famed actors as Edwin Forrest in *Richelieu* and Shakespeare's *Othello.* Tickets ranged from 50¢ to $1.50. Performances of the sprightly and tuneful works of Gilbert and Sullivan added variety to the programs.

Gus Jaubert, Lexington's famous burgoo maker, preparing a feast at Woodland Park. Seen in the background is the park's frame auditorium, built in the mid-1880's and razed in 1905. Photo courtesy of Mrs. John Swift.

Little wonder, then, that many residents were saddened when the Odd Fellows Hall went up in fire and smoke on the morning of January 15, 1886. Almost immediately, plans for a new opera house were made, but not in another Odd Fellows Hall, though that fraternal order did erect a three-story building on the burned out site. Herman L. Rowe was engaged as architect, and the new Opera House was built on its present site on North Broadway, completed in 1887 at a cost of $45,000. Lexington now had a plush, lavishly designed theatre of which it could boast. It opened on August 19 with Lizzie Evan in *Our Angel.* The theatre soon gained the reputation as one of the best one-night stands in the country, and a host of famous stars such as Maude Adams, Otis Skinner, George Arliss, and Helen Hayes played there. The American Opera appeared there, and the Boston Symphony left its Brahmin sanctuary to travel to Kentucky and play on this stage.

For Lexingtonians in the fall of 1888, nothing exceeded the excitement of a visit by Mrs. Lillie Langtry, the toast, if not the scandal, of the English and American stage. This stunningly beautiful actress was to star in *As in a Looking Glass.* As befitted such a celebrity, she traveled by train in her specially designed boudoir car, complete with its own dining room, kitchen, storeroom of fine wines, and special chef. Mrs. Langtry arrived safely from Cincinnati and set the town agog as she strolled about viewing the sights. However, the admiring Lexingtonians were embarrassed upon learning that the Langtry boudoir car was roughly handled while here. When being transferred from one line to another, it broke loose from the other cars of the train and ran down an incline, coming to rest at the bottom. The engine and cars behind her car thundered down upon it and gave her precious vehicle such a jolt that everything breakable and moveable inside was smashed — including almost every bottle of wine and brandy! The unfortunate chef was badly scalded and taken immediately to the hospital. It is doubtful whether the incident interfered with Mrs. Langtry's performance, but one can imagine her outrage at being so inconvenienced.

In 1882, Lell's Hall was built on the south side of Short Street, two doors west of Broadway. Featuring a beer parlor and restaurant on the first floor, with variety shows of the song and dance type presented on the second floor, Lell's catered mostly to a male clientele who favored a more robust form of entertainment. When the second floor was converted into a gymnasium a few years later, it became even more popular. At the turn of the century, Ed "Strangler" Lewis began his training here on his way to the world wrestling championship. Lell also erected his "European Hotel" around the corner on the west side of North Broadway.

For those wishing to play in an orchestra of their own, the Lexington Philharmonic Society was formed in July 1870, by gentlemen, both professionals and amateurs. They used the public library for their rehearsal hall, but do not seem to have developed sufficiently to present public performances.

Lexington claimed several notable artists at this time. Samuel Woodson Price had maintained a studio in the second story of the new post office on the northwest corner of Short and Broadway when he assumed the job as postmaster in 1869. He had completed his fine portrait of General George Thomas, and was continuing to paint well-received works, some of which were awarded gold medals at the 1872 Cincinnati Exposition. Removed as postmaster for political reasons in 1876, he established a studio downtown and shortly after moved to Louisville. He eventually became completely blind and died in 1918 at his son's home in St. Louis at age 90. He was buried in the Arlington National Cemetery.

Joel T. Hart, whose statue "Woman Triumphant" has already been mentioned, was Lexington's premier sculptor, but from 1860 until his death in 1877 he lived and worked in Florence, Italy. Though not among America's top sculptors, he was certainly one of Kentucky's best in the 19th century. His body of work was large and meritorious, including

full-length statues of Henry Clay, and busts of Cassius Clay, John Crittenden, Andrew Jackson, Benjamin Dudley, Zachary Taylor, and Robert Wickliffe. He was buried in the English cemetery at Florence near his friends Elizabeth Barrett Browning and fellow sculptor Hiram Powers. However, the Kentucky legislature appropriated sufficient funds in 1887 to have his body brought back to his native soil and buried in the Frankfort Cemetery.

Sculptor Joel T. Hart's masterpiece, "Woman Triumphant," stood in the rotunda of the Fayette County Courthouse in the late 1800's. The statue was destroyed when the building burned on May 14, 1897. Photo courtesy of Transylvania University.

The Swiss-born Edward Troye, one of the nation's greatest horse and animal painters, captured the images of so many legendary central Kentucky horses in the mid-19th

103

Lell's Hall, built in 1882, still stands at 412 West Short Street. J. W. Lell operated a beer parlor on the first floor and a theatre on the second. When erected it was considered Lexington's "most beautiful building." Photo courtesy of Transylvania University.

century that Fayette County and Lexington regarded him as one of their own. His death in 1874 at age 66 saddened all. The impressive monument marking his grave in the cemetery at Georgetown was erected in his memory by James A. Grinstead, Lexington banker and turfman.

Fairs and Court Days

The fairs resumed shortly after the war, although many of the old associations that originally sponsored them had expired and were replaced by new organizations. Of these, the most numerous were the Agricultural and Mechanical Associations which sprang up in the 1865-1900 period. Some of the fairs were organized by war veterans who emphasized the

festive rather than the educational aspects, and helped heal the wounds created by the conflict.

Harness racing became a regular event at these fairs as the trotters and pacers gained greater esteem.

By 1870, the old Fair Grounds at Maxwell Springs, used by the troops during the war, was gradually restored and fenced in. In 1876, the Kentucky Agricultural and Mechanical Society sold the grounds to the city for a park and purchased a 62-acre tract off South Broadway. Here they built a grandstand, laid out a race course, and on August 31 held the annual fair there for the first time. A floral hall, designed, according to the *Gazette* of August 14, 1880, by Phelix Lundin, but probably built by John McMurtry, was erected in 1882. The eye-catching octagonal structure still stands at the entrance to the famed trotting track called "The Red Mile."

The Fayette Agricultural and Mechanical Association for Colored People was organized in 1869 with Henry King as president, and was granted a charter by the legislature a year later. Believed to have been the first fair organized by Negroes, it was held in 1869 on the Newtown Pike. Twenty-five acres of land were then leased from the old Ficklin estate of M.C. Johnson on the Georgetown Road. Scheduled later at the Trotting Track at a different time from the white fairs, the colored fairs were very successful, and drew large crowds from an increasingly wide area.

In August 1883, President Arthur came to Louisville, stopping at Lexington on the way, to open the Southern Exposition, which introduced for the first time widespread use of electric lighting. The economic depression of the early 1890's radically reduced the number of fairs in Kentucky, and by the turn of the century they began to change character. Some fraternal societies and private organizations, such as the Elks, began to sponsor fairs in Fayette and Scott counties, and they became increasingly festive.

Of all assemblages which Kentuckians treasured well into the 20th century, none exceeded the county court days. The monthly meeting of county courts derived from the Virginia system of jurisprudence, and further back, to England itself. But the legal reason for court day was soon swallowed up in the

"County Court Day" on Cheapside after the turn of the 19th century. The monthly "Court Days" were declared a public nuisance in 1921 and discontinued shortly thereafter. Photo courtesy of Transylvania University.

diversity of activities which brought rural and urban Kentuckians together. James Lane Allen, who as a Fayette County youth attended many such days, wrote that their popularity reflected the character of the men who came (and the rough-and-ready features of the day almost dictated male dominance). It was, Allen thought, because the Kentuckian

> loves the swarm. The very motto of the State is a declaration of good-fellowship, and the seal of the Commonwealth the act of shaking hands ... The Kentuckian must be one of many ... must see men about him who are fat, grip his friend, hear cordial, hearty conversation ... Hence his fondness for large gatherings: open-air assemblies of the democratic sort — great agricultural fairs, race courses, political meetings, barbecues and burgoo in the woods ...

In the early 19th century, this conviviality was marked by athletic contests such as wrestling,

sledge-throwing, foot races, and pugilistic matches. Then, as the day wore on and the drinking became heavier, brawls of a less sportive kind occurred. As the years went by, auctioneers began to sell horses and cattle. By the end of the Civil War, county court days on Cheapside became marked less by athletic contests and horse racing and more by talking, horse trading, cattle buying, the swapping and buying of almost anything, and campaigning — all in a chaotic atmosphere of crowded animals and humanity, tobacco chewing, cigar smoking, and whiskey drinking.

The merchants and tavern keepers prospered from court days, but many of the local citizenry, not immediately involved, began to rebel. On a hot summer's day the stench was such as to "cause a strong, well man" to vomit. Rain might lay the dust, but it turned the area into a stinking, muddy swamp. By

1870, the local government was being pressured to relegate cattle sales to the outskirts of town, or at least to provide cattle pens. But when the city initiated such a policy, the merchants protested and the authorities relented temporarily. The growing cosmopolitan and genteel character of the town ultimately precluded the continuance of cattle and hog sales and they were finally prohibited at the downtown location. The tug-of-war continued into the 20th century and court days here were not officially abolished until 1921.

Building Expansion

The influx of new residents, including a sizable number of Irish, changing housing patterns, fluctuating economic development, and political realignments all added to the complexity of the post-Civil War problems. The "Athens of the West" which had lived on its remarkable accomplishments of the antebellum period — achieved largely by 1830 but cherished and fostered until the Civil War — now confronted a new era of uncertainty. Would it once again be able to generate those forces of cultural and educational attainment, and to what extent could it expand the economic base on which such achievements in part depended? Or should Lexington and Fayette County concentrate on modernizing and developing the town into a major economic and transportation center, competing with other emerging midwestern cities?

The immediate postwar years saw some energetic economic activity, but the decade of the 1870's was largely a static period with constant comments by the press and merchants of economic depression. The local newspapers in 1873 spoke graphically of the depressed condition of central Kentucky — trade diminished, merchants complained, laborers were out of work, farm and city properties had no purchasers. The previous three years had seen interest rates climb to 10 percent. Citizens called on the town government to cut costs.

Despite some stagnation in Lexington's economy, there was a notable degree of activity in the construction of buildings, especially churches. In the period between the end of the war and 1880 this included the new white First Baptist Church on the old Main Street

cemetery site but facing West Short Street, St. Paul Catholic Church across the street, the Centenary Methodist Church on the corner of Church and Broadway, the Second or Upper Street Baptist Church, and the Second Christian Church on Constitution (Second) Street. New hotels were built, such as the Ashland House (later the Reed and Drake) on Short Street between Mill and Broadway, and the Nicholas Hotel (also called the Florentine, Leonard, and Henry Clay) on Main Street. The Fayette National Bank Building and Higgins Block were erected on the northeast corner of Upper and Main streets. Jackson Hall was constructed between Vine and Water streets,

St. Paul Catholic Church, dedicated on October 16, 1868, is located on West Short Street at the head of Spring Street.

106

Lexington's sixth and last market house, Jackson Hall, was erected in 1897 in the block bounded by Limestone, Upper, Vine and Water streets. The market occupied the entire first floor and for many years the city offices were located on the second floor. The building was razed in 1941. Photo courtesy of Burton Milward.

with the Market House on the first floor and the town offices and much-used all-purpose hall on the second floor.

John McMurtry, Cincinnatus Shryock, Herman L. Rowe, and Phelix Lundin were among the most active of the architects at this time. Depending on the type of project, the styles reflected the continuing influence of the Gothic, the Renaissance Eclecticism, and the Italianate.

Born abroad and trained in Germany, Rowe worked in several places in the United States before coming to Lexington in 1880 to assist in the construction of the new buildings of the Agricultural and Mechanical College. Later, he designed the Opera House and the Carnegie Library, as well as Argyle Hall for the Campbell-Hagerman College for girls on West Second Street.

The Boom of the 1880's

It was the decade of the 1880's that saw a real boom in the economic progress of the city. A telephone service, an expanding railroad, electrification, a municipal waterworks, and a street railway system appeared in this period. All signs seemed promising for Lexington's development into a major metropolitan center. A Chamber of Commerce was organized on November 2, 1881, to foster business growth.

Essential to this modernization and expansion was reform of the structure and operation of the city government. The traditionalist and boss-controlled domination was challenged first in 1880 by a group of reform-minded councilmen, including Calvin Morgan, brother of the Confederate raider, and

Moses Kaufman, a bright, cultured and enterprising businessman and Lexington's first German and Jewish councilman. They persuaded the Council to pass a motion permitting the popular election of the mayor. Young Claude M. Johnson won the election and he, in turn, spurred on the reform movement. Johnson, the son of Rosa Vertner Johnson, the noted Bluegrass poet, was a druggist. Elected by the people three successive times until he declined to run again in 1887, he was succeeded in 1888 by Charles W. Foushee, a respected merchant, who served two terms.

Despite vigorous opposition from Dennis Mulligan and his supporters, who feared the loss of their political control, the General Assembly amended the city charter in 1882 to provide that not only should the mayor be elected by popular vote but all city officials as well. The Lexington electorate approved the new charter on May 25, 1882. However, the attempt to incorporate a provision permitting the city government to go into debt to build a waterworks failed at this time.

Water System Finally Built

Lexington was in real need of a water system. Cisterns, wells, and springs were the only available water supplies, and the spreading pollution of many wells by nearby privies caused increasingly severe outbreaks of typhoid fever. These sources were also vulnerable to drought such as occurred in November 1869, which caused a city-wide water shortage.

As early as 1875, Lexington newspapers were urging that a city water supply be developed, but no action was taken. Severe fires, like the one that destroyed the Phoenix Hotel in May 1879, underlined the need for ample supplies of water for fire protection.

Private companies indicated an interest in constructing an adequate waterworks, but Dennis Mulligan attacked these overtures as involving the city in too much indebtedness which would require higher taxes. He also implied that the private contractors would profit most from such a project.

Another severe drought in the fall of 1883 forced the city government to take action. A contract was made with the Lexington

Hydraulic and Manufacturing Company, organized by Gilbert H. King, General William Preston, and Colonel R.H.S. Thompson, to construct and maintain "a waterworks in the city to supply residences with pure, wholesome water for public, private, and manufacturing use." The contract specified that the works be completed within a year from December 1883, that 200 double discharge hydrants be installed throughout the city, for which the city would pay $10,000 annual rent, and that the water supply be sufficient for a population of 30,000 at 50 gallons per capita a day. A Lexington Waterworks Company was chartered by the General Assembly in February 1884, to provide the means of financing the construction.

The Lexington Hydraulic and Manufacturing Company employed convict labor in July 1884, to start digging a reservoir on the south side of the Richmond Road, to be called Lake Ellerslie after the name of Levi Todd's historic estate across the road. The use of convict labor caused some controversy, but economy dictated the choice and the first of the city reservoirs was thus excavated. Three more reservoirs were dug in 1893, 1902, and 1906. These proved to be sufficient until Lexington's worst drought in 1930 when the reservoirs nearly went dry, and in desperation a pipeline was quickly constructed from the Kentucky River to the pump house.

On January 30, 1885, the waterworks were placed into operation with dramatic displays. On that wintry afternoon a crowd gathered on Main Street near Cheapside to watch firemen shoot a column of water as high as the weather vane of the new courthouse. Later the people swarmed out to the waterworks for the dedication ceremonies. At long last, this much-needed facility was completed and Lexington moved ahead in its modernization program.

A year later the city charter was again substantially changed. In the spring of 1886 the General Assembly amended the charter to vest the city's legislative power in a Board of Councilmen and a Board of Aldermen, to be known jointly as the General Council. Since the minimum required age for an alderman was thirty and that of a councilman twenty-four, it may be presumed that the Board of Aldermen, familiarly known as the "Upper Lords," was to

Many of Lexington's finest homes stood along High Street in the 19th century. Among them was the residence of Mrs. William Rodes at the southeast corner of High Street and Rodes Avenue. Photo courtesy of Mrs. Horace Wilson.

act as a senior body to check any rash actions by the council.

This 1886 amended charter also specified that no police or fireman should take part in any election other than to cast his vote. This would certainly have reduced the power of the party bosses to control elections, but obviously other devices were employed. The poll tax, however, was still preserved, which kept the number of voters participating in city elections to a low level.

The changes in the city charter had thus made it possible for the city government to initiate and implement programs for the improvement of the city that had been so long delayed. The construction of the waterworks was the first major accomplishment.

New newspapers appeared. The *Lexington Daily Press* was founded in October 1870, by Hart Foster and Henry T. Duncan as Lexington's first daily paper. In January 1895, it was consolidated with the *Lexington Transcript,* which had started in 1876 and had

been edited for a time by Judge James H. Mulligan. These combined papers were renamed the *Morning Herald* under the notable editorship of Desha Breckinridge, and in 1905 the name was changed permanently to the *Lexington Herald.*

Meanwhile, the *Statesman* and the *Gazette* continued their careers from before the Civil War. In March 1888, Samuel J. Roberts organized the Leader Printing Company to publish the *Lexington Leader* (first known as the *Kentucky Leader)* as a Republican daily to counter the Democratic papers in town.

A wide diversity of businesses had developed, including a large number of mercantile and grocery enterprises, and many manufacturing plants producing, among other items, awnings, baskets, bricks, carriages, cigars, hempen products, finished lumber, paint, saddles, soap, tinware, and woolen goods. Lexington attracted more new businesses in the 1880-1890 decade, some of which flourished as did the Lexington Roller Mills, producers of

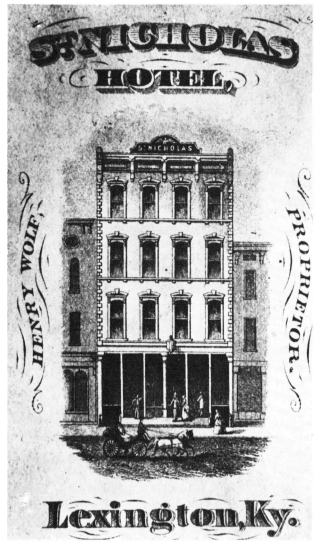

The St. Nicholas Hotel was erected in 1820 on the south side of Main Street, several doors west of Limestone. It was later known as the Florentine, Leonard and Henry Clay hotels. The building was razed in July 1947. Advertisement courtesy of Transylvania University.

the famed "Lexington Cream" flour, and the Van Deren Hardware Company. Others soon faded, such as the unusual Lexington Morocco Tannery. The Lexington Spoke Wheel Factory moved from Chattanooga to Lexington in 1885 and opened a new plant on Bolivar Street at the head of Mill Street. The site was somewhat controversial, being on part of the old Maxwell Cemetery where many of the early settlers had been buried. The cemetery had fallen into disrepair, and the factory was permitted to construct its building there, some of the tombstones being broken up and used in the foundation. Many of the bodies buried there remained and excavations for a 1914 tobacco redrying plant unearthed bones.

Railroads were essential to Lexington's economic prosperity since it depended on them for the flow of agricultural goods, manufactured products, passengers, and later, coal. In 1880 there were four railroads in Lexington. The oldest was the Louisville, Cincinnati & Lexington (the historic Lexington & Ohio Railroad) which became part of the sprawling Louisville & Nashville network. A second was the Elizabethtown, Lexington & Big Sandy Railroad, which had been chartered in 1872 and was acquired by the Chesapeake & Ohio system in 1880. A new depot was erected on the corner of South Limestone and Water streets behind the Phoenix Hotel. The third was the Kentucky Central Railroad which had been formed in 1875 to take over the Maysville & Lexington and the Covington & Lexington lines. Its depot was located on the west end of Short Street near the Lexington Cemetery until arrangements were made for joint use of the C & O depot. The fourth was the Cincinnati Southern Railway, which in 1877 had completed its line from Cincinnati to Lexington and farther south to Somerset. Skirting the southern edge of the city, it built a depot on South Broadway near Angliana. To cross the Kentucky River, this line built High Bridge near Wilmore, 317 feet above the water — a remarkable engineering feat using the new "cantilever" principle. It was, perhaps, the earliest such bridge in the country.

In 1886, the Kentucky Union Railroad, Lexington's fifth railroad, was organized to establish an important connection with the mineral and timber resources in southeastern Kentucky, and the line was extended to Clay City that first year. By 1891 track construction between Lexington and Jackson was completed for a total of 92 miles. The Kentucky Union reorganized in 1894 as the Lexington & Eastern Railroad and ultimately was absorbed by the L & N.

One other railroad built out of Lexington in this decade was the Louisville Southern, organized in an effort to break the L & N monopoly on this area and traffic between Lexington and Louisville. In 1889, the first train arrived at the Cincinnati Southern passenger station, having made the trip from Louisville via Shelbyville, Lawrenceburg, and Versailles. This route necessitated building another high bridge over the Kentucky River at

Horse and mule-drawn street cars were used in Lexington from 1882 to 1889, when they were replaced by electric cars. This photograph was taken in front of the street car company's stable on Vine Street in 1887. Photo courtesy of Burton Milward.

Tyrone. The line was later taken over by the Southern Railway.

The Coming of the Street Railway

Public transportation within the city was practically nonexistent until the 1880's. Compact in character, Lexington was what demographers would designate as a pedestrian city, that is, most of the residents lived within a mile or two of the center of town. Obviously, many Lexingtonians had their own horses and carriages, for convenience and display if not out of necessity. The local press boasted of the number of handsome equipages pulled by spirited horses that appeared on the city streets. A stable was a necessary appendage to any sizable residence. For those who either could not or would not purchase their own horses and carriages, there were scores of livery stables scattered throughout the city. Here a saddle horse or a horse and buggy might be rented for a modest fee. Drivers were available if needed. Close by the Phoenix Hotel was one of the larger livery stables, Treacy and Wilson, which provided service for hotel guests in the same manner as automobile rental agencies do today.

As the city pushed outward to the suburbs, many residents, especially women and older citizens, had no inclination to either walk or drive downtown. They wanted some form of public transportation. Elsewhere, cities of Lexington's size had long since established such transportation. But the Bluegrass town was to catch up quickly. City omnibuses, actually oversize horse-drawn stagecoaches, were put into operation on May 23, 1874. Licensed by the city, F. M. Beck operated a line which ran from Woodlands on the Richmond Road to the downtown depot. The charge was set at five cents by the city and the hours were 6 a.m. to 10 p.m. Another omnibus line established in 1880 ran from Woodlands to the Lexington Cemetery, but failed after six months due to lack of patronage. A few "cabs" or "hackneys" tried to operate independently but with little success.

In 1882, the *Daily Press* supported the effort of some local businessmen to organize the Lexington Railway Company, later called the Lexington Street Railway Company to avoid confusion with the steam railroads. In seven months this company had laid down nine miles of track on Main, Broadway, Limestone,

On July 17, 1880, "Professor" N. W. Lake, noted pedestrian, completed the feat of walking 390 miles around the courthouse square in 390 hours. Photo courtesy of Transylvania University.

Third, and Race streets and a small section on Vine. The company bought thirty mules and fifteen wooden cars, and the first mule car began to operate on August 12, 1882, an event which the paper called "a magnificent success," even though all the cars were not yet in use. Looking today at pictures of the small cars with one or two sleepy-looking mules in the traces, one is tempted to smile and wonder how these amusement park-like contraptions succeeded. They did have their problems. In their desire to economize, and anticipating a relatively small return from their investment, the managers sacrificed quality in equipment, rails, and mules. On steep grades some male passengers had to get out and walk to the top and board again.

Then, on September 11, 1883, a severe fire destroyed the car barns and stables on Race Street above Grinstead Street, killing 59 mules and 14 horses, and burning 14 cars. The company acted quickly, however, and within a month mules and cars had been replaced. Another fire in January 1887, destroyed a building and six cars but no animals were lost.

While the mule and horse-drawn car lines were not lucrative at first, the system was an asset to the city. Once a street car line was established, people began to build in the suburbs and real estate values rose.

In April 1889, the Belt Railway Company was organized as an adjunct to the Belt Land Company. The company was interested, as the title implied, in real estate on the circumference of the city. In their scheme was a belt-line railway circling the city, connecting the various railroads coming into Lexington. It was the company's intent to use electricity to power the cars. The Passenger and Belt Railway, as it was later called, constructed its lines with heavy T-shaped rails so that the electric cars could move more rapidly and carry heavy loads. A three-story brick powerhouse was built on the south side of Loudoun, between North Broadway and North Limestone Street, to supply the necessary power. On September 1, 1890, the first electric powered car ran from the car barn on Loudoun to the Phoenix Hotel. The "trolley car" system would gradually replace the animal-drawn cars in the 1890's.

Electricity and Telephones

The age of the gaslight was also coming to an end. Gaslights had illuminated Lexington streets for years, fueled by gas made at the Lexington Gas Works on Main Street between Spring and Patterson. European scientists had developed an effective arc light, dramatically demonstrated at the 1876 Philadelphia World's Fair. In the fall of 1879, Edison had produced his incandescent light bulb with carbon filament. Soon home, business, and street illumination would become revolutionized.

In Lexington, the Weston Electric Light Company was chartered in July 1882, and set up its modest power plant in a Vine Street room near South Broadway. Soon a few arc lights began to appear on Main Street replacing the gaslights. A year later the operation was moved to the old police station building on Water Street. In December 1882, a salesman for the Edison Electric Light

Company appeared in town and sold some 200 lights to the Phoenix and about 100 to Lell's Hotel. In 1886, Asa Dodge and C. H. Stoll bought the Weston Company, increased production, and consolidated it with the rural Excelsior Company.

On April 16, 1890, the Central Electric Company was organized, absorbed the Weston Company and moved its power plant to a site next to that of the Belt Electric Line Company on Loudoun Avenue.

Lexington ignored the need for a sanitary sewer system in this decade, though rather primitive storm sewer drains had been constructed at various strategic locations in the city. Without a sizable municipal water supply, a sanitary sewer system made little sense, and the knowledge of scientific sewage treatment was decades away.

Adding to the modernization of the standard of living of Lexingtonians in this decade was the introduction of a telephone system. Alexander Graham Bell had patented his famous invention in 1876 and it immediately became tremendously popular. The story of its establishment in Lexington is a confused one, but it appears that the East Tennessee Telephone Company, an affiliate of the Bell Telephone Company, which later became Southern Bell, had established an exchange on the third floor of a building on Cheapside by the spring of 1880. It was run by two male telephone operators who covered both the day and night schedules. Equipment was so primitive that single wires could not carry complex loads, so a maze of wires funneled out of one window in the Cheapside building along a series of poles down Main Street. The local press immediately complained about the cost of $50 a year and urged the company to reduce it to $15 or $20.

In 1884, Moses Kaufman, Judge Jere Morton, and others established the Overland Telephone Company, likewise located in a Cheapside building. Competing companies continued to appear during this period, seeking franchises from the city. However, by the turn of the century, the East Tennessee Telephone Company was successful in buying out or checking its competitors, with one exception. In 1899, Desha Breckinridge and other Lexingtonians decided to challenge this monopoly by organizing the Fayette Home Telephone Company and received permission from the city in July of that year to erect lines. In March 1901, they moved their offices into the McClelland Building, which had been recently completed on the northeast corner of Upper and Short streets. They competed intensely with the East Tennessee Company, and created a confusing dual telephone system until 1912, when the Fayette Home Telephone Company acquired the assets of its competitor and established an exchange in the remodeled Upper Street Baptist Church on the southwest corner of Church and Upper streets.

Chamber of Commerce Formed

The Chamber of Commerce, formally organized in November 1881, conducted a far-flung and intensive campaign to induce new mercantile and manufacturing enterprises to locate here. The Chamber persuaded George W. Ranck, onetime editor of the *Observer & Reporter* and author of the only history of Lexington at that time, to compose a review of Lexington as of 1882. No one was better qualified to write this *Guide to Lexington, Kentucky* (1884). The Chamber also elected Ranck its president.

The city officials had encouraged the introduction of telephones, electricity, and the construction of street railways, though they had little financial resources to underwrite or subsidize these projects. To assist in railroad expansion, they set up a special election in May 1888, to secure voter approval to subscribe $100,000 of capital stock for the Louisville Southern Railroad. Later, they submitted for voter action a referendum to give the Elizabethtown, Lexington and Big Sandy 25 acres of city land and $25,000 to set up machine shops within one-half mile of the city limits.

A perennial task of the city fathers was to improve the city streets and to brick more sidewalks. Streets like Main were paved with flagstones, later with brick. Some streets were paved with wooden blocks, and others macadamized. Brick streets became popular, however, in the late 1890's. To assist in making these streets level, and especially in packing down new macadamized material, the city in 1886 invested in a giant steam roller called by

A massive steam roller known as a "Willipus-Wallipus" was used in the construction and repair of streets in the late 19th and early 20th centuries. Photo courtesy of the University of Kentucky.

the fanciful name of "Willipus-Wallipus." This impressive mechanism fascinated many a sidewalk observer with its puffing, steaming and rumbling before falling through the covering of an old street cistern on East High Street. It required a mighty effort to extricate the monster, but the endeavor succeeded, for the city talked about repairing and reusing the Willipus-Wallipus in 1894.

A city fire department had been established at public expense in 1865, consisting of a chief engineer, a driver of the horse reel, one fireman and one pipeman. The cost to the city in 1864-65 was $310.48. The chief's salary of $100 was doubled the second year because the council was convinced "his duties are onerous." In 1864, an expensive ($6,000) steam fire engine was purchased at a time when the total city revenues were only $15,000, but this engine could throw "a stream horizontally for 225 to 230 feet." The city purchased in 1886 a Silsby suction steam engine and the number of pipemen was increased to four. The city officials were responsible for digging large cisterns at strategic spots downtown and keeping them filled with water. For a few years

after, the city was free of large fires. The city's net loss from fire, for instance, in 1870 was only $10,500.

This good fortune ended abruptly in August 1871, when two disastrous fires wiped out sections of downtown. One started in the Barnes and Woods drug store at Main and Upper, and destroyed eleven business establishments before being brought under control. Shortly after, a fierce fire erupted on the west side of North Broadway between Main and Short, spreading west and north to Short Street, demolishing 18 buildings. This led to a decision to build an additional cistern on South Broadway near Water Street, 20 feet in diameter and 18 feet deep. A continuing problem was keeping these cisterns filled, especially during dry weather, and even these reserves were soon exhausted if a major fire occurred.

In the wake of these two fires, action was taken to strengthen the fire department. The Lyon Engine House was sold, and two hand engines and old apparatus were discarded. The Central Fire Station on Short Street was established, containing in its inventory two steam fire engines, one hose reel, two ladder wagons with six ladders, four hand hooks, two fire axes, and 2,300 feet of hose. Five horses were kept available and 50 cisterns were scattered throughout downtown. This was an inadequate fire protection force for a town of Lexington's size, and anyone living or owning a business in the downtown area must have been acutely conscious of the danger of fire. The numerous livery stables, stuffed with hay and straw, were the most likely tinder boxes.

On May 25, 1875, the nightmare became a reality. Fire started in the livery stable of Davis and Adams on the corner of Limestone and Short streets. Only quick and heroic action saved 29 of the 40 horses, and the escaping frightened animals ran wildly through the streets before panting to a stop on the edge of town. Only one of the steam engines was functioning, but the firemen and their equipment arrived quickly on the scene. A brisk wind fanned the fire into a devastating conflagration, sending huge showers of sparks into the air and threatening every shingled roof

within half a mile. Able-bodied citizens grabbed buckets and spent the night helping extinguish incipient fires. Fearful that the whole town was threatened, telegrams were sent to Cincinnati and Louisville for help, unrealistic though such appeals might have seemed. The roof of the old brick courthouse was set ablaze in three places, but was finally extinguished while frantic efforts were made to save the official records by removing them from the building to the courthouse yard.

Owners of shops removed their stock, and lawyers their records from their offices. The Phoenix Hotel was endangered when its shingled roof caught fire several times. Only a change in the wind saved the town, and the one engine moving from cistern to cistern finally brought the fire under control. The blaze caused $60,000 to $100,000 damage, including the livery stable, the St. James Hotel, J. M. Tipton's agricultural implements store, several carriage factories, saddlery shops, W. C. Goodloe's new office building, numerous small shops, and Paul Conlon's saloon. Conlon, one of

A steam fire engine and hose reel are seen in this 1886 picture in front of the city fire station on West Short Street. Photo courtesy of Mrs. Clifton L. Thompson, Jr.

the best-loved Irishmen in the city, and one of Dennis Mulligan's close associates, had just been appointed fire chief a few months earlier. With his own property on fire, he undoubtedly exerted himself to extinguish the blaze. On his suggestion, firemen were now placed on constant duty at the firehouse, and a dormitory was provided for them on the second floor.

Moses Kaufman proposed a telephone alarm system which was installed in 1880. It was replaced a few years later by an independent telegraph alarm system, and boxes were positioned throughout the town in 1884.

Before the advent of the automobile, the mobility of the fire engines depended on horses. Their health was crucial, therefore, and a crisis developed when a horse epidemic designated as "epizooty" swept through the town in November 1872. In May 1882, the citizens were dismayed to learn that all city fire horses were "down with pink eye."

The completion of the waterworks in 1884 and the installation of hundreds of hydrants greatly improved fire protection, and the cisterns were abandoned.

In 1888, the General Assembly passed an act establishing a Board of Police and Fire Commissioners for Fayette County to supervise more effectively the appointment of personnel and the general operation of these departments. George W. Muir was made chief engineer (the title of Fire Chief being temporarily discontinued). During his seventeen-year administration, various improvements were made. A new central fire station was erected on the south side of Short Street between Limestone and Upper in 1888. As the city grew, reel houses were built as needed: the first was known as No. 2, on Woodward (now Maple) Avenue and Sixth streets; No. 3, on Pine Street west of Broadway; No. 4, the Vogt Reel House, on Jefferson between Second and Third streets; and No. 5, at Woodland Avenue and Maxwell Street. Muir introduced various devices to speed the response of firemen and equipment to a fire, including a pole extending from the sleeping quarters to the ground floor.

"A policeman's lot is not a happy one," sang the chorus in Gilbert and Sullivan's *The Pirates of Penzance* to a Lexington audience at the Odd Fellows Hall Opera House. Any city patrolman in the audience would have agreed.

Lexington, though not a crime-ridden town, had the usual violations and inebriates to worry its law enforcement staff, which was modest in size.

An 'Augean' Structure Replaced

In 1867, Benjamin McMurtry was elected city marshal with a single deputy, and watchmen for the city's four wards. With the influx of blacks into the city after the Civil War and the presence of Negro Union soldiers in town, tensions ran high for a few years. Explosive situations developed when peace officers occasionally arrested some of the Negro troopers, and the commanding officer came fuming down to the jail to demand the soldiers' release. Only when the Union troops departed was this tension somewhat reduced.

The separation between the day and night policemen was eliminated in 1882 and they became a single force under the Chief of Police, who had a complement of fourteen men.

In the early 1870's there was a growing public demand that policemen wear some distinguishing uniform. In response, policemen wore black caps with the word "Police" on the band in front. In 1884 each policeman was given a $50 uniform allowance and began to wear uniforms similar to those used in other cities.

The *Daily Press* reported in 1889 that the city had "a new patrol wagon used in hauling prisoners to the workhouse. It is bright red and looks almost nice enough to ride in." The patrol wagon was badly needed, as the practice of dragging drunken men though the streets or carting them in wheelbarrows was burdensome to officers and a distasteful sight to the public.

Unfortunately for the well-being of the force, the Watch House or Police Headquarters had been situated for decades on Water Street in a building located directly over the Town Branch. For some reason, the stream had not been arched over under the floor of the station and as the Town Branch had become virtually an open sewer, the stench in the Police Headquarters was formidable. A prisoner confined in one of the Watch House cells might justifiably have complained of having to endure "cruel and unusual punishment." When the new station was built, it was located on the same site, but at least the stream was arched over.

John McElroy (police chief, 1891-97) and Beecher T. McCoy wearing the first uniforms of the Lexington Police Department, ca. 1885. Photo from Police and Fire Departments, City of Lexington, *1914.*

An 1873 ordinance prohibiting prostitutes from riding in open carriages through the city streets caused even more commotion. Laura Palmer, arrested for violating the ordinance, protested vigorously against the discriminatory character of the law and threatened to carry the case to the highest court.

As the cases multiplied and the need for better facilities for the courts and county offices increased, there was talk of a new county courthouse in the late 1870's and early 1880's. The county's third courthouse, constructed in 1806, appears in etchings and photographs as a rather attractive structure. However, we know from the comments of numerous visitors and persons using its facilities, such as Henry Clay, that the interior

was far less appealing. Lawyers, judges, jurors, and spectators consistently condemned it. It had been bitterly criticized and vilified as far back as the 1830's. The post-Civil War Lexingtonians carried on the tradition. Painting helped this "grim, unsightly building," confessed the *Gazette* in 1867, but nothing could really change "this old and weather-beaten hall as a hopeless and hideous nuisance." With public opinion favoring a new structure, it seemed to be mostly a matter of money as far as the authorities were concerned. In 1878, an act was passed "to authorize and provide for the erection of a new Court House and Clerk's office in Fayette County." Three years elapsed before a committee was appointed to act. In 1882 plans were made to tear down this "Augean structure that stands like a petrified nightmare in the middle of our city with the pseudonym of a Court House."

In October the demolition began. Meanwhile, six architects submitted plans to a courthouse committee on which Cincinnatus Shryock was an advisor, and the design of Thomas W. Boyd was approved. Work was temporarily delayed, however, when the bids came in too high for the Council's liking; but finally an arrangement was made with William E. Bush, a contractor, to erect the courthouse on Boyd's plans. It soon became apparent that this complicated Renaissance-Eclectic structure, with its towering superstructure 100 feet above ground level, would cost more than anticipated, and so the superstructure, which was to have been made of stone, was instead constructed of timber and covered with tin to resemble masonry, a change that proved disastrous later.

While construction was underway, the old Grand Masonic Hall at Walnut and Short streets was used for court sessions. Though largely completed in the fall of 1884, the new courthouse was not entirely furnished until the following spring and then some of the lawyers were displeased with the furniture the architect had chosen.

Fayette County had its new courthouse for only thirteen years. On the morning of May 14, 1897, an employee, climbing to the belfrey to wind the clock, accidentally dropped a match and fire started in the wooden-domed pavilion. The fire quickly engulfed the superstructure, and within a few hours the entire building was

gutted. Most of the court records were saved, but some of Jouett's portraits, along with other papers and law books, went up in smoke. The large bell in the belfrey came crashing down on Joel T. Hart's statue, "Woman Triumphant," destroying his masterpiece.

The job of replacing the burnt-out shell was quickly undertaken. Fayette County's fifth courthouse was designed by Lehman and Schmitt, a Cleveland firm, in the popular Richardsonian Romanesque style of the day. It was built by Albert Howard and George Clark and completed in 1900. In 1966, it underwent a complete interior renovation to make space for more courtrooms and offices.

In 1883, another service provided by the federal government was expanded for the convenience of Lexingtonians. This was the

inauguration of free mail delivery. Prior to that time, persons picked up their mail at the post office. A new post office was completed in 1889 on the northwest corner of Walnut and Main streets. Parcel post delivery service apparently was not in operation at the time, there being a private Lexington Parcel Delivery organization which advertised that it would deliver parcels anywhere in the city.

Educational Progress

The public schools statewide suffered badly during the Civil War, and public concern for their improvement was casual. The General Assembly pursued an erratic course in legislating for the administration of public schools and the tax measures needed to support them. For a period, taxes for black schools

118

were separated from those for white schools, much to the injury of the former. By the mid-1880's, this differentiation was abolished, but the creation of a segregated school system saw the expenditure of public funds heavily favoring the white schools. Building costs and teachers' and staff salaries show marked differences between the two systems.

Public education for blacks in Lexington and Fayette County after the Civil War depended largely on the activities of the Freedmen's Bureau and benevolent associations. The first black school in the post-Civil War period was started in 1867, largely due to the efforts of a concerned and energetic black leader, the Reverend James Turner. Securing aid from the American Missionary Society, which sent white female teachers to Lexington, and with general expenses paid by the Freedmen's Bureau, classes were started in the so-called "Ladies Hall," the former Methodist Church on Church Street, which had been purchased by the Negro women. An unexpectedly large enrollment of black children necessitated construction of a new school on Corral Street in 1869-70. In 1874, a new state law required that all taxes collected from black taxpayers, except those applied to the care of paupers, plus money received from sale of federal lands, be applied to black schools. This was to continue until the per capita expenditures equaled that appropriated from state and local taxes for white pupils.

By 1882 the city had three black schools: the Corral Street school, Pleasant Green School, and the Fourth Street School. The Missionary Society operated the one at Ladies Hall until it closed in 1883. The Fourth Street School was eventually moved to a new building at Fifth and Upper.

Of the 41 school districts in the rural areas, at least five were for black pupils, usually located at the sites of new freedmen communities established on property given by former slaveowners. These included Maddoxtown on the Huffman Mill Road, Bracktown on Leestown Pike, Cadentown on Liberty Road at Todds Road, Uttingertown on Royster Road, Coletown on Shelby Lane, and Fort Springs on the Versailles Road. All remained operative until the consolidation period of the early 20th century.

The community's fourth courthouse had a short life of only thirteen years, being the victim of a devastating fire on May 14, 1897, that resulted from a carelessly dropped match. Most of the courthouse records were saved, however.

One of the major advances for black education in Lexington was the establishment of the Chandler Normal School to meet the demand for black teachers. Miss Phoebe Chandler of Massachusetts donated enough money to purchase four acres of land between the Georgetown and Newtown Pikes on which a building was erected in 1889. The building was designed by Vertner Tandy, a black architect (son of William Tandy, a successful Lexington contractor) who later moved to New York City and achieved national recognition. Providing education for black pupils through the eighth grade, the Chandler school later added four more grades. The quality of education at

Chandler made it one of the city's best schools, from which most of Lexington's outstanding blacks graduated. Enrollment declined after the expansion of the public school system. The supply of black teachers was enhanced by the establishment of a state Colored Normal School which became Kentucky State College.

The white public school system benefited from the leadership of such men as James O. Harrison, city superintendent from 1848 to 1873, and county superintendents B. N. Grehan, Thomas Bullock, and E. F. Darnaby. The most notable was Massilon A. Cassidy, a former lawyer and teacher from Tennessee who became superintendent of both the city and county systems in 1885. He served in this capacity until 1892 and as county superintendent until 1903, when he again became city superintendent. An innovator, Cassidy began the consolidation of the small one-room schools. He built the first large consolidated elementary school, Picadome, in 1888, started the first kindergarten at Dudley School in 1892, and opened the first high school in Lexington in 1905 at the old Morton School.

Grandiose University Plan

At the higher education level in Lexington, there were significant developments. Transylvania University, the glory of Lexington's golden age, had declined to a high school during the Civil War years. Its buildings were commandeered as hospitals by the Union troops. The imposing Medical Department building had been destroyed by fire in May 1863. The future was bleak and uncertain until John Bowman, an energetic Mercer County farmer with a stirring educational vision, appeared on the scene. A graduate of Bacon College, he led a campaign to create a new school in Harrodsburg called Kentucky University under the control of the Christian Church. Kentucky University appeared to have a bright future after it opened in 1858, but the destructive impact of the Civil War depleted its classes, and the main building, used by Union troops, went up in flames.

Near the end of the war, Bowman, undaunted, proposed to the Transylvania trustees that the schools merge under the name of Kentucky University and be located on the relatively undisturbed Transylvania campus. He envisioned a major state university there, and to this end persuaded the General Assembly not only to legalize the union of Kentucky University and Transylvania, but also to place the new Agricultural and Mechanical College, established February 22, 1865, a product of the Morrill Land Grant Act of 1863, in this university complex.

His persuasive powers worked similar magic in the Lexington community, which contributed $100,000 for the purchase of Henry Clay's "Ashland" and the adjoining "Woodlands" estate as a campus for the A&M College. The Transylvania campus was maintained as the center for the liberal arts college and the revived law department. A College of the Bible also was made a department of Kentucky University to provide a seminary for future Christian pastors. Wilbur Smith's new downtown business school was dovetailed into this grandiose operation as the Commercial Department of Kentucky University. It was the most exciting and promising educational venture Kentucky had seen since the days of Horace Holley, but the scheme had a major flaw. Bowman was attempting to mix oil and water, building a state university on a denominationally controlled base.

For the first five or six years this amazing educational amalgam prospered. Lexingtonians, confronting the post-Civil War doldrums, were cheered by its success, and saw in it an opportunity for a renaissance of the "Athens of the West" distinction. It was not to be. Ominous rumblings were heard within the Disciples brotherhood about Bowman's leadership and direction. He was also embroiled in a struggle with the Main Street Church over the independent organization of another Christian church in Lexington. From around the state came criticism at having a nonsectarian A&M state college under sectarian administration. Both nonsectarians and spokesmen from other denominations besieged the General Assembly to detach the A&M College from Kentucky University. The result was a disaster for Bowman's dream.

The Disciples set up their own legally independent College of the Bible. The General Assembly succumbed to public pressure and separated the A&M College from Kentucky University in 1878. Bowman was replaced with leadership acceptable to the church, and Kentucky University continued successfully as a modest-sized liberal arts college with a law department that operated until 1912. Its connection with Smith's Commercial College, a marriage of convenience at best, gradually waned and disappeared. In the late 1890's and early 1900's, Kentucky University made arrangements with one or two Louisville medical schools to award Kentucky University diplomas to their graduates, thus creating the illusion that the Transylvania Medical Department had been resurrected. No medical education took place in Lexington or on the Kentucky University campus, however, and the school soon ended this practice.

During this period, intercollegiate sports were beginning to develop. In addition to baseball, the new games of football, and later basketball, appeared. The first recorded intercollegiate football contest in this region of the South was played on April 9, 1881, between Kentucky University and Centre College on a field later known as Stoll Field of the University of Kentucky. Each team had fifteen players and little protective equipment. This mishmash of rugby and football entertained the crowd for an afternoon, with Kentucky University emerging the winner by a mystifying score of 13 3/4 to 0.

In 1908, Transylvania resumed its historic name in order to avoid confusion with its stepchild, the A&M College, which wished, quite rightly, to assume the title of State University, and in 1916 the present name of the University of Kentucky.

The Agricultural and Mechanical College, however, had a long, hard road to travel before it arrived at the university stage. Kentucky University officials had agreed to allow the A&M College to use until 1880 the facilities at "Ashland" and "Woodlands," which legally belonged to Kentucky University. Lexington contributors to the A&M College were dismayed to learn this. Soon the A&M College would have neither buildings nor a campus, and its only income would be a minuscule interest from the endowment created by the sale of federal lands under the Morrill Land Grant Act of 1863.

Other communities vied for the chance to lure the state school to their area, Bowling Green being a major contender. Lexington citizens were determined not to lose the school. Furious at the Kentucky University officials, who they believed had betrayed them (and, indeed, some of the trustees heartily desired A&M's departure to eliminate its competition), Lexington did all in its power to outbid Bowling Green. The city offered the A&M College the Lexington City Park (old Fair Grounds) as a campus, plus $50,000 in bonds. The General Assembly authorized acceptance of the offer and the A&M College was officially incorporated. An 1880 act was passed, authorizing a special tax to finance the A&M College's operation, a landmark action which guaranteed a steady, if modest, revenue for the state school. The establishment of a Normal School in 1880 as a part of A&M's complex paved the way for admission of women students, and the institution became coeducational.

First A & M College Building

The cornerstone for A&M's first building on its present campus was laid in October 1880, and by February 1882, the buildings were completed on the high rise of land overlooking a pond at what is now the intersection of Limestone and Euclid Avenue. The first president was James K. Patterson, born in Glasgow, Scotland, in 1833. Crippled for life by an accident as a young boy, Patterson used a crutch, but this in no way hampered his full participation in an active life. His family had emigrated to America in 1843, and Patterson, largely self-taught, began his teaching career at Hanover College. Here he married, and later moved to Stewart College in Clarksville, Tennessee, where he became professor of classics. He was preparing for the Presbyterian ministry when the Civil War interrupted those plans. When Stewart College closed, he moved to Lexington to accept the principalship of the Transylvania High School, the only active remnant of this once proud university.

With the creation of Kentucky University in 1865, Patterson continued on the faculty as professor of classics in the liberal arts college and as professor of history at the new A&M

College. In 1869 he accepted the position as head of that institution and remained until his resignation in 1910. His dedication and commitment to the college was complete, and the survival of the institution was due on more than one occasion to his sacrifices. In 1881, when the funds for the new buildings were exhausted, he pledged his own personal savings as security for a bank loan.

Patterson's control over the A&M College was, for decades, almost absolute, and he had strong faculty support. His authoritative administration was challenged on various occasions by the boisterous spirits of the students and these incidents brought unfavorable publicity to the school. On the whole, however, the school functioned as an orderly institution, concentrating on the traditional curriculum of the classical and scientific studies. A sizable preparatory department was established to compensate for the lack of an effective statewide public school system, a situation that brought to the campus many students who were inadequately prepared for college work. The enrollment in the Normal and Commercial departments, and in the short courses in agriculture, helped swell the total.

Despite its name, the Agricultural and Mechanical College paid little attention to agriculture until a new building in 1907 to house the College of Agriculture promised greater concentration in that area. More emphasis had been given to engineering, even in the Kentucky University days, and in 1891 the establishment of the Department of Mechanical Engineering met with immediate success. A Mechanical Hall was completed in 1892 to house the department.

Most important in relating the institution to the agricultural and farming constituency of Kentucky was the Agricultural Experiment Station which was established in 1885 in crowded quarters, but expanded later, thanks to federal funding under the 1885 Hatch Act. Such services as testing the composition and efficacy of new fertilizers and issuing helpful bulletins to farmers in language they could understand became especially popular with the state legislators. The original Experiment Station Building, occupied on campus in 1890, was replaced by the 1905 structure on South Limestone.

In 1908 the old A&M designation was changed to "State University, Lexington, Kentucky." A law school was added that same year. When Patterson retired in 1910, to be succeeded by Judge Henry Stites Barker, he could look back with great satisfaction on his contribution to the successful development of Kentucky's state university.

The establishment of the A&M College and its gradual development into a major state university, and the continued operation of Transylvania University with its rich historic legacy, contributed significantly to Lexington's reputation as the leading educational, if not cultural center, in Kentucky.

New Private Schools

Neither the emergence of Kentucky University and the A&M College, nor the expansion of the public school system signaled the end of private education in Lexington. Not only did a number of the antebellum schools continue to operate in the post-Civil War period, such as Sayre Female Institute, St. Catherine's, St. Paul's and St. John's, and the Lexington Female College, but new ones appeared. The most enduring of these was the women's school established by James M. Hocker, a local banker. Known as the Hocker Female College, it was housed on the west side of North Broadway between Fourth and Fifth streets in an impressive $100,000 structure built in the prevailing eclectic Renaissance Italianate style. When a sizable donation was received from William Hamilton in 1878, the school was renamed Hamilton College. In 1889, Kentucky University became a major stockholder, and in 1903 assumed complete control of the school. Under President Burris Jenkins, it was administered as a junior college, the first two-year college in Kentucky. It remained a popular and high quality women's college until its demise in 1930. The building was converted into a woman's dormitory for Transylvania students, later known as Lyons-Hamilton Hall. The building was razed in 1962.

In the quarter of a century following the Civil War, Lexington had experienced substantial social, political, and economic changes. James Lane Allen's colonel and his servant Peter might have been dismayed at the

University of Kentucky campus showing the Administration Building, ca. 1900. Photo courtesy L & N Railroad archives.

difference and unable to adjust to this transformed society. However, many Lexingtonians welcomed the reform of their city government, and the introduction of the street railway, waterworks, electricity, telephones, and more railroads. Both blacks and whites were forced to work out a new and liveable relationship. Negroes, faced with the handicaps of a suddenly precarious and unfamiliar way of life, and being forced to depend heavily on their own resources while their rights were severely restricted in many areas, nevertheless managed to develop a vital and independent black community.

The city also changed in appearance as an expanding building industry erected new churches, downtown business structures, and impressive private residences. Some Lexingtonians hoped for, and expected, great growth in the city's population and manufacturing enterprises. Though the city's population grew at an impressive rate of 30 percent in the decade of 1880 to 1890, and 22 percent and 33 percent in the two decades thereafter (the rural county grew more slowly), the economic ligaments of Lexington as a major retail, wholesale, and transportation center remained practically unchanged. The rapidly expanding production of burley tobacco

created the opportunity for Lexington to become a major entrepôt for this crop and enterprising buyers, sellers, and warehousemen capitalized on this.

The ease with which many ex-Confederates returned to Fayette County and resumed their careers assured a continuity of family names and influence that preserved to some extent the traditional character of the town. The Breckinridge family best symbolizes this. Not only did John C. Breckinridge live out his last years here, but the son of the Reverend Robert Breckinridge, William Campbell Preston Breckinridge, a veteran of Morgan's campaigns, became the most popular orator for the Democratic party campaigns in the postwar decades, an influential editor of the *Lexington Herald,* and a Congressman. His son, Desha, carried on as an outstanding editor of the *Herald,* and his daughter, Sophonisba, became one of the notable women in America.

Among those carrying on the tradition of public service into the 20th century were Henry T. Duncan, Richard C. Stoll, and Laura Clay, daughter of Cassius.

Lexington at this time, and for some decades to come, remained a town proud of its traditions while seeking ways to expand its economic growth and prosperity.

Graves & Cox as it appeared in the late 19th century when the store was located at the southeast corner of Main and Upper streets. With owners George K. Graves (center) and Leonard G. Cox is a black employee, Frank Justice.

Chapter VI

1890/1920

Life at the Turn of the Century

Surrounding the hustle and bustle of Main Street, the opening and closing of new businesses, the installation of a city waterworks, and the clanging of the electrified streetcars of this busy town was a magnificent panorama of the nation's finest and most picturesque horse and livestock farms. The relationship between the urbanites, the farmers, and the elite of the great estates began to undergo subtle but significant changes after the Civil War, especially as some of the old family ties which had interlocked town and farm began to disappear. The influx of out-of-state money and owners into the breeding and racing of horses intensified that change.

Even the most town-bred Lexingtonian who may rarely have visited a horse farm or attended the races sensed the beauty and tradition these estates and activities added to the Bluegrass environment. Yet many townsfolk were not fully aware of the truly unique character of the farms and horses which brought international acclaim to the region.

One of the earliest and most famous of the Bluegrass horse farms was Woodburn Farm in Woodford County, purchased by Robert Alexander and developed by his son, Robert Aitcheson Alexander. In 1856 Woodburn was fortunate in obtaining the great stallion Lexington. This outstanding horse, bred by Dr. Elisha Warfield of Lexington, had been sold to Richard Ten Broeck who took him south. After having won a series of brilliant races, Lexington began to go blind and Ten Broeck returned him to Midway, Kentucky, to begin

stud service. Soon after, Alexander purchased Lexington for Woodburn Farm, where he became one of the most successful sires in American Thoroughbred history.

An historic farm, originating in John Breckinridge, Sr.'s Cabell's Dale of the 1790's, was acquired in 1827 by David Castleman who named it Castleton and built a splendid mansion there in 1840. Among other enterprises, Castleton Farm bred Kentucky's renowned saddle horses. One of the great sires of the saddlers was Denmark, foaled in 1839 near Danville, and the fame of these fine horses was so great that they were in constant demand for Confederate and Union cavalry during the Civil War. Morgan's extraordinary escapades may well have depended on his men possessing some of these outstanding animals.

In 1903 James R. Keene, the so-called "Silver Fox" of Wall Street, bought Castleton and expanded the farm. Under the next owner, David Look, in 1911, Castleton focused on trotters until Mrs. Frances Dodge Johnson (later Mrs. Frederick Van Lennep), owner of the notable Dodge stables in Michigan, bought Castleton and established it as a premier American saddle horse and Standardbred farm. The great five-gaited Wing Commander, under the masterful hand of the remarkable Earl Teater, not only won numerous championships but also sired prize-winning progeny.

Walnut Hall, located on an old French and Indian War land grant, was named by Matthew Flournoy whose son rebuilt the present mansion. The farm was enlarged under the ownership of Lamon Harkness in 1892, and became an outstanding producer of top-notch Standardbreds.

Fairlawn Farm, situated at that time on the outskirts of Lexington at the end of North Broadway, was bought in 1873 by Colonel William T. Withers, a veteran of Vicksburg, and became a widely known trotting horse farm, though it is now entirely engulfed by Lexington's urban expansion. The mansion has been occupied for some years by the Thoroughbred Press.

A colorful and unusual entry into this world of fine breeding and high stakes was Price McGrath, a poor lad from Woodford County who gambled his way to a fortune in New York, winning $105,000 in a single evening. He returned to his beloved Bluegrass, established McGrathiana Stud and began to breed horses. McGrath became the proud owner of Aristides, of Lexington lineage, who won the first Kentucky Derby in 1875. The parties at McGrathiana were legendary. After McGrath's death in 1881, Colonel Milton Young bought the farm and became a foremost breeder. Later, the farm was renamed Coldstream, and is now owned by the University of Kentucky.

Elmendorf was bought and named in 1881 by Daniel Swigert whose ability as a Thoroughbred breeder was proved in Spendthrift and other horses which won four Kentucky Derbies. It was Elmendorf that attracted the eye of the wealthy James Ben Ali Haggin. The Mercer County boy had gone West and made a fortune in gold, silver, and copper, and developed a large ranch in California with 2,000 Thoroughbreds; but the call of the Bluegrass, and of his youthful fiancee, Margaret Voorhies of Versailles, brought the widowed magnate to Lexington where he bought Elmendorf. Here he erected the imposing $1,000,000 marble mansion called "Green Hills" as a present for his bride. It was dedicated October 22, 1902, with an elaborate party. Not many were surprised when the aging tycoon in 1913 built the Ben Ali Theatre on Main Street especially for his wife when she found her Opera House box inadvertently occupied by strangers.

Expanding his estate to some 8,000 acres, Haggin made Elmendorf a spectacular Bluegrass farm with the finest buildings, the most proficient operation, and a farm that was as productive in crops as in horses. After Haggin's death in 1914 at age 93, the huge estate was gradually divided. Joseph Widener of Philadelphia bought the original core of the estate, including Green Hills, which was never lived in after Haggin's death. Widener later tore down the mansion, leaving only the steps and columns of the original entrance.

Close by Elmendorf was Greentree Stud, which came into prominence in 1895 when John T. Hughes, a nephew of the previous owner, expanded the farm and achieved fame through his breeding of matched pairs of carriage horses and prize-winning Saddlebreds.

With a phenomenal talent for buying and selling horses, John E. Madden entered the field as an amateur from Pennsylvania. A man who could uncannily sense a horse's potential, Madden mastered the technique of buying horses inexpensively, training them as winners, and selling them at a handsome profit. He invested the money in a Bluegrass farm named Hamburg Place, after a famous trotter. Breeding both Thoroughbreds and Standardbreds, his farm produced five Kentucky Derby winners and five Belmont Stakes winners. Today, Hamburg Place is a thriving Thoroughbred farm under the management of Preston and Anita Madden, whose scintillating pre-Derby parties have become a notable feature of that festive season.

Idle Hour Farm

In the sporting and gambling tradition of Price McGrath, Colonel Edward R. Bradley, a successful bookmaker and casino operator, invested heavily in the horse farm industry in 1910 by buying the Ash Grove property on the Old Frankfort Pike and expanding it into the impressive Idle Hour Farm, which produced four winners of the Kentucky Derby. The annual one-day charity racing meet at Bradley's private track as a means of raising money for Kentucky orphans was a memorable feature of Idle Hour. After his death, the farm was sold and divided into King Ranch, Darby Dan, and Danada farms.

Among the wealthy non-Kentuckians investing in Bluegrass farms was Harry Payne Whitney, who in 1917 purchased part of the

Multimillionaire James Ben Ali Haggin started building Green Hills in 1897 on his Elmendorf Farm on the Paris Pike. This 40-room mansion, shown here under construction, was the scene of lavish entertainment. It was razed by a later owner in 1929 and only the columns and the front steps remain. Photo courtesy of Mrs. Clifford Amyx.

Haggin estate. Under his son, C. V. Whitney, the farm has produced many Thoroughbred stakes winners for well over half a century. Among these was Regret, the only filly to have won a Kentucky Derby until 1980 when Genuine Risk accomplished the feat. In 1966, Whitney sold a portion of his farm to John Gaines, who has made Gainesway a flourishing, well-known Thoroughbred breeding operation.

Probably no horse farm is more familiar to Lexingtonians than Calumet. Located on Versailles Road, it is one of the most visible of Bluegrass horse farms to visitors arriving by air at Blue Grass Field and to those driving by automobile to the spring and fall meets at Keeneland. In 1924, William Monroe Wright, founder of the profitable Calumet Baking Powder Company of Chicago, united a number of historic farms into the farm he named for his company. By 1980, Calumet under his son,

Warren Wright, Sr., and the latter's widow, Mrs. Gene Markey, had produced eight Kentucky Derby winners, two Triple Crown winners, 146 stakes winners and 34 division leaders — an unparalleled record. Whirlaway started the famous Calumet roster of Derby winners, with Citation achieving equal fame. Calumet's prodigious sire Bull Lea produced a remarkable number of stakes winners for many years.

Spendthrift also has become a renowned Thoroughbred breeding establishment. The controlling figure of this operation comes from one of the most distinguished families of Fayette County — the Leslie Combses — starting with the old general who was a leading citizen and lawyer of Lexington for many years in the early part of the 19th century. His fine residence on Main Street (where the old Lafayette Hotel building now stands) was a

Floral Hall, an octagonal building erected in 1882 at the trotting track and fair grounds on South Broadway, was used for exhibits during annual fairs. The building is still standing at the entrance to the Red Mile track. Photo courtesy of the University of Kentucky.

showplace. General Combs was also a horseman, as were many affluent gentlemen of his generation, and was at one time president of the Kentucky Association that established an official race course in Lexington. Another progenitor of Leslie Combs II, creator of the present-day Spendthrift, was Daniel Swigert. Neither the General nor Swigert could have dreamed of the scope of syndicated breeding operations which Combs has developed at Spendthrift since 1937. With his son Brownell Combs II, Leslie Combs II formed the syndicate that purchased Nashua in 1955. The syndicated ownership of stallions now has become a familiar technique in the breeding of thoroughbreds, and the prices continue to escalate. In 1981, a Northern Dancer colt, Storm Bird, who had had a spectacular racing career in Europe, was syndicated for a record-breaking $28 million. Storm Bird now stands at Ashford Stud Farm, outside of Versailles.

In adjoining Bourbon County, Claiborne Farm has been owned and operated by generations of Hancocks. In 1947, Nasrullah, one of the greatest stallions of this century, was acquired by Claiborne and has sired such champions as Nashua and Bold Ruler. The phenomenal Secretariat is now standing at stud at Claiborne. Another of the Hancocks, Arthur B., III, bred the 1982 Kentucky Derby winner, Gato del Sol, at his nearby Stone Farm.

The most popularly known name among Kentucky horses is, of course, Man o' War, whose statue greets visitors at the entrance of the spacious Kentucky Horse Park in suburban Lexington. Along with Will Harbut, the horse's groom and constant companion for over 25 years, who called Man o' War the "mostest hoss in the world," the famed racer, who won 20 of his 21 starts, became an international star. "Big Red," as he was affectionately called, humiliated his opponents by coming to the wire so far ahead of them that soon few would contest him. Thus his owner, Samuel D. Riddle, put him into stud in 1921 on Faraway Farm. His most famous offspring was War Admiral.

The Kentucky Futurity, established in 1893, and run at the Red Mile, the oldest American stakes race for harness horses, and the Bluegrass Stakes for Thoroughbreds, which is contested at Keeneland, are high points each year in the racing season and in the social life of Lexington.

The most colorful link between the Bluegrass horse world and England is the Iroquois Hunt Club, founded in 1880, which carries on the tradition of foxhunting. Members of the club assemble in scarlet-coated splendor for the formal hunts and the annual "Blessing of the Hounds" by the Episcopal Bishop. With Grimes Mill as its picturesque headquarters, the Hunt Club carries on an ancient art with grace and charm.

The 'Billy' Klair Era

Lexington moved into the Gay Nineties, but the name was a misnomer for millions of Americans who suffered from the impact of a deep economic depression for much of that decade.

The city government was headed by a series of able mayors. One of the most distinguished was Henry T. Duncan, a founder of the *Lexington Daily Press* and a city

councilman for many years before serving two terms as mayor in 1894-95 and 1900-03. Joseph Simrall, who served between 1896 and 1899, was one of Morgan's men during the Civil War and had served as a member of the Board of Aldermen, a director of the Northern Bank, and a school board member. Thomas Combs, mayor from 1904 to 1907, was a member of the enterprising Combs family that had established the Combs Lumber Company in Lexington in 1895, one of the largest and most prosperous such firms in the city. Following his terms as mayor, he was elected a State Senator and became a director of the Federal Reserve Board of Cleveland.

Of all these mayors, Duncan was the most memorable because of his courage and integrity in investigating and exposing inefficiency and corruption in the city government. He also instituted a number of improved methods for disbursement of funds and for greater efficiency of operation of the various departments. Longtime officeholders who owed their jobs to patronage rather than competence were naturally upset.

By the time of Duncan's second term as mayor, 1900-03, he found the chief opponent to his reform program was the 26-year-old William (Billy) Francis Klair, a native

Lexington's first electric street car in its initial run in 1889 is seen in front of the Phoenix Hotel. Photo courtesy of Burton Milward.

129

Lexingtonian of great energy, ambition, and political skill, who proved to be more adept at forming and expanding a Democratic party bloc in the city than his predecessor, Dennis Mulligan. Though German by ancestry, Klair was a Catholic and had married into an Irish family, thus securing the important support of the Irish Democrats. Active in politics from an early age, he won the election in 1899 to the state House of Representatives and began to widen his political connections throughout the state. His influence in the General Assembly resulted in sizable appropriations to the A & M College and to the Eastern Kentucky Hospital (Lunatic Asylum).

Klair exerted a strong political influence in Lexington and Fayette County government for almost three decades. Two of his inner circle, Thomas Combs and John Skain, were elected mayors. A bald man who smoked a cigar, Klair was well liked, admired, and heartily supported by the Democratic party loyalists. He opposed woman suffrage because he believed it posed a threat to his political control, especially if the Negro women voted in any sizable numbers, for they were staunch Republicans. His stand on this issue arrayed him against Laura Clay and the various women's rights organizations. Apart from the suffrage issue, however, he sided with the women and other reformers in opposing the liquor and gambling interests, and in supporting a number of civic improvements, especially in the areas of education, child welfare, and health.

Reflecting a national trend in the Progressive Era — when reform parties in numerous cities were being organized in response to the sensational exposes of municipal corruption by journalists such as Lincoln Steffens — Henry T. Duncan, his son, and other leading reform-minded citizens in Lexington organized a so-called "Fusion Ticket" in the fall of 1909 to challenge the reelection of Klair to the General Assembly. This Fusion Party, composed of independent Democrats and Republicans, chose Henry T. Duncan, Sr., to run against Klair, and also selected tickets for city and county offices.

In a hotly contested election, the Republican-Fusion Party ticket won all but one of the Fayette County posts, but lost to Klair's nominees for the city offices. Klair's majority

over Duncan for state representative was 132 votes. It is noteworthy that over 3,000 black voters supported the Republican-Fusion candidates, which represented the largest percentage of the votes they received.

Regardless of party affiliation, the City Council and Board of Aldermen faced an agenda of problems, some new, some a continuation of old ones. The streets were always in need of improvement. Some of the Council, having visited other cities in Ohio and Indiana, were convinced brick streets were preferable, and throughout the 1890's a number of Lexington's thoroughfares were covered with bricks. It was noisy pavement, however, and thus creosoted wooden blocks were used on Cheapside and some side streets. While deadening the sound, the wooden blocks proved troublesome in other respects as they became extremely slippery during wet weather, proving hazardous to both man and beast. They also tended to wash out, leaving treacherous holes. The remaining streets continued to be macadam or dirt.

End of the Turnpikes

The most significant new development was the termination of the historic turnpikes and their irksome tollhouses. The Civil War had been a disaster for Kentucky's roads. The turnpike companies found it difficult to make a profit and pay dividends to their investors. After the war, the great expansion of railroad building competed with roads for new investors as well as traffic. There was a growing popular dissatisfaction with the toll road system; attacks on tollhouses and tollkeepers across Kentucky became rampant. In 1881, the tollhouse on Parkers Mill Road burned and arson was suspected.

The state began to divest itself of turnpike stock and authorized cities and counties in 1892-93 to finance the purchase of these roads by special tax levies, or to take over abandoned roads or those for which the charters had been forfeited. In 1895, the people in Fayette County were given the opportunity to vote on a proposition to buy the turnpikes, which they approved. An 1896 act expanded these powers as the state decided to provide free highways and gravel roads. No longer would travel to

The Kentucky Association Race Track was located in the vicinity of Fifth and Race streets from 1828 to 1933.
Photo courtesy of Kitty Portwood.

nearby towns be plagued by tollhouses and tollgates. The construction of the interurban railways made toll roads even more impractical. Yet, for almost a century, the turnpike system had provided Kentuckians with a much improved road system.

Little progress was made to improve the storm water drainage system for downtown. Recurrent flooding was endured by hapless merchants who suffered occasional losses of goods in their basements, but the expense of installing an adequate system was so staggering that everyone agreed to postpone taking action.

Fires, Hangings and 'Disorderly Houses'

The Fire Department continued to be improved and modernized, if only on a modest scale, and substations were built in outlying parts of the city. In 1904, William A. Jesse succeeded Chief Muir, and remained at that post until 1928. Gradually, motor-powered vehicles replaced horse-drawn equipment. The full modernization of this department, however, would not come until after World War II. Fire remained a perpetual menace.

In April 1906, a disastrous fire struck the Kentucky Association Race Track complex. Occurring in a crowded residential area, the fire spread rapidly, fanned by a high wind. It swept through 18 houses and threatened to wipe out northeast Lexington until the wind fortunately changed direction, or lessened, allowing the fire department to bring it under control.

On January 11, 1916, fire gutted the recently built Ben Ali Theatre on Main Street, causing an estimated $100,000 damage. A month later, the Broadway Christian Church went up in flames. But the most destructive downtown fire in this period occurred on the morning of May 21, 1917, when fire ravaged most of the block bounded by Short, Limestone, Church and Upper streets, destroying the five-story Merrick Lodge on the corner of Short and Limestone, along with livery stables, business houses and a few residences. In addition to the Merrick Lodge, the greatest loss was the Second Presbyterian Church on Market Street whose tower was set ablaze by a cloud of sparks, causing the entire building to burn.

The Board of Police and Fire Commissioners, established in 1886, had helped create a more reliable and efficient police organization and in January 1908, a detective force was established. A series of police chiefs held that office until Jerry J. Reagan was elected in 1902. This able and courageous man served Lexington well in this position until his death in 1928.

In addition to the police wagon acquired in the 1880's, the Police Department was the fortunate recipient of a handsome, roomy, and well-equipped ambulance given by Mrs. Maria Hunt Dudley. A gray horse, which formerly served the Fire Department, was assigned to draw the vehicle. Unfortunately, when the fire bell rang, the ambulance driver was hard put to keep the old gray from charging off to follow the fire trucks!

Statistics on crime in Lexington appeared in the official reports, not all of which are easily available. In 1894, for instance, the report stated that the majority of arrests were for drunkenness (646), assault and battery (361), forgery (84), grand larceny (61), gambling (46), house breaking (50), and cutting and wounding (105). There were only two murders and one rape. The press warned, "beware of footpads," reflecting the fact that in 1892 highway robberies were becoming more frequent in the Lexington vicinity.

Crimes of violence always caught the attention of the press. A notable encounter between two highly respected members of the community occurred on November 8, 1889, when Colonel Armstead Swope and Colonel William C. Goodloe, who had become enemies over political differences, met at the new post office on the corner of Main and Walnut streets. Their letter boxes were adjacent, and insulting words sparked a brawl in which Swope shot Goodloe in the abdomen while Goodloe perforated Swope with thirteen stab wounds from a hunting knife. The injuries were fatal to both men.

Capital crimes, whether committed by blacks or whites, were punished by hanging. Today, when executions are rare, the frequency of hangings in former days in the county jailhouse yard is surprising. Though the size of the yard limited the number of observers, many others sought strategically located upper-story windows or rooftops to view the spectacles.

Such was the case when Tom O'Brien was hanged for the murder of his estranged wife, Betty Shea. She was a servant in the John Woolfolk residence, now the Whitehall Funeral Home, when O'Brien slipped into the house one

Jerry J. Reagan, chief of the Lexington Police Department from 1902 until his death in 1928. Photo from Police and Fire Departments, City of Lexington, *1914.*

night and murdered the woman. A portable gallows capable of being assembled easily was in use at the time. The newspapers reported that "the gallows arrived yesterday from Georgetown . . . Seven men have been executed on it . . . The instrument, said to be designed by Cincinnatus Shryock, is a little colored by time and the elements, but looks like it was good for many years yet."

That was probably the last hanging at the historic old Megowan's jail on the northwest corner of Limestone and Short streets, for, after a long delay, a new county jail was erected and occupied in 1891, a few hundred feet to the east along Short Street. One other institution in the county was established as a part of the detention system. This was the Kentucky House of Reform for juveniles, which was provided for by an act of the General Assembly and built at Greendale in 1899.

A persistent problem for the police was the control of prostitution. From the 1790's, prostitution had existed in Lexington, either as an individual operation or institutionalized in the bawdy houses, or "disorderly houses," as they were generally called. Records of arrests for operating disorderly houses appear early, but there does not seem to have been a consistent or persistent attempt to stamp them out entirely. For one thing, the police of the undermanned force were too busy with public drunkenness, brawls, and robberies. However, a new policy was tried in 1911 when the city ordered more policing of the redlight district, and required the "girls" to register with the police through the head of the house in order to check juvenile involvement.

By the post-Civil War period, certain sections of town could be identified as redlight districts. One of the oldest was the so-called Babylon Block, existing before the Civil War in a row of buildings extending along Water Street from Limestone to Ayres Alley. One journalist, writing in 1888, recalled that while the block had disappeared with the growth of the railroads in that area, it had once deserved its name for its "tinsel splendor and carnival of vice; its mad, reckless life . . . its forced gayety and its hidden misery eating away at the hearts of the poor, shameless women who dwelt within its borders . . ."

Judge Charles Kerr informed a grand jury in 1911 that vice was rampant in the city, that a redlight district had existed in Lexington for over a hundred years, and that many other "houses of assignation" were scattered throughout the city.

Most famous of all such establishments in Lexington and the central Bluegrass region was that of Belle Breezing, who operated here from about 1876 to 1917. A Lexington girl who, while in her teens, chose the "primrose path" as a remunerative career, she practiced her trade in what had been the Robert Todd home on West Main Street before opening her own "sporting house" on North Upper Street, between Third and Fourth streets, in the early 1880's.

Belle's reputation won her the status of a "madam," and with money from a wealthy client she built her famous establishment, a three-story brick, 27-room mansion on the southwest corner of Wilson and Megowan (now Northeastern) streets. It soon became one of the most lavish and expertly conducted bordellos in the South. So discreetly did Belle administer her affairs that notable and rich individuals frequented her establishment, especially during the racing season, and she became a wealthy woman.

Her house was located near the center of the redlight district known as "The Hill." Belle felt in no way confined to her home, nor saw any need to hide out. She took her weekly "earnings" to the bank in a plain paper bag,

This forbidding looking structure is the Fayette County Jail erected in 1891 on East Short Street near Limestone Street. It was demolished in 1978. Photo courtesy of Transylvania University.

Belle Breezing, Lexington's best known "Madam," is pictured here in the parlor of the "finest sporting house north of New Orleans." Her famous establishment was in operation from 1876 to 1917. Photo courtesy of E. I. Thompson.

attended the races at the Kentucky Association Track, and kept her eyes and conversation confined to her small coterie, although many in attendance knew her identity.

Despite citizens at public meetings in 1911 demanding that action be taken against both owners and operators of houses of ill repute, it was not until World War I that the activities at Belle Breezing's house and other bordellos were brought to an end. This happened when the military authorities at Camp Stanley on the Versailles Road ordered such places "off limits" to both officers and men, which effectively closed down Belle's house. She lived in semi-retirement until her death in August 1940, and was buried in the Calvary Cemetery on West Main. Even *Time* magazine took note of her passing, describing her as "a famous Lexington bawd who ran the most orderly of disorderly houses." The building became a rooming house, and in December 1973, was almost destroyed by fire. The fame of the house was such that souvenir hunters scrambled

for what remained, including the very bricks of the structure.

Doctors and Hospitals

Not until after the Civil War did Lexington see the establishment of a hospital. In 1877, Sister Euphrasia and five other sisters of the Order of Charity came from the Mother House at Nazareth to take charge of a hospital that the Sisters of Mercy had started earlier in the vicinity of St. Paul Catholic Church. It proved to be inadequate and they rented the Alford residence on Linden Walk, where at first they could accommodate only six patients.

Through the efforts of Dr. Waller O. Bullock, Sr., a member and often president of the Board of Health, and Father Tom Major, a large house on West Second Street, west of Jefferson Street, was bought in 1878. Twelve patients were taken in. Two English agricultural specialists visiting Lexington in 1879 reported the existence of St. Joseph Hospital and the fact that the city paid $150 annually to the hospital for the privilege of sending temporary paupers there. Private patients were admitted on payment of $5 or $6 for lodging and care, but the patient paid the additional cost for the doctor and medicine. Indigent patients were taken care of by the hospital's charity fund. Many doctors donated their services for the poor.

A three-story brick building was erected in 1887 to increase the capacity and facilities of St. Joseph Hospital, with an annex added in 1898. In 1908, another annex was completed with operating rooms, some private rooms, and improved quarters for the sisters. A Nazareth training school for nurses was organized in 1918, with the first students graduating in 1921. On February 11, 1929, the main building burned but was rebuilt immediately. Frequent benefits and picnics for the hospital were given at Woodland Park and the Kentucky Association Race Track.

The Protestants meanwhile became involved in a hospital project. The Women's Guild of Christ Church provided the leadership and the money to purchase in 1889 the H. H. Gratz property, including the Farmer Dewees "White Cottage" on East Short Street, and converted it into a Protestant Infirmary. It was divided into men's and women's wards, with bathrooms and an operating table. The community at large was asked to contribute to its support, and one missionary group in the city offered to provide a much-needed brick pavement in front of the infirmary as long as each brick bore the name of the donor.

A Negro ward was soon added. In 1895 an addition was designed by Aldenburg and Scott and erected in 1896. This large, three-story, stone-trimmed brick structure of rather unusual design, which is still standing, became the main part of the hospital and contained a fine operating room.

By 1899, the infirmary became nondenominational, receiving the support of many churches, and was renamed the Good Samaritan Hospital. In 1905, the hospital acquired the property of W. H. McCorkle, formerly the James O. Harrison estate, on South Limestone Street as the site for its new building, which was dedicated on July 3, 1907. The Southern Methodist Church took over the hospital in 1925, and the United Methodist

Church — the final product of several mergers — today operates the institution, which is in the midst of a large building expansion program.

The Eastern Lunatic Asylum, which eventually changed its name to Eastern Kentucky Hospital for the Insane, had greatly increased its capacity when the General Assembly in 1867 appropriated $150,000 for an additional 250 rooms. The institution had grown from one building in the 1820's, to "a small city," said one reporter in 1901. In that year, 144 employees were caring for 1,000 patients. A 200-acre farm adjacent to the wards, which was worked in part by the patients, furnished much of the produce, meat, and dairy products for the residents.

Dr. T. T. Wendell, an outstanding Negro physician, devoted a lifetime to meeting the medical needs of the community. Though he served both white and black patients, he attended mainly blacks at Eastern Kentucky Hospital. In August 1906, he directed a musical concert at the Main Street Auditorium (the old Main Street Christian Church) as a benefit for the Negro wards at St. Joseph, Good Samaritan, and Eastern Kentucky hospitals. In that same year a much-needed building was erected for Negroes, and some decades later one of the new buildings at Eastern Kentucky Hospital was named for Dr. Wendell

Annual Mental Asylum Ball

Of all the dances and balls given throughout the year in Lexington, none compared with the annual grand ball at the mental asylum. Charitable in origin and purpose, the unique character and location of this event, which was always splendidly conducted, was attended by the best families. Since a number of the more orderly patients were permitted to attend as well, the diversity of the participants and the special environment of this dance created one of Lexington's most unusual social events.

There were other institutions supported privately or by a church, including the historic Orphans Asylum. In 1894, the Rescue Home, or "The House of Mercy," was organized to give asylum "to that unfortunate class of women, fallen in sin, who are desirous of leading a better life and express a wish for reformation," namely, unmarried pregnant girls. The Board of Managers was composed of a representative from each of the Protestant, Catholic, and Jewish churches. A house on Fourth Street was bought from the Belt Line Railroad for about $6,000, with contributions from the Fiscal Court and the City Council, as well as private subscriptions. Workmen, some donating their services, repaired the building. Applications exceeded capacity. This institution, now known as the Florence Crittenton Home, is still operating on the same site.

Widows' and Orphans' Home

Meanwhile, the Odd Fellows established a widows' and orphans' home at Jefferson and West Sixth streets. They erected a four-story brick building with an octagonal tower which was dedicated in 1898, and this, along with a two-story residence on the property, provided the facilities. An additional building was erected in 1909, and in 1927, the two earlier buildings were replaced with a four-story brick boys' dormitory. The Odd Fellows constructed another facility in Eminence, Kentucky, when the Lexington home became too crowded.

Another private sanitarium for the treatment of nervous and mental disorders was opened by Dr. R. D. Chenault on South Broadway, which he called High Oaks. After his death in the early 1890's, Dr. Silas Evans and Dr. George Sprague operated it for Mrs. Chenault. In 1912, when she sold the property to a tobacco company for a warehouse, Dr. and Mrs. Sprague purchased an 83-acre tract farther out on Harrodsburg Road, and erected a sanitarium, still called High Oaks. This facility functioned until 1945 when it was sold to the Sisters of Charity of Nazareth and became the new site of St. Joseph Hospital.

Tuberculosis, or consumption, as it was commonly called, was a terrible killer in the 19th and early 20th centuries, and the Bluegrass area, despite its reputation as a healthful environment, had a high percentage of tubercular cases. The newest treatment at the turn of the century consisted of fresh air, sunlight, nourishing food, and proper exercise, a therapy most notably featured at a Saranac, New York, sanatorium. On this model the Bluegrass Sanatorium was established in August 1917, on the Georgetown Pike, due in part to

the vigorous support of Madeline McDowell Breckinridge, about whom more will be said later. In the following three years, 381 patients were admitted, of whom four died while there, and twenty-five died who left before being offically discharged. It was equally supported by the city and the county, while those who could afford to pay something were charged accordingly. The financial stability of the sanatorium was substantially enhanced by a gift of $125,000 from Leo Marks in memory of his father, Julius Marks, a Lexington businessman from 1875 to 1901. Leo Marks had moved permanently to Columbus, Ohio, in 1892 to operate a furniture business, but he maintained an interest in Lexington and owned a horse farm on the Paris Pike. In response to this gift, the facility was renamed the Julius Marks Sanatorium.

It is hard today to realize how elementary medical practice was at the turn of the century. Even a half century after Transylvania had closed its Medical Department, only modest progress had been made in surgery and little or none in internal medicine and drug therapy. When Dr. Waller O. Bullock registered his diploma with the Fayette County Clerk in 1897 to practice medicine, it was a pleasant town of about 35,000, he later recalled. There were about 50 doctors, two of whom were black, and most of whom were

> graduates of the Louisville schools or shall I say 'diploma machines.' Notwithstanding this fact, there were a considerable number of able, studious, and skilful practitioners ... Most of the doctors of that day considered that when they got their diplomas they were finished physicians and required no further study in books and consequently the average was pretty low.

Most were general practitioners with a set of surgical tools and a limited supply of medicines, few of any true efficacy. Though knowledge of bacteria was widespread, as was the need for sterilization, effective anti-infection solutions were unavailable. Despite the fact that the doctors "treated the patients more than they did the disease," they were loved and honored by all.

With the arrival in 1887 of Dr. David Barrow, a former student at Kentucky University (Transylvania) and a graduate of the Medical Department of the University of

Main Street looking west, showing the Phoenix Hotel on the left, ca. 1915. Photo courtesy of the L & N Railroad archives.

Louisiana (now Tulane University Medical School), who had served as an intern at Bellevue Hospital in New York, the latest in surgical techniques was introduced into Lexington. When he formed a partnership with Dr. Bullock and his own well-trained son, Woolfolk Barrow, in 1916, a new era in medical treatment was about to begin. Though interrupted by the war, this partnership was to form the basis for the present Lexington Clinic, which in the post-war years helped advance medical treatment in the community. Dr. Benjamin F. Van Meter, an outstanding surgeon, and Dr. John W. Scott, a brilliant internist, along with Drs. T. H. Kinnaird, W. E. Bannister and others, added to the group of medical practitioners who, working under difficult handicaps, provided the best treatment then possible for their patients. Also, the organization and functioning of the Fayette County Medical Society created an esprit de corps that was beneficial to the physicians.

Lawyers and Judges

It is unfortunate that no history of the Fayette Bar Association appears to have been written, nor has there been a comprehensive study made of the lawyers and judges in Lexington and Fayette County in the post-Civil War period. For the historian, this poses a problem of evaluating the outstanding legal professionals during these decades. The eulogistic obituaries of deceased lawyers and judges are not the best guide to an impartial judgment, but it can be said with some degree of confidence that the Fayette County bar and bench included many distinguished individuals.

Judge King Swope recalled in a column written for the fiftieth anniversary edition of the *Lexington Leader* in 1938 that, of the outstanding members of the bar in the previous three or four decades, only George B. Kinkead, E. L. Hutchinson, J. S. Botts, and Charles Kerr were still living. He also stated that in the 1880's Fayette Circuit Court was a term court and the judge literally "rode the circuit" in various counties. In 1893, however, the Fayette Circuit Court was made an independent circuit consisting of the county alone, and became a court of continuous session, the first judge being Watts Parker. After his death in 1911, Parker was succeeded by Charles Kerr, who later became a federal judge in the Canal Zone before returning permanently to Washington, D. C., to practice law. He was succeeded, in turn, by Richard C. Stoll and King Swope.

The Schools

The schools, as always, remained of keen interest to the citizens. The annual school report of 1894 expressed satisfaction with

> the fast disappearance of that prejudice which, without reason, has existed in the South against the public school. The opening of each session brings us new pupils who have never attended the public schools before.

The value of a public school education was that it recognized no caste or class distinction, the report went on (racial separation was apparently not regarded as discriminatory). The city superintendent, William Rogers Clay, who had taken over when Massilon Cassidy became county superintendent in 1892, expressed his concern about the overcrowding of classes, the desirability of employing experienced teachers, and the need to introduce more practicality into the curriculum. He urged the establishment of a manual training school and suggested that the State College build a school of eight grades to give practical training in actual teaching to the young, inexperienced students in its normal department. The Davidson School, close by the college campus, he thought might be used for that purpose. He also said Lexington could be proud of its colored schools, which had the same course of study as the white schools.

The white schools at that time were Davidson, Johnson, Dudley, Harrison, and Morton, while the colored schools were the Fourth Street, Constitution, and Patterson. The Chandler School was, of course, one of the most important black schools, but was not a public school. Meanwhile, work on the Dudley School annex was proceeding. Public school enrollment increased from 1,700 in 1880 to 4,860 in 1900, but many children never attended school.

The black schools in the 1890's received excellent leadership from Green P. Russell, who had studied at Berea, considered law, and then decided he could provide greater service as a teacher. He started at the small black Fayette County school at Chilesburg before accepting an appointment as principal of the Fourth Street School in 1890. He later became supervisor of the city's black schools, holding both positions concurrently. Mayor Duncan was so impressed by his work that he recommended to the General Council that they name the black high school after Russell. Russell later became president of Kentucky State College.

Russell School remained the only public high school for blacks until Dunbar was built in 1922. The county black students wishing high school training had to attend Chandler School until Douglas High School was built on Price Road in 1929.

Russell School was fortunate in being able to recruit a fine contingent of black teachers, many of them graduates of Chandler Normal School, Berea, or Northern colleges. Their education and dedication soon made them leaders in the black community along with ministers, successful businessmen, and a few professionals.

Under Massilon Cassidy, who became city superintendent in 1903, the first white high school was opened at the historic Morton School on Walnut Street in 1905. Then, in 1909, he supervised the construction of the first school designed specifically as a high school. with Herman L. Rowe as architect. It was erected on the site of the old Morton School. In 1917, a new Lexington High School was opened at the corner of Limestone and Fourth streets (present site of the Lexington Junior High School), and the Morton building became the Morton Junior High School.

The most remarkable educational project in this period was the brainchild of Mrs. Madeline McDowell Breckinridge. This outstanding woman was descended on her father's side from Judge Samuel McDowell, leader of the many Danville conventions that led Kentucky to statehood, and a grandniece of Dr. Ephraim McDowell. On the maternal side, she was the great-granddaughter of Henry Clay. In 1898, she married Desha Breckinridge, son of W. C.

Madeline McDowell Breckinridge, wife of Desha Breckinridge, editor of the Lexington Herald, *was one of Kentucky's most prominent philanthropists and a leader in the women's suffrage movement. This protrait by Dixie Seldon hangs at Ashland. Photo courtesy of Henry Clay Memorial Foundation.*

P. Breckinridge and the scion of one of Lexington's most famous families. Despite formidable physical handicaps, including tuberculosis which eventually killed her, this attractive, magnetic person lived a remarkably full life devoted to a wide variety of reform projects. These culminated in her leadership role in the woman's suffrage movement when she assumed the presidency of the Kentucky Equal Rights Association in 1912, replacing the indomitable Laura Clay. Prior to this, she had been a charter member of the Lexington Civic League, an organization devoted to the general betterment of city life, especially parks and recreation for children. She was founder of the Kentucky Association for the Prevention and Relief of Tuberculosis, and with assistance from other family members was influential in the establishment of the Blue Grass Sanatorium in Lexington.

In the latter part of the 19th century, hundreds of Irish immigrants had come to Lexington to work on the large-scale railroad building projects expanding in all directions from Lexington. The railroad companies quickly constructed cheap housing for their workers in the less expensive and less desirable sections of town such as Irishtown and Davis Bottom, adjacent to the railroads, and often near poor black neighborhoods. Some of the Irish set up grocery stores serving their own and the blacks. Thanks to the political patronage of men like Dennis Mulligan, a number of the Irish secured jobs on the police and fire departments. Some reached top posts, as in the case of Paul Conlon in the Fire Department, and J. J. Reagan in the Police Department. Irish names eventually appeared among Lexington's mayors.

Mrs. Breckinridge, aware that many of the newly arrived immigrants were illiterate and poverty-stricken and unfamiliar with American ways, conceived of a project to build a school in their community that would serve both children and parents. This was the era of the settlement house in a number of major cities, the most famous being Jane Addams' Hull House in Chicago. Mrs. Breckinridge's contacts with wealthy and civic-minded people in the East and Midwest enabled her to solicit funds for her plan, starting in 1908. The Lexington Board of Education contributed $10,000. This, added to other contributions, including a $30,000 donation from Robert Todd Lincoln, eldest son of the President, made possible the erection of the school, completed in 1912 and named Lincoln School after its largest financial supporter.

Lincoln School, located on West High Street and De Roode Street (it was originally called the West End School), provided classrooms, a laundry, cannery, swimming pool, and both afternoon and evening programs for the parents of the day students. Elizabeth Cloud, who had been trained at Hull House, was the first principal and remained there until the early 1920's.

Beginning in 1905 with the appointment of Mrs. Nannie Faulconer as county school superintendent, a post she held until 1921, great strides were made in improving the atomistic system of 48 schools scattered among 41 school districts. Under the old system, all local supplies had to be bought by the local district, so either a generous parent helped, or the teacher had to buy coal, chalk, erasers, etc., out of a meager salary. Having read about consolidated school systems in other states, Mrs. Faulconer proposed such a scheme to the school

Early county school bus, the first purchased for the Greendale School, showing Mrs. Nannie G. Faulconer, superintendent of Fayette County Schools, at the left. Greendale became the first consolidated school in 1910. Photo courtesy of Mrs. Joseph Barker.

board. When questioned on the matter of expense, she pointedly called attention to the difference in the quality of housing for young school children and that for expensive race horses. Support was forthcoming to build five grade schools between 1911 and 1916. The Board voted to consolidate Greendale, Old Cane Run, Tyler, and Donerail schools into one location on the Georgetown Pike where an interurban line provided transportation. On January 15, 1910, Greendale, the first consolidated school in Kentucky, was dedicated on Spurr Road, not far from Georgetown Pike. Athens and Picadome schools were completed in 1912 and Russell Cave and Faulconer four years later. All five of these new consolidated schools were constructed on the same general plan and with the same exterior appearance. None of the original buildings now exist. The original Greendale was replaced by Linlee in 1927. The new name — an amalgam honoring both Lincoln and Lee — was adopted to avoid confusion with the state reformatory for boys in the same vicinity.

Other programs Mrs. Faulconer initiated were: a transportation system using horse-drawn wagons until a motor bus was acquired in 1916; and a vocational education program that included shops in each high school, as well as homemaking instruction, and garden plots which furnished food for the school lunch programs. She also organized a county beautification program which initiated extensive tree planting along roadsides.

In the early spring of 1921, Mrs. Faulconer resigned when inept handling of finances and post-war economic problems brought the county system to the verge of bankruptcy. There was no money to pay the teachers. Professor George Baker, a University of Kentucky education instructor, was selected to replace her.

During the four years Baker was in office, he established the first uniform salary schedule, plus incentives to encourage teachers to continue their education, and by 1929 all county teachers were college graduates and were teaching in their major fields. Baker also created an unusual circulating library for the county. Housed in his office, the library contained some 5,500 volumes, many of which were autographed by their authors, such as Gene Stratton Porter, Zane Grey, James Lane Allen, Irvin S. Cobb, and Booth Tarkington. Under his successor, Miss Mattie Dalton, the Parent-Teacher Associations, begun in the 1920's, were extended, and teachers were encouraged to join national and state teachers' associations.

In addition to the private and parochial schools already mentioned, two new private schools of special merit were established at the turn of the century. One was organized by Ella M. Williams, daughter of Professor Samuel M.

Williams, who headed Sayre Female Institute from 1859 until his death in 1869. A graduate of Sayre, Miss Williams started her own school in September 1895, in the old Second Presbyterian Church parsonage at 177 North Upper. A number of prominent families sent their children there. Crowded for space, Miss Williams combined her school with that of the Misses Annie and Mary McElhinney and in 1900 moved to a commodious and impressive two-and-a-half-story red brick antebellum residence at 355 North Broadway. Here, anywhere from 75 to 110 pupils arrived by foot, horse and buggy, bicycle, or streetcar. Her successful school operated until 1914, a year before Miss Williams died.

In 1903, Professor Barton C. Hagerman, principal at Hamilton College, purchased the old Thomas January (or Tobias Gibson) house on West Second Street to establish the Campbell-Hagerman College for Girls. He engaged Herman Rowe to design dormitories for the school, and the old house was soon flanked by two four-story brick structures. The one to the east was called Argyle Hall and featured a tetrastyle Ionic portico. The Hagerman School was a major competitor of Hamilton College until it closed in 1912, after graduating nearly 200 young ladies.

The Universities

Transylvania University, having resumed its traditional name in 1908, functioned successfully as a small, liberal arts college. It had become coeducational in 1889 with some prodding from Laura Clay and the Equal Rights Association. The example of coeducation at State College across town showed its practicality. Burris Jenkins and Richard Crossfield provided the most significant presidential leadership during these years. In 1895, the College of the Bible had built an imposing structure on the campus, facing Broadway, and adjacent to Old Morrison, indicating the close relationship between the college and the seminary. Though legally independent, these two schools occasionally had the same president and shared faculty and classes. College life was changing here, though, as it was across the country. Athletics, both intramural and intercollegiate, were becoming increasingly important as were fraternities and sororities.

The most dramatic incident on the Transylvania campus in the first two decades of the 20th century was the so-called "heresy trial" which was instigated by a disgruntled seminary student who thought the teachings of the new faculty, especially of Alonzo W. Fortune, William Clayton Bower, and Elmer Snoddy, were too liberal and unorthodox. He circulated a broadside among the alumni, Disciples of Christ members, and curators, airing his views. This conservative element raised such a hue and cry that the curators were compelled to hold a court of inquiry, examining the faculty members cited and the accusations against them. The charges against the faculty were not successfully sustained, however, and the liberal tradition of academic freedom at Transylvania was preserved.

Across town, the State University was now operating under the new administration of Henry Stites Barker. In 1911 the institution had fifteen buildings located on its 53-acre campus plus the Agricultural Experiment Station with its 243 acres. Under President Barker, a graduate school was formally organized, and in 1913, a School of Journalism was added. The university football and basketball teams enjoyed winning seasons but the baseball team was losing its popularity.

The Experiment Station continued to be one of the most active agencies of the university, producing many diverse pamphlets and bulletins for distribution to farmers throughout the state, informing them of the latest advances in tobacco raising, care of hogs, cattle, and poultry. The Colleges of Mechanical and Electrical Engineering, Civil Engineering, and Mining Engineering were also active, their various deans publicizing their contributions to the welfare of the Commonwealth.

Enrollment at the State University increased from 582 in 1910 to 998 in 1916. Yet, with all of these positive signs of progress and accomplishment, the Kentucky legislature continued its historically parsimonious financial support of the university.

By 1917, conflicts developed between the administrators in the various divisions of engineering and agriculture, intensified by an attempt to consolidate these divisions into a more efficient unit. Criticism of President Barker grew, and a committee was appointed which made a thorough investigation of the

The University of Kentucky, or State University, as it was then known, had fifteen buildings in 1911 on its 53-acre campus, plus the Agricultural Experiment Station with 243 acres. Photo courtesy of The Filson Club.

situation. Its list of recommendations were accepted for the most part by the Board of Trustees. Barker resigned, and after a careful search for a new president, an excellent choice was made in Frank L. McVey, a Yale Ph.D. in economics who had established a fine reputation as scholar and administrator as president of the University of North Dakota.

McVey assumed the presidency in September 1917, and despite the unsettled conditions of the war years made an effective transition. Within a few years, his leadership and the implementation of the recommendations of the investigating committee placed the university on a more harmonious and progressive course. Its services to the community and state expanded and improved, and the scholarly quality of the faculty was markedly increased.

The institutions of higher learning had historically been the important pillars of Lexington's claim to being the "Athens of the West." In the antebellum period, Transylvania

University had provided that contribution. Though the State University, or the University of Kentucky as it was renamed after 1916, did not achieve real distinction until the McVey administration, its presence and that of Transylvania added an educational aura and intellectual dimension to the Lexington community that fostered the historic tradition.

Lexington's Cultural Life

Supplementing these educational centers were other cultural activities that enhanced the cultivation and sophistication of Lexington. Theatre, music, art and letters were hallmarks of such cultivation. The new Opera House was the theatrical center, and from its opening in 1887 it provided Lexingtonians with top stars and some of the best dramatic fare the American stage had to offer. It was not all heavy drama, for minstrel shows and an occasional vaudeville show alternated with Shakespeare. The building was renovated to expand its capacity in 1891. Gilbert and Sullivan remained popular, *The Gondoliers* being performed here in 1892, and later *The Mikado.*

Less successful were the attempts to fill the house by having famed prizefighters like John L. Sullivan and James "Gentleman Jim" Corbett fumble their way through contrived theatrics. John Philip Sousa's renowned band performed here. It was a testimony to the theatre-goers' tastes that Richard Mansfield's performance of *Cyrano de Bergerac* and Thomas Keene's *Julius Caesar* played to packed houses, people standing all night in line to purchase tickets. Joseph Jefferson's classic portrayal of *Rip Van Winkle* was equally popular. Lillian Russell, like Lillie Langtry earlier, caused great enthusiasm, especially among the male clientele.

The coming of the motion picture, however, would gradually begin to erode the popularity of the legitimate theatre.

Lexington also could claim a few stage celebrities of its own. The one who received most national acclaim was Carolina Louise Dudley, born in a stone house on West Main Street in 1863. Better known as Mrs. Leslie Carter, she was trained and given her first role by the great David Belasco in New York. Almost overnight this glamorous, red-haired, green-eyed actress became the toast of Broadway, and also was said to have taken London by storm.

Ada Meade Saffarans of Lexington became a musical comedy star at the turn of the century, and was so popular in her home town that the Hippodrome Theater was renamed the Ada Meade in her honor in 1914.

Lexington's musical culture was enhanced by concerts by the Boston Symphony, Cincinnati Symphony, and smaller ensembles during this period. Locally, a community chorus of 100 voices presented Handel's *Messiah* in 1903. Performances of this immensely popular oratorio had been presented in Lexington on a smaller scale in the antebellum period. The existence of a chorus of such a size was new, however, and encouraged the formation of smaller choral and instrumental ensembles.

Of the new conservatories of music, such as Mrs. Sallie Johnson's in the historic Combs residence on Main Street, by far the most famous was that of Anna Chandler Goff. She,

along with Professors Fred Lyman Wheeler and Bruce Reynolds, and portrait painter Sudduth Goff, bought Duff Hall of the old Hagerman College on West Second Street and converted it into an arts club. Miss Goff later operated her Lexington College of Music here. No one did more to foster fine music in Lexington than this dynamic, colorful impresario who brought to the new Woodland Auditorium in the period from World War I to the 1930's world-famous artists, including Paderewski, Heifitz, Josef Hofman, Rachmaninoff and many others.

Saxton and Trost's bands were not only barbecue and picnic music-makers, but were capable of performing first-rate programs, thus adding to the community's musical resources. The local Lexington Symphony Orchestra was apparently functioning in January 1907, as the *Herald* reported a concert by this group.

Though Lexington suffered from a lack of notable native artists at the turn of the century, evidence of a community's interest in art is also manifested in the acquisition of distinguished art works. Lexington had a few affluent patrons of art works, the most prominent in the post-Civil War period being John B. Wilgus.

Born in Lexington in 1824 into the most modest circumstances, Wilgus exemplified the typical Horatio Alger hero as he worked his way up from a poor lad hauling bricks to a successful grocer, president of the City National Bank, an organizer of the National Exchange Bank, and an investor in railroads and gas works. In 1855, he bought the residence of Mary Todd's grandmother, Mrs. Robert Parker, on West Short Street, tore it down in 1870-71 and built the present structure with its four-story tower overlooking the town. He also had designed a special polygonal pavilion as a gallery for the display of his art collection. For years his love of beauty motivated him to acquire a respectable number of oil paintings and a few pieces of sculpture. He enjoyed holding open house to provide an opportunity for any who cared to see his collection. Unfortunately, after his death in January 1887, the collection was dispersed through an auction held at the more spacious quarters of W. R. Milward, funeral director, on Main Street between Mill and Cheapside.

Lexington had always shown an exceptional interest in literature, dating back to the 1790's.

The Civil War, not surprisingly, dampened both literary and educational activities, not only in Kentucky but nationwide. After the war, the literary interest gradually revived. How many promising poets and novelists were lost on the battlefields we will never know, but by the 1880's a new generation was appearing. Representative of that group was Lexington's James Lane Allen. Born in Fayette County and educated at Kentucky University (Transylvania), he made a living teaching, both at his alma mater and elsewhere, until his writing consumed his entire energies. By the 1890's, Allen's stories had been published in *Harper's Magazine.* His haunting, almost nostalgic evocation of the beauties of the Bluegrass, woven into stories alive with colorful and often historic characters, won him a national audience. His stories about James Moore and "King" Solomon have been referred to. The controversial *The Reign of Law* was centered in Lexington and Transylvania. One of his most popular novels, *The Choir Invisible,* which headed the national best-seller list for months, was set in Lexington of the 1790's.

Allen moved to New York in the 1890's and stayed until his death in 1925. He was, up to that time, Lexington's most distinguished author. It is fitting that a memorial fountain he gave to the children of Lexington should occupy a prominent place in Gratz Park, provided by money he left in his will.

Though not a native of Fayette County, nor a longtime resident of the area, John Fox, Jr., was another Kentucky best-selling novelist of the era. He grew up in Bourbon County and spent a year at Transylvania before transferring to Harvard. Like Allen, Fox fashioned his novels out of Kentucky material. *The Little Shepherd of Kingdom Come* was set not only in eastern Kentucky, which provided the title, but also in the Bluegrass and Lexington. Later made into a play, it delighted audiences at the Opera House.

Another of Lexington's literary celebrities was Rosa Vertner Jeffrey. Brought to Lexington by her adoptive parents in 1838 and schooled at the Episcopal Seminary, she married Claude Johnson, a wealthy Lexingtonian, in 1845. A beautiful, charming woman, she was one of the social and literary leaders in the community. One of her sons, C. M. Johnson, was elected mayor of the city. After her husband's death in 1861, she moved to Rochester, New York, for a few years, where she married a Scot named Alexander Jeffrey. They returned to Lexington permanently, living a good part of that time in the Wickliffe house at Second and Market Streets.

In 1896, Henry Schange (center) advertised 5-cent milkshakes at his sidewalk fruit and ice cream stand at the southeast corner of Main and Mill streets. The Schange family later operated the popular Schange's Candy Kitchen.

144

The cornerstone for the present two-story, cut stone Lexington Public Library building was laid on June 8, 1903. Herman L. Rowe was the architect for the structure, whose $75,000 cost was largely offset by a gift from Andrew Carnegie. The building is located in Gratz Park. Photo courtesy of Transylvania University.

Her first literary works were poems published in George Prentice's *Louisville Journal* in the antebellum period and a volume of poetry published in Boston in 1857. After the war she wrote several novels, a five-act comedy, and what is probably her best volume, *The Crimson Hand and Other Poems* (1881). Though not as gifted a writer as Allen or Fox, she was nevertheless Lexington's resident poet laureate and was among the earliest Southern women to attract some national attention as a literary figure. The special poem she wrote for the unveiling of Hart's "Woman Triumphant" in the courthouse added to the lustre of that occasion.

Despite its promising beginning in 1795 as a pioneer venture in forwarding the cause of learning through a community library, the Lexington Library had a star-crossed and checkered career. Christopher Morley's peripatetic *Parnassus on Wheels* would have been hard-pressed to keep up with the physical meanderings of this institution, not to mention its fluctuating financial and operating status. It wandered from the Transylvania classroom to Andrew McCalla's drug store, the old statehouse, and the Kentucky Insurance Company between 1795 and 1837, but did boast of possessing some 6,000 volumes at that time. It then fell upon hard times, losing support and subscribers (it did not become a free public library until the end of the century). Closed for a while, it was briefly revived in 1846 when it shared Transylvania's old 1827 Medical Department Building with the city officials and the Odd Fellows. In 1854 a fire seriously damaged both books and building. The trustees of the library then purchased a building on Jordan's Row across from the courthouse, and here it resided for about 21 years. Meanwhile, a faction of the Upper Street (later Hill Street) Methodist Church bought the damaged Medical Hall for $300 and used it as a chapel until they disbanded and in time sold the building to the Library Association. Here the library operated until a generous gift from Andrew Carnegie enabled the present structure to be erected in 1905.

That the library in 1890 was not a flourishing institution was reflected in the

Transcript's comment that of all of Lexington's charities the library was the most neglected.

> As to the library, that poor old fossil of a prehistoric age, where rat-eaten tomes mock at the so-called classic shades of Lexington. What can we say to stir up enthusiasm among literary pockets? Or pockets unliterary? A good public library would pay well in this community.

The city finally bestirred itself in 1898 with Mayor J. B. Simrall's encouragement and amended the city charter so as to allow the establishment of a public library. There is little doubt that Mary K. Bullitt prodded them into taking this action. Described as "one of the most cultivated and refined women in Kentucky ... Her mind a storehouse of knowledge and information," Miss Bullitt, an energetic and attractive woman who was one of the early society editors of the *Herald,* had become dedicated to creating a truly "public" library. The city officials appointed her librarian in 1898, a post she held until 1911. During her incumbency, Andrew Carnegie, one of the richest men in the world, was disposing of his fortune, a substantial part being used to build libraries. The first was erected at his birthplace in Dunfermline, Scotland.

Lexington received a grant from Carnegie of $50,000 in 1902, acquired the lower section of Gratz Park from Transylvania, and employed Herman Rowe to design the new library. In marked contrast to the style in which he had designed the Opera House fifteen years earlier, Rowe, as Clay Lancaster states, gave a "controlled classic treatment" to the library plan. The impressive structure "features wide steps leading up to a colossal Renaissance portico of four Corinthian columns with reliefs in the pediment." The interior featured high windows and ceilings with a marble stairway leading to an upper rotunda, giving quite an aura of grandeur. It was opened in June 1905, and remains one of the finest public buildings in Lexington, though in serious need of repair.

An interesting sidelight concerning the transfer of the books to the new library was a plan to fumigate all the volumes before moving them so as to prevent disease from being spread to the patrons!

Architecture

All of these activities — the stage, music, art, education, literature, and the library — contributed a significant dimension to Lexington's cultural life. To this should be added the architectural achievements of the community. The very permanence of buildings, fires and the ravages of time notwithstanding, makes them the best hallmarks of an age, expressing as they do the style of life, and the affluence, or lack of it, of the people who lived in earlier eras. It is perhaps an American characteristic that in many towns public structures were slighted and private residences emphasized in the architectural quality of buildings. In Fayette County, the great estates, beautifully situated in the magnificent Bluegrass meadowland, framed with endless miles of white or black plank fences or the skillfully crafted field-stone fences, are a delight to the eye. In town, the fine private homes clustered around Gratz Park and Old Morrison, stretching north and south along Broadway, Upper, Mill and Limestone, and the streets and courts radiating from them, bespoke of wealth and an aesthetic sense that reflected the social status, dignity, and pride of their owners.

The area surrounding downtown, especially High Street and what is now designated as the Northside, was the home of many distinguished figures. The houses they erected during a century and a half reflect a wide range of styles — the Federal, Greek Revival, neo-Gothic, Italianate, Renaissance Eclecticism, and Richardsonian Romanesque. The diversity that emerged in the World War I period and the 1920's defy any categorical definition. Some houses were grandiose in concept and size, others modest and tranquil. To walk downtown today along these streets is to walk through historic periods, to sense the changing eras of the town as manifested in its stone, brick and frame forms. Even the less immediately visible streets with their rows of cramped frame structures, mostly occupied by Lexington's less affluent white and black citizens, reveal an integral part of that history.

Many of these buildings were designed by Lexington architects, or by local builders working from books of architectural styles. Lexington could list with pride such men as Matthew Kennedy, Gideon and Cincinnatus Shryock, John McMurtry, Thomas Lewinski, Phelix Lundin, Herman Rowe, and Vertner Tandy, to name some of the more prominent in the 19th and early 20th centuries.

The mercantile and banking edifices, interspersed with the small, cramped shops and hand industries ranged along the major streets of downtown, were not, as a group, as architecturally distinctive as the private residences surrounding them. The post-Civil War period saw the move to taller buildings such as the Carty building on the historic southwest corner of Main and Mill, and the Fayette National Bank and the Higgins Block on the northeast corner of Main and Upper, which replaced such classic structures as the Bank of the United States on Short Street. After the turn of the century, the massive courthouse was flanked by the City National Bank, the McClelland Building, and finally, the blockbuster of the town's traditionally low skyline, the new 15-story Fayette National Bank, designed by the famous New York firm of McKim, Mead, and White, erected in 1912-14. One of the most impressive structures on Main Street was the 1907 Union Station which was given an attractive setting appropriate to its size.

The towering style set by the Fayette National Bank was echoed a few blocks east by the 12-story Lafayette Hotel (1920-21), designed by Chris C. and E. A. Weber of Cincinnati and Fort Thomas, Kentucky. It was built by Mason and Hanger, soon to become one of the most distinguished engineering and construction firms in the country, whose main offices are still located in Lexington.

Adding to the architectural diversity of Lexington were the many new churches built in this period. Most visible to downtown was the spacious Richardsonian Romanesque Central Christian Church, erected in 1894 by the congregation of the Main Street Christian Church on the site of the old Grand Masonic Hall, at Short and Walnut streets.

Newcomers to the established denominations already functioning in town were the Jewish congregations and the Christian Scientists — one of ancient lineage, and the other a native American sect whose leader, Mary Baker Eddy, was still living.

Persons of the Jewish faith were an early and significant part of the Lexington community, but due to their lack of members no temple or synagogue was erected for more than a century. Among the leaders was Benjamin Gratz, a member of a distinguished Philadelphia family. Living graciously in the stately house facing the park that bears his name, Gratz not only enjoyed a successful business career but became an influential figure in various community activities, including long and devoted service to Transylvania. In the post-Civil War era, Moses Kaufman exhibited a similar business acumen and was likewise a leader in community affairs and a public official.

As late as the turn of the century the number of Jewish families was small. Not until 1903 was the first congregation of Reformed Jews organized through the efforts of I. J. Miller, Fred Lazarus, and Simon Wolf. A rabbi from Chattanooga came once or twice a month to hold services in the Odd Fellows Hall on Main Street. The congregation, adopting the name Adath Israel, at first rented, then in 1905 purchased, the Maryland Avenue Church from the Evangelical Germans who had built it. A gift of $25,000 from Leo Marks, matched by an equal amount from the congregation, made possible the erection of the present temple on North Ashland Avenue, the first services being held in the building in October 1925.

Though the *Daily Press* reported in December 1874, a rumor that a synagogue was to be established in Lexington, it was not until a quarter century later that a small group of Orthodox Jews began meeting in the Merrick Lodge Hall. When a sacred Yom Kippur service was inadvertently interrupted by the lodge members in the fall of 1911, the Jewish families determined to purchase a building as their synagogue, and they acquired the former Maxwell Street Presbyterian Church on West Maxwell and Jersey streets. Under the leadership of David Ades, Beryl Kravetz, Sol Kahn, Nathan Rogers, and Joe Rosenberg, the Ohavay Zion Congregation was incorporated on April 17, 1912.

The Christian Science Church was founded in October 1900, and eventually constructed a building on East Main Street.

The Congregational Church, which was strong in New England, provided a number of teachers and workers for the Freedman's Bureau in the Bluegrass area following the Civil War. In the early 1890's a black Congregational church was organized and a stone building was constructed on the south side of West Short Street opposite St. Paul Catholic Church. When the Chandler School closed, this small Congregational Church agreed to administer the community project at the Chandler building with financial assistance from the American Missionary Society. Eventually, the church moved from the West Short Street sanctuary to the Chandler site.

Thus, the decades that bridged the end of the 19th century and the beginning of the 20th century saw Lexington challenge the traditional political control of the city, improve its schools, foster its cultural life, and expand economically, especially in the establishment of tobacco markets.

Rising Importance of Tobacco

Tobacco had been an important crop for Kentuckians since pioneer days, and in the 1890's it replaced hemp as the major money crop. Even before Kentucky statehood, tobacco, packed in hogsheads, was shipped down the Ohio and Mississippi rivers, to the New Orleans market; and at home, tobacco was a medium of exchange and a substitute for money.

So important was it that the Virginia Assembly enacted legislation to improve the quality of export tobacco, and in 1783 authorized establishment of inspection warehouses, where tobacco bound for New Orleans would be received. The receipts issued by the warehouses quickly became negotiable documents. Later, hogshead markets were established in Louisville and Cincinnati, and within a few years local dealers began buying the leaf directly from growers, who thus were spared cost and trouble and obtained their payment more quickly.

Fayette and many other Kentucky counties gained a distinct advantage after 1864, when a new variety of tobacco, known as "white burley," was discovered on a Brown County, Ohio, farm, where it was grown from seed produced as "a freak of nature" in Bracken County, Kentucky.

In the early 1900's, a change occurred that was to revolutionize the marketing of burley and make Lexington the world's largest burley sales center. The looseleaf auctioning system had been practiced in Virginia for many years, and Charles W. Bohmer, who was familiar with that plan, came here in 1904 and, along with W. J. Loughridge of Lexington, D. D. Jones of Woodford County and others, organized the Burley Loose (sic) Tobacco Warehouse Company. They erected a frame sales house on South Broadway where the R. J. Reynolds Tobacco Company later built a redrying plant (now the University of Kentucky's Reynolds Building). The first sale was held here — the first looseleaf sale in the Burley Belt — on January 9, 1905.

In the 1890's tobacco replaced hemp as Kentucky's major money crop, and Lexington eventually became the world's largest burley market. These horse-drawn tobacco wagons are waiting to unload at warehouses on South Broadway.

At the same time, W. L. Petty of North Carolina, had come to Lexington to establish the city's first tobacco redrying plant on Chair Avenue, off Broadway. He was, naturally, one of the chief buyers in that first season, along with Reynolds, the American Tobacco Company, United States Tobacco Company, Hancock and Company, T. H. Kirk and a number of individuals.

In 1906, two new sales floors were opened by Silas Shelbourne and by Luther Stivers and Morgan Gentry, and in ensuing years the number of sales facilities increased, most of them being developed along South Broadway. While accurate figures for the first sales season are not available, the Lexington market in 1907 sold 18,347,805 pounds for an average of $10.93 a hundredweight.

Lexingtonians also cherished the continuing existence and prosperity of the fabled horse farms which gave the area a special distinctiveness. Some were disturbed that the ownership of these farms was shifting from the historic families who founded them to wealthy individuals from outside Kentucky. The fear that this would result in a significant change in the style of operation or appearance of the farms proved unfounded. Most of the new owners, who invested large sums of money to expand acreage, improve facilities, and substantially upgrade the quality of horse breeding, revealed as great a dedication to the preservation of the distinctive Bluegrass character of their estates as did the earlier owners.

There was obviously a marked difference in their relationship to Lexington. Coming from New York, Philadelphia, Chicago and other major metropolitan centers, the new owners had no special family connections with the town. Consequently, some did not make their horse farms their permanent homes.

The impact of the expanding horse farm industry on the economy of Lexington and Fayette County was beneficial. Hundreds of residents were employed on these farms, and large quantities of goods and services were purchased from Lexington businesses. As the tourist trade increased, many visitors came primarily to attend the races and to see the cultivated countryside, with its impressive farms and mansions, and the graceful horses that grazed in the fields.

Increasingly, as urban Lexington grew and the town's activities absorbed the time and interests of the citizens, the horse farms became a less familiar feature of the city-dweller's life, though always remaining an integral part of the total community.

Miss Laura Clay, daughter of Cassius M. Clay, was prominent in the suffrage movement, Democratic politics and public affairs in the 1890's and the early part of the present century. Photo courtesy of Paul Fuller.

Chapter VII

1880/1920

The Struggle for Democracy

One change gradually taking place in Lexington after the Civil War was the status of women. Under the leadership of such notable women as Laura Clay, Madeline McDowell Breckinridge, and Sophonisba Breckinridge, the male-dominated society was being challenged. In January 1888, the Fayette County Equal Rights Association was founded, whose purpose was "to advance the industrial, educational and legal rights of women, and to secure suffrage for them by appropriate State and National Legislation." The very breadth of its objectives was a tactical device designed, in part, to divert attention from the explosive voting goal which was regarded by many of both sexes as too radical. Thus, over the years, ERA members might on various occasions be supporting the Women's Christian Temperance Union, coeducation at state and private colleges, improvement of local schools, and health programs for children. They campaigned to change the prevailing state laws that gave a husband almost absolute control over his wife's property, her wages, and their children, and prevented women from serving on juries.

In 1838, Kentucky had permitted women in certain categories to vote in county school districts for school trustees and, later, for school taxes, but even this was repealed in 1902 because more Negro women were going to the polls than were white women.

The male opposition was adamant, but more liberal individuals such as editor Desha Breckinridge, on whom his wife doubtless had considerable influence, espoused some of the women's causes. Acting on the premise that the

way to a man's heart, if not his mind, was through his stomach, a Women's Rights Restaurant on Main Street was established in March 1893. It was advertised as one of the best in the city and open to both "Ladies & Gents."

Some headway was made in the Kentucky legislature in the 1890's regarding a woman's property rights, and eventually suffrage was achieved nationwide by the ratification of the Nineteenth Amendment in 1920.

Whatever differences Laura Clay may have had with other woman suffrage leaders, nationally and locally, over the best way to achieve their goals, she was the most dedicated and influential Kentucky woman in this crusade. Not only was she an organizer and first president of the Kentucky Equal Rights Association from 1889 to 1910, but she also was auditor of the National American Woman Suffrage Association from 1895 to 1911, a position of significant influence in determining policy.

The women could claim credit for winning the victory in the ratification of the Eighteenth Amendment in the previous year, which initiated prohibition.

Women in Lexington were active in many forms of charities, the founding of the Protestant Infirmary being an example. They helped to organize a free soup kitchen in January 1893, on Church Street, providing nourishment for at least 800 "poor, ragged people of both races," suffering from the impact of one of the nation's worst depressions. Charity concerts at the Opera House brought

Isaac Murphy, noted black jockey and three times rider of Kentucky Derby winners, was born in 1861, and died in Lexington on February 2, 1896. Photo courtesy of Clyde T. Burke.

in needed funds. In December, the women cooperated with the men in organizing the Union Relief Society to provide work for the unemployed and buy necessary items for the destitute.

Challenging the male dominance in the architectural field, Miss Magdalene McDowell designed homes in 1904 in the Aylesford subdivision on Maxwell Street and Linden Walk. Another Lexington woman, Mary Desha, granddaughter of Governor Joseph Desha and daughter of John Randolph Desha, a prominent Lexington doctor, started her career in town as a teacher, first in a private school with her mother and later at Dudley School. She moved to Washington in 1885 to take a government job, and when the Sons of the American Revolution vetoed a proposition in 1890 to admit women, she joined with two other women to organize the Daughters of the American Revolution and recruited Mrs. Benjamin Harrison, the President's wife, to be its first president. Miss Desha's hometown has since seen the organization of numerous distinguished D.A.R. chapters.

The first woman physician licensed to practice medicine here was a Negro, Dr. Mary E. Britton, a native of Lexington who started her career as a teacher in the 1870's. Later she received her M.D. degree from the American Medical College of Chicago and returned to Lexington to practice in 1902.

Mrs. Mary C. Love Collins, admitted to practice law in 1911, was one of the first women attorneys in Lexington.

One of the most brilliant women of Lexington in this era was Sophonisba Breckinridge. Born in 1866, a daughter of W. C. P. Breckinridge, she graduated from Wellesley College in Massachusetts, read law, and became the first woman to pass the Kentucky bar exam. Finding few clients in Lexington, she moved to Chicago to start a new career. She became the first woman to earn a Ph.D. in political science at Rockefeller's newly established University of Chicago, but her association with Jane Addams led her into the area of social service. She joined the faculty of the University of Chicago and later became dean of the Graduate School of Social Service Administration, helping found the *Social Science Review*. She energetically participated in a wide range of reforms — women's suffrage, improving factory conditions for women and children, juvenile courts, improving conditions in tenements, and supporting the rights of blacks, immigrants, and women generally.

During this period a growing number of women's groups were organized. Some, like the Business and Professional Women's Club, reflected the expanding role of women in American life.

Notable Lexington Negroes

There is little doubt that one of Lexington's best known Negroes in this era, not only in his hometown but at every major racetrack in America, was Isaac Burns Murphy. Born during the Civil War of ex-slaves and growing up among horses, first as an exerciser, then as a rider, Murphy had talents as a jockey that soon became dramatically apparent. His rare gift of judging a horse's ability and what was needed to win a race (he rarely used his whip), soon put him in the forefront as the nation's finest jockey. In twenty years from 1875 to 1895 he won 628 of 1,412 races, a

Dr. T. T. Wendell, a prominent black physician for whom a building at Eastern State Hospital was named. Photo courtesy of the Lexington Public Library.

Isaac Scott Hathaway (1872-1967), an eminent black sculptor, was born in Lexington and educated at the Chandler Normal School. Photo courtesy of the Lexington Public Library.

44.5 percent record that may never be equalled. Winner of three Kentucky Derbies, he also won four American Derbies in Chicago, and five Latonia Derbies when those races were more prestigious than those at Churchill Downs. A man of unimpeachable honesty, he resisted the importunities of gamblers, and with his winnings built a handsome home on East Third Street in Lexington. His reputation won him a permanent resting place near the remains of Man o' War at the entrance to the Kentucky Horse Park.

A far cry from a racing career was that of another black, Isaac Scott Hathaway (1872-1967). Born in Lexington, and a student at Chandler Normal School, he became deeply interested in painting and sculpture. After attending a number of art schools, including the Cincinnati Art Academy, he opened a studio in Washington, D.C. where he specialized in sculpting excellent miniature busts of prominent individuals, especially blacks such as Booker T. Washington and George Washington Carver. In 1946, the United States Treasury Department commissioned Hathaway to design the Booker T. Washington half-dollar,

the first American coin designed by a black of a black.

The famous jockey and the gifted sculptor were sources of great pride for Lexington and for the Negro community in particular. Equally important as ideals for many Lexington blacks were the business and professional men and women who, starting with little or nothing and burdened with the handicap of color, became successful and prosperous.

A remarkable volume entitled *Prominent Negro Men and Women of Kentucky* was published in 1897 by W. D. Johnson, editor of the *Standard* and a frequent adversary of H. H. Gratz, editor of the *Gazette.* It contained the biographies of numerous black Horatio Algers. One of these was Benjamin Franklin, a former slave of Judge George Robertson, who became one of Lexington's most prosperous barbers and chiropodists, serving some of Lexington's best citizens. By carefully saving his profits and by shrewdly investing his money, he accumulated a modest fortune and built an impressive residence at 560 North Limestone Street, designed in the Richardsonian Romanesque style of 1884.

There were enough such black businessmen in town to organize their own Business League on August 8, 1900.

Another former Fayette County slave, Jordan Carlisle Jackson, with little or no formal education, became an active editor of several Negro newspapers in Lexington, such as *The American Citizen,* copies of which unfortunately do not seem to have been preserved. He became one of the most skillful Republican politicians in the area, winning a seat as a delegate to the National Republican Party Convention in 1876 and again in 1892.

The first prominent Negro attorney in Lexington was J. Alexander Chiles, a native of Richmond, Virginia, who earned his law degree from the University of Michigan in 1889. The *Kentucky Leader* in November 1890, reported that in a trial for burglary held in Fayette Circuit Court the

> great novelty in the case was the appearance of Jas. A. Chiles, the colored lawyer, who recently came to this city from Richmond, Va. Mr. Chiles has the honor of being the first colored attorney who has ever argued a case at length before a jury in the Circuit Court in Fayette Co. He proved himself a fluent speaker, and made quite a lengthy plea for his client.

The first notable black doctor to practice in Lexington was Dr. John E. Hunter, a native of Virginia and a graduate of Oberlin College and Western Reserve Medical School. When he arrived in Lexington around 1880, he was the only black doctor until he persuaded other black physicians such as P. D. Robinson, J. M. Allen, and Nathan Ridley to join him. He built a number of houses, set up a free clinic on the corner of Short and Upper streets, and gained access to the hospitals. His son, Dr. Bush Hunter, has likewise devoted a lifetime of service to the Lexington community. The name of the present Hunter Foundation is a fitting tribute to the long years this father and son practiced in Lexington.

As of 1907, there were eight black physicians, three dentists, and four lawyers in Lexington.

The achievements of Negro business and professional individuals not only were a source of pride for the black community but also exhibited to a skeptical white community evidence of the black's ability to succeed in fields dominated by whites. Both blacks and whites agreed this was the best way to settle "the much agitated race questions," as the Lexington *Weekly Press* stated in 1890.

From the days of Peter Duerett and London Ferrill to the era of Peter Vinegar, black ministers had provided religious and community leadership. The flamboyant Vinegar, who died in 1905, was among the last of the ministers born as slaves in the antebellum period. A native of Woodford County, he moved to Lexington and became a tremendously popular revivalist, baptizing thousands during his ministry. Causing some dissension in one congregation, he ended up preaching in the old Lyon Fire House on South Limestone. With sermons entitled "Hell is Only a Mile From Lexington," "Damned Hot Day," and "Watch that Snake" (a reference to the human tongue), he attracted large audiences, both black and white. His funeral and burial in the Seventh Street Cemetery drew thousands, as Ferrill's had some fifty years earlier.

The so-called Colored Fairs continued to be the most successful events sponsored by the black community, increasing in size and popularity each year. The Colored A & M Society used the fairs not only as occasions to award liberal premiums for exhibits, black and white, but as incentives to greater industry and thrift among all classes. The fairs were so profitable that handsome dividends were paid to the stockholders in the association. The group was honored by being admitted as a member of the National Trotting Association, for many years the only Negro organization to enjoy such a distinction.

The black community was also proud of the Colored Orphans Industrial Home, established without white aid by a group of women led by Mrs. E. Belle Jackson, for orphans and a small number of aged and helpless women. The purpose of the home was to train boys and girls "for usefulness in this life and immortality in the life to come."

The Struggle for Civil Rights

Despite the achievements made by the Negro community, the pressures to maintain

Baptism taking place in the workhouse pond, located near Bolivar and Upper streets, 1898.
Photo courtesy of Transylvania University.

segregation mounted. During the Reconstruction period, federal laws and federal courts checked moves to establish discriminatory policies and practices, especially in public transportation and theatres. The Civil Rights Act of 1875 attempted to prohibit most forms of segregation in public areas, but in 1883 the United States Supreme Court found most of the law unconstitutional. Only Justice John Marshall Harlan, a Kentucky Republican and a Transylvania Law Department graduate, dissented.

The Supreme Court's invalidation of the 1875 Civil Rights Act sent a message to the state legislatures, and a flood of segregation laws began to pour out of the legislative chambers. The Kentucky General Assembly passed a separate coach law for public transportation vehicles in January 1892, despite the efforts of the Colored Citizens Protective League to prevent it. Following its passage, there was talk of a black boycott of merchants who backed the bill. On July 1, 1892, there was a mass meeting to protest the law at St. Paul A.M.E. Church, with Jordan Jackson as chairman.

The May 1896, decision of the U.S. Supreme Court in the *Plessey v. Ferguson* case, again with Harlan as the sole dissenting voice, established the "separate but equal" doctrine that legalized segregation until it was struck down in the hallmark decision of *Brown v. Board of Education* in 1954. In 1904, the Kentucky legislature passed the Day Law prohibiting the operation of "an institution of learning in which white and colored persons may be taught at the same time and in the same place."

Kentucky blacks, faced with these formidable barriers, did what they could to express their viewpoints in ways still available to them. They organized a Colored Republican League, and in Lexington an Emancipation Society was formed to celebrate Emancipation Day on January 1, 1894. This tradition was maintained for decades.

By October 1897, Lexington blacks complained about being denied the right to register to vote, but the local courts upheld the registrar's prerogative to make the decision in this matter. A year later, blacks claimed the right to be summoned as jurors in cases

155

Damage caused by the disastrous sleet storm of 1890 on Upper Street between Short and Main streets. Photo courtesy of the University of Kentucky.

involving a black, but Circuit Court Judge Watts Parker overruled them and the all-white jury prevailed.

Finally, from a different viewpoint, was the threat issued by the Daughters of the Confederacy and the Confederate Veterans Association to mount a boycott against the upcoming performance in November 1905, of *Uncle Tom's Cabin* at the Opera House because it was partisan history presenting a false picture of slavery.

The Turn of the Century

A Lexingtonian in 1920 reminiscing over the previous thirty years might have recalled the depression of 1893 and the soup kitchens on Church Street. There was the sleet storm of December 27, 1890, which iced the city, split trees, and pulled down every wire in town,

darkening and partially immobilizing the community for a week. There was the shock of learning that Lexington's distinguished U.S. Senator James Beck had died suddenly at the Washington train depot on May 4, 1890. Some Lexingtonians were disturbed by the rapid growth of the labor unions. On Labor Day in September 1894, there was a giant parade of Lexington's labor organizations down Main Street and out to Woodland Park for an all-day picnic and celebration.

Nor would Lexingtonians forget the scandalous affair of their own Congressman, W.C.P. Breckinridge, who was taken to court in 1893 by twenty-seven-year old Madeline Pollard on a breach of promise suit. The former Sayre Female Institute student said her illicit relations with Breckinridge dated back to her school years and that he had promised to marry her after his second wife died. Not only did the aging Confederate veteran lose the suit, he also lost his bid for reelection, thanks to the combined efforts of an aroused women's coalition and ministerial groups. More scandal filled the newspapers with the account of the wedding of Cassius Clay, the eighty-four-year-old Lion of White Hall, to fifteen-year-old Dora Richardson in 1894. Whether scandalous or not, downtown bystanders were treated to the unusual sight on August 11, 1896, of a group of unidentified girls parading in bloomers on West Short Street.

Perhaps some Lexingtonians could recall having eaten at the sumptuous new restaurant on Main Street that opened in 1894. It was the Navarre Cafe, operated by Riley Grannan, the former Louisville hotel elevator operator who had made a fortune as a bookmaker and gambler. He lavished part of his money on an eating establishment elegant enough for the wealthiest horsemen. Replete with special dining rooms, Brussels carpets, a French chef, heavy

silverware, and gaming rooms, the cafe unfortunately was too rich for the Lexington consumer and folded in 1902. It was used as an art gallery to supplement Lexington's first grandiose Exposition in December 1894, for local manufactures and other products of the Bluegrass. The Exposition was held in the former Main Street Christian Church, which was remodeled into a hall and auditorium, and a special bridge was built over Main Street, connecting the Exposition Hall with the Navarre Cafe. Large crowds turned out for the gala event.

Political campaigns always aroused a Kentuckian's heart, and the silver-tongued orator from Nebraska, William Jennings Bryan, stirred a large crowd to fever pitch at the Fairgrounds in September 1896. The 1890's were a politically turbulent period, reaching a climax with the assassination of William Goebel on January 30, 1900, in front of the old Capitol in Frankfort. The Democrats managed

Pedestrian bridge built across Main Street for the 1894 Exposition, looking west. On the left is the former Main Street Christian Church where part of the exposition was held. Photo courtesy of Transylvania University.

View looking west on Main Street from old Phoenix Hotel ca. 1910. Photo courtesy of Kitty Portwood.

to swear him in as Governor before he died, however, despite continued threats from armed Republicans roaming the town.

Few Lexingtonians would forget the startling news of the blowing up of the U.S. battleship *Maine* in Havana harbor on February 15, 1898. War fever spread throughout the country, and Congress declared war on Spain on April 20th. Theodore Roosevelt resigned as assistant secretary of the Navy to recruit his "Rough Riders." This was to be a "splendid little war," said John Hay, and Kentuckians of all political stripes and allegiances flocked to the banner.

The Second Regiment of the Kentucky State Guard mobilized on the Fairgrounds. Some troops camped at Woodlands, and a resident on Ashland Avenue later recalled how, as a young girl, she made and sold cakes to the soldiers. Later the army established two major camps: one at James Clark's farm on the Bryan Station Road, the other at the Weil farm on the Versailles Road.

Lucien Young, a Lexingtonian and a graduate of the U.S. Naval Academy at Annapolis, participated in the crucial naval battle at Santiago and later became a rear admiral.

The war was over in a matter of months. Troops both well and sick were returning before others had barely left. They flocked into the Lexington camps before being shipped south. On October 11, 1898, one of the soldiers from camp was killed in town by a guard when he failed to produce a pass and ran. There was a near riot and martial law was imposed for a night or two.

The colorful and eccentric Charles C. Moore livened this period. He was the town's annoying gadfly, spasmodically publishing his controversial newspaper *The Bluegrass Blade* in the 1890's, which challenged most accepted religious and political beliefs of the community. He so angered some readers that they assaulted him physically on the street. In 1894 Judge Watts Parker had quashed a blasphemy charge against Moore with eloquent judicial finality, but Moore's enemies were determined to muzzle him. On the flimsiest of evidence they secured a conviction in a federal court in Cincinnati on the grounds that Moore had sent obscene material through the U.S. Mail. For this, the gentle fellow was sentenced for two years to the federal penitentiary in Columbus, Ohio, where he promptly won the affection of both the warden and the inmates. President

McKinley, informed of the injustice of Moore's incarceration, pardoned him after six months. Moore came home to Lexington in July 1899, to receive a hero's welcome at the station, paraded triumphantly to the Phoenix Hotel and was eulogized by city officials and Josephine Henry, the ardent freedom fighter from Versailles. He then proceeded to write his memoirs in a volume entitled *Behind the Bars: 31498.*

One might have recalled, too, the sad moment when the studious George W. Ranck, Lexington's 19th century historian, was run down accidentally by an L & N train as he was walking the tracks in the west end of town on August 2, 1901. He was exploring Lexington's early site, as he loved to do, perhaps checking on the location of McConnell's Spring.

Nor could one soon forget that memorable evening of February 11, 1902, at the Phoenix Hotel where, at a dinner given in honor of visiting Kentucky legislators, Judge James H. Mulligan read his poem "In Kentucky." No sooner had he finished exclaiming "and politics — the damndest in Kentucky," than a thunderous ovation swept the hall, and the poem, of dubious literary merit, became as familiar to Kentuckians as "My Old Kentucky Home." The Mulligans were already famous. The judge's father was Dennis Mulligan, the local Democratic potentate, who had stirred up many a political tempest. After the Civil War, the elder Mulligan had bought land including the Maxwell Springs and built Maxwell Place in 1870 (now the home of the president of the University of Kentucky) for his son, James.

Judge Mulligan's second marriage in 1881 to Genevieve Morgan Williams of Nashville changed his life style dramatically, and Maxwell Place became the center of lavish parties. An exotic interlude occurred in Judge Mulligan's life when he accepted a position as Consul-General to Samoa. There he became a good friend of the frail Robert Louis Stevenson, who was living out his life halfway around the world from his native England. When the noted author died, Mulligan was one of the few white men to attend his funeral. He returned to Lexington with memorabilia of the author and as many volumes of Stevenson's as he could acquire.

A sensational case involving the attempted murder of the Mulligan family by an arsenic-laden meal in 1904 resulted in no convictions but so tore the family apart that it ended the judge's career.

Judge James H. Mulligan and his son Willoughby (Pete) on the grounds of his home, Maxwell Place, ca. 1906. Judge Mulligan wrote the now famous poem, "In Kentucky". Photo courtesy of E. I. Thompson.

More significant than political contests or murder trials in changing the character of Lexington was the appearance of the automobile at the turn of the century. Thomas B. Dewhurst of Lexington built a pioneer automobile with a small four-horsepower, air-cooled engine. Called the "Dewabout," this engine-powered buggy cruised down Lexington streets at a frightening fifteen miles an hour, scaring horses and pedestrians alike.

A local newspaper reported that in July 1900, a Lexington young lady had ordered a Victoria automobile. Two years later the Elks featured auto races at the Bluegrass Fair. In

Thomas B. Dewhurst, left, a local mechanic and bicycle dealer, is shown operating the "Dewabout" which he built. It was the first automobile on the streets of Lexington in 1900. Photo courtesy of Transylvania University.

1903, James Timmins of Lexington successfully tested his auto. In July 1905, there were enough car owners to start an auto club, and garages and car sales agencies opened on East Main Street.

In 1909-1910, a car manufacturer built a plant in Lexington's west end to produce a fine and expensive car called the "Lexington." Unfortunately, the company faced certain disadvantages here and moved to Indiana, though keeping the name Lexington for its product, the "Lexington Minuteman Six."

As a result of Henry Ford's Model T assembly line production techniques, this expensive new form of private transportation was so reduced in price as to bring it within the buying ability of the average citizen. The transportation revolution was underway.

So was the entertainment revolution. Thomas Edison's moving pictures were hypnotizing the country. The first motion pictures shown in Lexington were presented at the Opera House on December 15, 1896, when so-called "short subject" films were projected on the stage curtain between vaudeville acts. In the spring of 1905, the famous early film, *The Great Train Robbery*, was shown at Woodland Auditorium, and within two years movie theatres sprouted downtown. The earliest of these were nothing more than modest-sized rooms with movable wooden chairs, a noisy, hot, smelly projector and a small screen. But the magic was there and if the admission fee of five or ten cents was small, so was the film fare. Probably Lexington's first movie theatre was the Theatorium on Cheapside, joined soon

A street car crashed into a C & O train on Water Street after its brakes failed coming down the South Broadway hill on May 9, 1907. The motorman of the street car was killed. Photo courtesy of Transylvania University.

by the Princess, Blue Grass, Phoenix, Colonial, and the Star. The Strand, a more plush theatre, opened on Main Street in 1915.

Vaudeville, which was in its heyday and would continue to prosper into the 1930's, required adequate stages. Thus, the Hippodrome (Ada Meade), Ben Ali, Opera House, and the Majestic were the main houses featuring this type of entertainment.

Yet, as the automobiles and movies swept Lexingtonians into a new age, there were pauses for historic recollection and commemoration. Such was the dedication of a fitting monument in September 1908, to "King" Solomon, financed by a drive led by John Wilson Townsend. The Daughters of the Confederacy and the Kentucky legislature provided $15,000 for an equestrian statue of

John Hunt Morgan, created by sculptor Pompeo Coppini. There had been some debate as to whether Morgan ought to be astride his mare "Black Bess" or, as the sculptor thought, a more heroic stallion. The sculptor won out. The humorous legend that the crowd attending the dedication on October 18, 1911, conducted by General Basil Duke on the courthouse lawn, was horrified at the unveiling to see the unmistakable features of a stallion is just that — a legend.

The Great Crusade

In 1914, the dark cloud of the First World War descended on Europe. For most Americans, it was a distant, unfortunate event. They thought President Wilson's neutrality

The 15-story Fayette National Bank building at Main and Upper streets was designed by the New York firm of McKim, Mead and White and was for years Lexington's tallest building. It was erected in 1913-14. Photo courtesy of the University of Kentucky.

thought as well as in action as Wilson had advised the American people. Lexingtonians read the war news as they did the sports page, reacting occasionally to the stories of German atrocities in Belgium and the use of poison gas. While the sympathy with the Allies grew — the ties with Britain and France were strong — the stance of neutrality remained firm.

Moviegoers at the Ben Ali could see motion pictures of the battlefields. Some Lexingtonians contributed to the British-American War Relief Fund. Others were more concerned that the proposed Dixie Highway, eventually to connect Michigan with Florida via Cincinnati, should pass through Lexington.

Then came news of the torpedoing of the giant passenger liner *Lusitania* off the coast of Ireland by a German U-boat, with the loss of over 1,000 passengers, including 128 Americans. Cries of outrage were heard throughout the country. Desha Breckinridge, in editorials in the *Herald,* pledged to support President Wilson's sharp protest. The local editor wanted a strong policy adopted toward Germany but was not advocating entry into the war. Approaching the brink of war, the United States drew back. Talk of being too proud to fight and a stiff demand for an apology, reparations, and a promise to forego future U-boat attacks on passenger liners came from the White House. A year later Lexingtonians helped reelect Wilson on the slogan, "he kept us out of war."

In that same year, Henry Ford sent his celebrated, if ineffective, "Peace Ship" to Europe in hopes of helping bring the war to an end. Aboard was Lexington's Helen Bullitt Lowry, a former *Herald* reporter, who had been appointed Hearst Syndicate's International News Service official representative. After the war she joined the staff of the *New York Times.*

The resumption of unrestricted German submarine warfare in January 1917, ended all hope for peace. American shipping was being torpedoed. By February 8, Breckinridge was urging Congress and the President to take immediate action. Special patriotic rallies were held at Woodland Auditorium, and businesses and residents proudly displayed the American flag. Lexingtonians were ready when Congress,

policy the correct one. But for many Germans, Italians, Austrians, English, French, and Russians recently arrived on these shores, it was far more difficult to remain neutral in

Cheapside during World War I, showing troops and Liberty Bond signs. Photo courtesy of Burton Milward.

responding to Wilson's war message, passed a declaration of war on April 6.

On the evening of April 14 a giant rally of some 15,000 was held on Cheapside and the courthouse lawn. "Pulsing in their veins was a patriotic fire," remarked one reporter, as they listened to martial music and heard the exhortations of Spence Carrick, Colonel John R. Allen, and Governor A. O. Stanley. Black citizens planned a patriotic rally of their own and talked of forming a special Negro regiment.

Camp Stanley was established on the Lansing (Garrett W. Wilson) farm on the Versailles Pike where three hundred barracks were quickly thrown up. The Weil farm was again rented by the government as a camp.

Women paraded through the streets urging men to join up. Many University of Kentucky and Transylvania students left their campuses and enlisted, while others entered the Student Army Training Corp and remained in their dormitory-barracks on campus.

Mass meetings were held to sell Liberty Bonds. On June 5, eligible males registered for the draft, and in the first drawing the names of 75 from Lexington and 50 from rural Fayette County were drawn.

Women's organizations coordinated their efforts to produce a variety of woolen, cotton, and flannel apparel for the troops. They gathered thousands of magazines and books for the camps, prepared endless numbers of bandages, learned first aid, and some joined a nursing program for hospitals here and overseas.

The newspapers were saturated with war news. By October 1917, there was an acute shortage of sugar, and it was soon rationed. "Meatless" Tuesdays and "wheatless" Wednesdays were instituted. Local bakers experimented with "war bread" without lard and sugar, and special cookbooks were published containing recipes without crucial ingredients. A labor exchange program was put into effect to help solve the loss of skilled workers.

By January 1918, certain evenings were designated as "lightless" to save coal. The railroads had been taken over by the U. S. government and non-essential passenger travel discouraged.

German aliens were required to register although there were only eleven in Fayette County. Anti-German sentiment was intense, however, and was expressed in somewhat extreme, if not ludicrous ways. Selections of literature by German authors were scissored out of school textbooks, no German or Austrian music was played or sung, and even the harmless name of kindergarten was to be banned as a "Hun name" and replaced by "primary circle."

The Barrow Unit

One of the most remarkable community efforts in this war was the creation of the famed Base Hospital No. 40, more commonly known as the Barrow Unit. Dr. David Barrow, over military age and not in robust health, conceived the idea of a central Kentucky hospital unit composed of Kentuckians and administered by Kentuckians. Through Barrow's acquaintance with General Gorgas, the Surgeon-General, permission was granted to form such a unit under Barrow's direction, with Good Samaritan Hospital as the parent institution. The hospital unit was to have 1,000 beds, 33 medical officers, 200 enlisted men and five civilians, all under the auspices of the Red Cross. The project was enthusiastically supported by physicians and laymen alike. A reporter asked:

> What did millionaires, lawyers, farmers, barbers, students, hoboes, stud-poker artists and other individuals with long records and short bankrolls have in common in 1917? They were part of the "omnium gatherum" of the social strata who wore the hat cord of the Barrow unit.

Some of the best known citizens of central Kentucky volunteered for service in the unit. Among the Lexington doctors besides Barrow were Waller O. Bullock, Charles C. Garr, Samuel B. Marks, W. S. Wyatt, Harry Herring, W. D. Reddish, and George Wilson. There were also 75 enlisted men and 29 nurses from Lexington. The unit left March 1, 1918, for training at Camp Taylor. It was given a rousing send-off by a large crowd at Union Station along with "the sweetest benedictions of this community," as one editor remarked.

After a period of training at various camps, the components of the unit were assembled at Hoboken, New Jersey, in early July and sailed to Southampton, England. On arrival they helped to convert a spacious manor house at nearby Sarisbury into a hospital.

Everyone pitched in, and a reporter from the *Leader* who accompanied the unit, wrote back that Lexingtonians might be somewhat amused and surprised

> to see some well-known society favorites of the Blue Grass and former businessmen wielding the pick and shovel, pouring concrete, painting and whitewashing as though they had rather do that than spin out to the Country Club in white flannel and super sixes. As someone said, "Barrow Unit is right! Wheelbarrow unit!"

By such efforts the largest of American hospitals in England was ready for the flood of wounded pouring across the Channel during the final great offensive that broke the German resistance on the Western front.

Edward Jones, one of the enlisted men, wrote home in August 1918, that spirits were high. General Pershing's battle cry of "Hell, heaven, or Hoboken by Xmas," was widely quoted, Jones said. Though well fed, he "would give an arm for some fried chicken and corncakes." Among the patients were some Kentucky Negroes who were "tickled to know they are among Kentuckians."

In September 1918, Americans heard of another enemy as dangerous as the Kaiser's army. It was the deadly Spanish influenza, "the Spanish lady," as some called it. The powerful virus swept through the armies and populations of western Europe with catastrophic impact, killing and immobilizing almost as many American troops as the carnage in the trenches. As wounded soldiers returned to the United States, the flu struck New York and other major cities in epidemic proportions, spreading across the country like wildfire. There was no escape and there was no cure. Oldtimers recalled with dread the terrible cholera plagues of the previous century. For a while it seemed as if Fayette County might be spared. Louisville was reporting thousands of cases, especially at Camp Taylor, while none appeared here. Soon, however, the flu arrived in the first week of October 1918. The State Board of Health closed all schools, churches, recreational and amusement centers — any place where people congregated in sizable numbers. By the middle of the month, 170 cases and eight deaths were reported. Flu had swept through the troops at Camp Buell on the University of Kentucky campus. Residents in the county,

Some members of the Good Samaritan Base Hospital Unit No. 40, known as the Barrow Unit, which served in England in World War I. Dr. David Barrow, for whom the unit was named, is on the first row, fifth from the left. Photo courtesy of the University of Kentucky.

since they were naturally isolated, fared much better. By the time the epidemic was over — a matter of five or six weeks — well over 1,000 cases had been reported, mostly in Lexington, and at least 51 people had died.

This grim visitor was just departing when the welcome news of the armistice arrived. No one in Lexington would ever forget that day. It began early. At 2 a.m. on November 11 the *Herald* received the news. Signals flashed red from the top of the *Herald* building. Church bells began to ring. The Christ Church bells rang out the Doxology. Whistles blew and fire engine sirens shrieked. Some people wept, some sang. That day many allowed themselves the extra luxuries of rationed sugar and butter. Mayor James Rogers announced a holiday for the afternoon to allow thousands to join in a giant parade on Main Street, led by the University of Kentucky band. For a moment everyone forgot the influenza ban. A bonfire was lighted that night on Cheapside, on top of which was an effigy of the Kaiser. Only by 2 a.m. the next day did the weary but happy celebrants finally wend their way to bed.

Across the sea, Jones of the Barrow Unit was equally excited. "Such another day was never known in all history," he wrote. Though the war was over, the hospital continued to tend the wounded and flu patients. Then on March 20, 1919, the Barrow Unit sailed for the United States. On their way to Louisville's Camp Zachary Taylor for demobilization, they stopped in Lexington where they were met by an exuberant crowd. Here the men detrained and in smart, disciplined fashion marched up Ayres Alley onto Main Street and headed for the courthouse. A remarkable quiet settled over the crowd as their beloved hospital unit marched by. When the unit dispersed at Cheapside, great cheers went up from the crowd, and relatives and friends welcomed home their loved ones.

This historic organization was memorialized years later in 1957 when the new Army Reserve Training Center was named for David Barrow.

Now the cheering and celebrations ceased. The Great Crusade was over. There remained the task of creating a lasting peace.

Heavy rains in the summer of 1932 flooded the Town Branch sewer and water covered Main Street causing heavy damage. This perennial problem was finally solved when the voters approved a storm sewer bond issue in 1933. Photo courtesy of Robert E. Parris.

Chapter VIII

1920/1945

Prosperity, Depression and War

Shortly after New Year's Day 1920, Lexingtonians read in the local press the news of the widespread raids conducted by Attorney General A. Mitchell Palmer on aliens suspected of harboring radical ideas. When the United States entered the First World War, President Wilson had predicted that intolerance would become resurgent among the American people. Great national crises, he warned, tend to create a repressive attitude among the people toward those who disagree with the established credo. The Bolshevik Revolution in Russia intensified that fear. People suspected "Reds" of fomenting the numerous strikes erupting across the country and of poisoning the minds of the young with radical ideas. The Ku Klux Klan enjoyed an unprecedented revival both north and south of the Mason-Dixon line. Catholics, Jews, foreigners, and blacks were the main targets.

Lexingtonians were consoled to learn that while federal agents had made arrests in Louisville, none were initiated here. The Department of Justice informed the community that no such action was necessary because "Lexington stands out as one of the one-hundred-percent all-American cities." The smugness the residents might have felt at this characterization was soon shattered by a tragic event.

In early February 1920, Lexington headlines grimly reported the murder of ten-year-old Geneva Hardman in the South Elkhorn neighborhood. The police and bloodhounds quickly tracked down Will Lockett, a Negro army veteran, who confessed to the crime. He was taken to Frankfort for safekeeping to escape the threat of a lynch mob. The authorities justifiably expected trouble when Lockett was brought to Lexington for trial on the morning of February 9 in the Fayette County courthouse, with Circuit Judge Charles Kerr presiding. Police Chief J. J. Reagan, knowing his force inadequate to handle a mob, had called 97 members of the State Guard under Adjutant General James Deweese to assist him. They deployed themselves inside and outside the courthouse, mounting several machine guns on the courthouse steps.

As expected, a large crowd, many of them from out of town, gathered early on Main Street in front of the courthouse. They were in an ugly mood, determined to rush the building and seize Lockett. The trial had no sooner started than the noise of the crowd grew louder and spectators in the courtroom rose to leave. Judge Kerr rapped for order. The bailiffs drew their pistols and the trial proceeded.

Then the mob attacked, some firing as they came. The troops opened fire, killing four immediately, mortally wounding another, and injuring more than fifty others. This action effectively prevented further assaults. The trial went on. Lockett was quickly found guilty and sentenced to death in the electric chair at Eddyville penitentiary. Judge Kerr permitted no one to leave the building until U. S. Army troops from Camp Taylor arrived by train within a few hours. The town was placed under martial law for over a week.

Members of the Kentucky State Guard protected the courthouse as a mob gathered on Main Street on February 9, 1920, when Will Lockett was tried for rape and murder. Later in the day, the mob rushed the courthouse, and troops killed five and wounded over fifty others. Photo courtesy of Transylvania University.

This melodrama received nationwide publicity, not only because of its violent character but also because it was the first time in a Southern town that troops had fired on and dispersed a lynch mob. A *New York Times* editorial praised Lexington for its commitment to preserve law and order, though the cost was high.

Unfortunately, Lexington was the exception. A month after the Lockett riot, a mob attacked the jail in Paris, took a Negro prisoner to a nearby county and lynched him. The *Lexington Herald* condemned the action. A year later in March 1921, a Negro was lynched at nearby Versailles.

The Ku Klux Klan, condemned by the Lexington press, nevertheless continued its nefarious activities. The masked, white-garbed figures burned a wooden cross on the Negro baseball field opposite Douglas Park in January 1923, set off some dynamite charges, and vowed to stay in Lexington to see that law violators, bootleggers, "murderers of character," wife-beaters, and seducers of innocent women were properly punished. More fiery crosses appeared on the roads leading out of Lexington, and a state convention of the Klan was held in

the city but parades were forbidden. By the mid-1920's the activities of the Klan diminished.

The Anti-Evolution Campaign

The nationwide search for security in a time of disintegrating traditional views and values was also reflected in the anti-evolutionist crusade fostered by William Jennings Bryan in speeches in Lexington and elsewhere. The Reverend John Porter of a local Baptist church led the campaign here. Thirty-seven states considered laws banning the teaching of Darwinian views on evolution in the schools. Oklahoma, Tennessee, Mississippi, and Arkansas passed such laws. In 1922, the Kentucky legislature considered enacting a similar law and President Frank L. McVey of the University of Kentucky spoke eloquently against it. The bill lost in the Senate and failed by only one vote in the House. For the next few years, the anti-evolutionist forces continued to badger the General Assembly to pass the desired law. In 1925 the nation read about the famous trial of John Scopes, a University of Kentucky graduate and science teacher in the

Dayton, Tennessee, school, who had broken the Tennessee law. The nation's radio and newspapers covered the seamy encounter between Clarence Darrow and the aging Bryan, whose death a few weeks after the trial seemed to symbolize the demise of the issue.

Prohibition

For many Kentuckians, however, involved neither in the Lockett riot nor the evolution controversy, the implementation of the Eighteenth Amendment to the U. S. Constitution had a more immediate and personal impact. No statistics exist on how many Fayette Countians were drinkers, how many teetotalers. From pioneer days, the family still and the local distillery were familiar landmarks of the region. Was not bourbon a creation of the Bluegrass? Had not many farmers experimented with grape-growing and wine-making before natural enemies wiped out grape cultivation? Was not one of the largest structures on Main Street, the Lexington Brewery, erected in 1898? Was not one of Kentucky's largest distilleries, James E. Pepper's, operating at full capacity on the Old Frankfort Pike? Now all this was to change

along with the closing of scores of saloons scattered along Lexington's streets.

Prohibition became official at midnight on January 16, 1920. Most imbibers filled their cellars and storage rooms with as much wine and liquor as they could afford. The federal enforcement officials soon became visible, seizing a truck carrying 100 cases of whiskey from Covington to Louisville. Local residents now found their caches of liquor prime targets for thieves. Some of the confiscated whiskey was given to local hospitals for "medicinal" purposes. Some doctors began to issue a larger number of "prescriptions" to their patients. They resented, if not ignored, a ruling limiting them to 100 such prescriptions a year.

Soon the production of moonshine became a national, state and local pastime. Kentuckians were masters of the craft. Arrests in town were frequent, starting within a month after liquor sales stopped. The first arrest resulted from the raid of a restaurant on North Limestone where the owner was charged with using a mash made of raisins.

Legal distilleries, which operated under federal permit, were prime targets for hijackers, causing uneasy night watchmen to fear for their safety. On March 18, 1920, several

The Lexington Brewing Company on the south side of Main Street, opposite Dewees Street, opened for business in 1898. It was demolished in 1941. Photo courtesy of the University of Kentucky.

masked men entered the office of the Old Tarr Distillery on Manchester Street, tied up the watchman, and stole 94 cases of whiskey. In July 1921, another masked band made off with 100 cases from the Southeastern Express Company, where confiscated whiskey was being stored.

Bootlegging became big business, although some of the operations were small. Two whites and two blacks, alighting from an L & E train from eastern Kentucky were met at 2:15 a.m. by police, who discovered them carrying a suitcase containing six hot water bottles and two glass containers filled with moonshine. Police found certain areas of town especially dangerous when attempts were made to stop illegal whiskey traffic. Such was "The Jungle" around Fifth and Smith streets where shoot-outs occasionally occurred. Specially designed cars with storage areas under seats, under the floorboards or in doors, brought in supplies to specified drop-off spots, many of them on Limestone Street. It was almost impossible to stamp out the traffic.

Proponents of prohibition, however, pointed with pride to the decline in the number of arrests for drunkenness and the closing of the offensive saloons, yet few who wished to acquire alcoholic beverages had difficulty securing them. Meanwhile, the city government looked about for new tax sources to replace the income lost from saloon licenses.

Civic and Economic Progress

In March 1920, the Governor signed the suffrage bill implementing the Nineteenth Amendment, though that document was not officially ratified until August. Women could now participate in Presidential elections. On May 3, women were part of a large crowd gathered for the Democratic Convention on Cheapside. Women's names were placed in the jury wheel for the June term of the Federal District Court. Kathleen Mulligan, daughter of Judge James H. Mulligan, was appointed Lexington municipal judge, 1928-29, the first woman to sit as a judge in Kentucky. She also served as the first woman vice-president of the Fayette Bar Association. Mrs. Cecil Cantrill, the former Florence Shelby, a woman with a most distinguished lineage, became involved in politics in the 1920's. Securing the support of

Lexington's Democratic political boss, "Billy" Klair, she successfully ran for the state legislature in 1933. Mrs. Cantrill continued her political activities, becoming the first woman city commissioner in 1936, running on the "Home Town Ticket." She was reelected two years later, and during her terms of office was named mayor pro-tem.

Thus, another dimension was added to the changing society of the 1920's. The fears of many men that the American political scene would undergo radical transformation because women could vote were hardly justified. The Presidential election of 1920 was the first barometer, and if the women supported Wilson progressivism and the League of Nations, it was hardly visible in the landslide vote for Republican Harding and "normalcy."

Lexingtonians were shocked at the unexpected death in August 1923, of President Harding, the silver-haired editor from Ohio, but the mourning period was cut short by the equally shocking exposure of the Teapot Dome

A Democratic political rally on Cheapside in the 1920's. Photo courtesy of Mrs. John Swift.

scandals that followed. They could depend on honest "Cal" Coolidge, the tight-lipped Vermontor, who had said that "the business of government is business," and voted for him in 1924.

That business was the main concern of people seemed true enough on Main Street. C. Frank Dunn, the energetic sparkplug of Lexington's Board of Commerce, delighted in listing Lexington's assets and trying to convince new businesses to locate here. The Lexington newspapers agreed. Lexington was as prosperous as at any time in its history, they claimed. There were fewer vacant residences and stores. Even former saloons had been converted into stores.

In the 1921 City Directory appeared the names of businesses, some of which had been established for nearly a century and are still familiar to Lexingtonians today. Among the most historic were the W. R. Milward Funeral Home, begun in 1825 as a furniture store, and the Transylvania Printing Company, formed in

1872. Among the clothiers, offering what were then sometimes called ladies' or mens' furnishings, were Graves Cox, Philip Gall, and Kaufman for the men, and Embry & Company, Lowenthal, B. B. Smith, Mitchell, Baker, Smith, and Paritz for the ladies. Among the larger department stores were the names of J. D. Purcell, Wolf Wile and Company, and Mitchell, Baker, Smith. Furniture stores included the elite C. F. Brower, Leet Brothers, L. L. Roberts, and Wheeler. Fine tailoring could be had at the Main Street shop of Philip Angelucci. The Kerr brothers also provided funeral accommodations, and flowers could be secured from Honaker, John Keller, or the Michler Brothers. Among the druggists were Will Dunn, Lee Cassell, Charles Curry, Hubbard and Curry, and McAdams and Morford. Jewelry and fine silver could be obtained from Victor Bogaert, Harry Skuller, or P. Villeminot. Soon Barney Miller would be joining the East Main Street dealers in auto supplies, sports equipment, and that novel

171

product — the radio. For the musically inclined, Candioto Piano Company was in operation, Mike Levas' "Coney Island" hot dog stand (now Levas' Restaurant) served a delicious weiner on a bun with a spicy chili dressing. Laval would clean carpets, and Van Deren, Clark, and Smith-Watkins would take care of hardware needs. The Hillenmeyer Nursery, located in the Sandersville area since 1846, would meet landscaping requirements.

Building supplies and construction were provided by Perry, Combs, McCormick, Smith-Haggard, Congleton, and des Cognets. Iron and blacksmith work could be obtained from the Saunier Brothers. There were, of course, many other firms, some of which have long since disappeared from the scene.

Lexington for most of its history had an abundance of banks. The rapid occurrence of their founding, prospering, failing, or merging is something to wonder at now in this age of a relatively small number of large banks in the community. Obviously, it was easier to organize a bank in earlier days with modest capitalization and a family clientele. By 1920 this was beginning to change. Of the nine bank' existing in 1917, most would merge or disappear within the next decade or two.

One of the most important mergers occurred in 1929 when the First & City National Bank and the Phoenix National Bank were consolidated under the name of First National Bank & Trust Company, with William H. Courtney as head. Within two years this bank absorbed the Fayette National Bank and moved into the latter's high-rise building. The Second National Bank, founded in 1882, whose offices had been on Cheapside for a century, is now Lexington's second oldest bank. Other familiar banking names at this time included the Bank of Commerce, Security Trust Company, Union Bank & Trust Company, and Title Guaranty & Trust Company, which became the Citizens Bank & Trust Company in 1931. Central Bank and Trust Company was originally the Central Exchange Bank, an outgrowth of the Southern Industrial Loan Company, founded in 1938.

In the 1920's Lexington appeared to enjoy full employment especially in residential home construction. New subdivisions, such as Ashland, Liberty Heights and Hollywood Terrace, were opening up as the street railway and the automobile provided access to outlying areas.

Lexington was closely tied to neighboring towns by the electric interurban railway lines built in the early 1900's. These lines, owned for the most part by the Kentucky Traction & Terminal Company which was headquartered in Lexington, provided inexpensive and convenient travel from Lexington to Paris, Georgetown, Frankfort, Versailles, and Nicholasville. The long, orange-yellow interurban cars, sometimes designated the "Yellow Peril" because of frequent collisions with animals, pedestrians, and automobiles, brought many customers to Lexington to avail themselves of the city's retail and recreational resources. The interurban lines were discontinued in 1934 when the Kentucky Traction & Terminal Company went bankrupt.

1922 Economic Outlook

In 1920, Lexington was facing, as it had in 1880, the possibility of a major expansion. The Board of Commerce ordered a survey prepared by a Chicago firm analyzing the assets and deficiencies of Lexington for future growth. Completed in 1922, the study pointed out that greater Lexington, with a population of about 42,000 (the 1920 U. S. Census gave Fayette County 54,644), had a positive national reputation out of all proportion to its size. This was due to its natural beauty, fine horses, and traditional hospitality. Economically, its main assets were its horse industry, a flourishing tobacco market, access to Eastern Kentucky coal fields, the presence of two universities, a strategic railroad center, good hospitals, and an ample number of good hotels.

Lexington, the report said, could continue to live as it did now and enjoy a "tolerable prosperity."

> But if the constructive imagination of her people can be aroused, and the physical advantages capitalized, there is no other city on the American continent with a fairer prospect for the coming years.

However, naturally favorable conditions were no guarantee of success. The human factor — the "enterprise" — was needed.

Lexington, according to the report, had its handicaps, too. Large-scale manufacturing had no tradition here. There was a shortage of skilled labor. Banks were not accustomed to industrial financing, said the report, "and local investors are much sounder judges of good

One of Lexington's first buses in 1927. The metal device protruding from the front of the bus was known as a "cow-catcher". Photo courtesy of the University of Kentucky.

horses than of good manufacturing projects." It was noted that some industries had started here and then departed. There were always the small excuses but the major one seemed to be "the unconscious indifference of the community to manufacture." With its huge tobacco market, Lexington was a logical spot for a large cigarette manufacturing industry. There was none. Other handicaps to attracting new people and new industry were the poor sanitary and housing conditions in certain sections of the city, areas where new housing for industrial labor might be located.

The city's death rate was unusually high for a community boasting of its healthful environment. The future water supply was questionable, the fire department inadequate, the public school buildings third-rate, the classrooms overcrowded, and playground and park space severely limited.

The report was a remarkable appraisal in many ways, though few of the recommendations were ever implemented. Lexington, in many respects, was what the people wanted and there seemed to be no overwhelming urge to change.

Advances were made in some areas, however. Overcoming considerable resistance, both individual and business, Lexington passed

a zoning ordinance putting restrictions on new buildings. The city was divided into five residential districts and all new building in these areas required official permission except for residences, schools, and churches. The County Fiscal Court rejected a zoning plan for the suburbs and rural areas.

The city also moved to break out of its geographical limitations by attempting to annex the developing housing areas bordering the city limits. The residents in these areas who benefitted from some city services were not enthusiastic about annexation because the tax burden was lighter in the county. This was to be a familiar feature in Lexington's history for over half a century as the courts upheld the residents' right to resist annexation. It was a major impediment to Lexington's urban progress.

Other improvements included a move to expand the sanitary sewers to the poorer housing areas, and the discontinuation of County Court Day on Cheapside, an action requiring formal declarations by the Fayette Circuit Court in 1921 and 1922. Along with the demise of Court Day was the closing of the city market house. Modern markets were making the old market house obsolete, though a petition with 2,500 signatures protested the action.

The city also embarked on an ingenious recycling scheme to increase revenue. This was the establishment of a municipal "piggery" on the Old Frankfort Pike. Here several hundred pigs were fattened on garbage collected by the city and sold at an impressive profit, netting some $5,000 in 1924 on a modest investment.

By 1929 more than 14,000 motor vehicles were operating in Fayette County. The traffic problem created by this growing volume was partly solved when intercity buses were forbidden on Main Street between Walnut and Broadway, and a union bus station was established in the Johns Building on Walnut Street. Four-lane traffic also eased the flow on Main Street and the completion of the West High viaduct unplugged another bottleneck.

In other areas, the city officials moved with measured and deliberate pace under the leadership of Mayor Thomas Bradley (1920-28), lawyer and city attorney, and James J. O'Brien (1928-32), city clerk. Despite the fact that a $500,000 bond issue was passed, surprisingly, by the citizenry following World War I to build a city hall and a municipal auditorium, it was not until December 1924, that the city commissioners named Frankel and Curtis as architects for the complex.

There was considerable disagreement on where the new facilities should be located. One group of citizens favored use of the Old Main Street Cemetery lot west of the First Baptist Church, which stretched to Jefferson Street. Sketches were made of an imposing city hall and auditorium, beautifully landscaped, overlooking the warehouses and railroad tracks to the south. Others concentrated on the site adjacent to Central Christian Church (actually the old Davenport and Morton properties) facing Main Street at the head of an especially constructed Esplanade. In the end, neither site was chosen. Instead, approval was given to a location abutting Central Christian Church on Walnut Street facing Barr Street, which was widened to provide a more impressive approach to the structure.

Municipal Building Completed

By 1928, the municipal building was finally completed, and city officials whose offices had been moved about town for a century and a half had a permanent facility. The dimming, unhappy memories of meeting in Jackson Hall, accompanied by the roar of roller-skating from the adjacent rink, were happily replaced with pleasant quarters in this impressive yellow brick structure with its columned limestone portico. Ultimately, the need for more space resulted in the erection in 1963 of what Clay Lancaster called "a boxlike addition," obliterating the architectural distinctiveness of the original facade.

To the dismay of everyone, the cost of the city hall left little for a municipal auditorium which did not become a reality until fifty years later, despite endless columns of newsprint discussing the project and urging its necessity for a progressive community. The $4 million Memorial Coliseum, dedicated on Memorial Day 1950, served partially as an auditorium but it was a University of Kentucky property and sports center on the university's campus. The Lexington Center, completed in the late 1970's, came closer to the original goal, but the character of that complex was markedly different from what an earlier generation needed or envisioned.

The 1922 report predicting a possible water shortage in Lexington began to haunt the city in the fall of 1930 when a severe drought reduced the reservoir water supply to critical levels. Fear that a major fire might break out with no water to fight it led city officials to issue a ban on unnecessary water use. The city also secured a court order forcing the water company to lay a pipeline to the Kentucky River. Within two months the seven-mile line was laid, special pumps installed, and by December the water ban was lifted. The Kentucky River has been an increasingly important source of Lexington's water ever since.

One historic problem city officials had wrestled with since the founding of the town was the flooding of the Town Branch. Since these crises occurred only occasionally, the tendency was to postpone action. By the 1920's, Main Street was lined with hotels, stores, restaurants, and theatres, yet the storm sewer system remained woefully inadequate. The expense of constructing a satisfactory system was high and only a bond issue could provide the necessary funds. Such action required a referendum and voter approval, and, predictably, the voters consistently defeated it.

Nature tried its best to change the voters' minds. On June 29, 1928, five inches of rain raised water two feet deep on Main Street from Ransom Avenue to Broadway, damaging shops, storage areas, and especially the basements of the Lafayette and Phoenix hotels. Three weeks later a less devastating downpour covered Main Street.

On November 7 the voters approved of Herbert Hoover for President (Al Smith's Catholicism and pro-liquor stance doomed him), and the new city manager system of city government, but voted down a bond issue for a new storm sewer system.

On August 2, 1932, the worst flood in Lexington's history followed an 8.06-inch rainfall, 7½ inches cascading down in seven hours. Water over three feet deep surged along Main Street and into the stores, hotels, and theatres, filling every basement, and forcing a number of families living in homes in low-lying areas to flee. Damage was estimated at more than $1,000,000. The health officials warned of typhoid fever and thirty-six cases were reported, four of them fatal. The downtown business

Lexington's City Hall on Walnut Street was completed in 1928. The handsome facade has since been covered by an addition to the front of the building. Photo courtesy of the University of Kentucky.

community united in a campaign to persuade Lexingtonians to pass a bond issue for an adequate storm sewer system. Yet on November 9, the voters decisively voted for Franklin D. Roosevelt as President and again rejected the bond issue. Eventually, the adamant opposition of the electorate was worn down, and a bond issue was passed in 1933. A supplementary federal grant of $1,443,000 for sewer construction guaranteed completion of this long overdue project.

The Public Schools

It was fortunate that the citizens of Fayette County and Lexington were not as indifferent to their schools as to the storm sewer problem. In November 1920, they voted for a $400,000 bond issue to erect a new junior high school and a black high school as school enrollment climbed to 4,923 white students and 1,579 black students. The white junior high school erected on the old H. E.

Ross property on South Limestone Street was completed in 1923 and named for Jefferson Davis. The new Negro high school, built on the west side of Upper Street between Fifth and Sixth streets where the Bluegrass Commission Company had once stood, was also completed in 1923 and named for the well-known Negro poet, Paul Lawrence Dunbar. The principal was Professor W. H. Fouse who had provided excellent leadership in black education in Lexington. In his first annual report he stated:

> This building marks a new epoch in the educational history of the colored people of Lexington since we are now using the 6-3-3 plan of organization ... used in no other colored school in the state of Kentucky.

This system, also used in Lexington's white schools, was the division into primary, junior, and senior high schools. Under Fouse, whose emphasis on quality was matched by Superintendent M. A. Cassidy's, Dunbar became the first high school for blacks in Kentucky to qualify for admission to the Southern Association of Colleges and Secondary Schools. It also spelled the demise of the Chandler Normal School which gradually phased out its traditional curriculum, and by 1926 was being used as a training school for men and boys who wished to learn a trade in furniture-making and repair. It also maintained a kindergarten.

Meanwhile, during the superintendency of Mattie Dalton, a high school for blacks in the county school district was built in 1929. Located on Price Road, it was named for Frederick Douglass, the famed Negro abolitionist.

Crowded conditions at Lexington High School led to the construction of Henry Clay High School, which was completed in 1928 at Walton Avenue and East Main Street where for years the Redpath Chautauqua had pitched its tents.

In 1926, Russell Cave High School burned and a new elementary and high school building replaced it. Athens High School was dedicated in 1929; and in that same year, Colonel D. Y. Dunn was named superintendent for the county schools. His aim was to complete the consolidation program initiated by Mrs. Faulconer. Bryan Station High School was built in 1932, temporarily closing Russell Cave and Linlee schools. In 1939 one of the most modern high schools in the South opened when Lafayette replaced Picadome. The Southern Association was so impressed by Lafayette's program that it requested a published account to be widely distributed through the South.

In 1930, the Lexington Board of Education appointed Henry H. Hill as the new city superintendent. A tract of ten acres on Tates Creek Pike was chosen in May 1934, as the site for the new M. A. Cassidy elementary school. Kenwick School on Henry Clay Boulevard opened in the fall of 1937, and Morton Junior High School, adjacent to Cassidy, in 1939. The demolition of the abandoned old Morton School building at the corner of Walnut and Short streets now made this historic educational site available for commercial development.

The Opera House was converted into a movie theatre in the 1930's. Photo courtesy of the University of Kentucky.

The Kentucky Theatre on East Main Street was promoting its cooling system in 1930. The theatre is still in operation. Photo courtesy of the University of Kentucky.

The Arts and History

Life in Lexington in the "Roaring Twenties" was considerably less "roaring" than that found in parts of America's larger cities. Women's hair was cut shorter, and the skirts were in the more fashionable "flapper" style. Some indulged in cigarettes. Yet the town was hardly a setting for Scott Fitzgerald's *The Great Gatsby*. Movie houses prospered here as they did everywhere, and if the ads reflect the film fare being offered, some of it was surprisingly steamy, causing comment by more than one editor. The Hays code in the 1930's to assure the American public of less lurid cinema substantially changed what was thought appropriate for citizens to see. Despite Red scares, anti-evolution controversies, woman suffrage, and prohibition, life in Lexington remained relatively unchanged.

Thanks to Anna Chandler Goff, the quality of concerts at the Woodland Auditorium compared favorably with those offered in the largest American cities. It was a privilege for a town of Lexington's size — and at an edifice as unpretentious as Woodland Auditorium — to hear Geraldine Farrar, the New York

Philharmonic, Madame Schumann-Heink, Harold Bauer, Fritz Kreisler, Sergei Rachmaninoff, Jascha Heifetz, and the young virtuoso Vladimir Horowitz. It is also a tribute to this determined impresario that she brought to Lexington the outstanding Negro tenor Roland Hayes and the rising Negro contralto, Marian Anderson, and provided ample room for both blacks and whites to hear these artists. In 1932, the Community Concert Association of Central Kentucky was organized, utilizing the auditorium of the Henry Clay High School.

Though the Opera House was struggling to survive, Shakespeare was still being presented in the early 1920's. Reginald DeKoven's musical, *Robin Hood*, with its ever popular song, "Oh, Promise Me," which for years would be heard at weddings, drew large crowds. Sizable audiences also turned out for the dramatization of Fox's *The Little Shepherd of Kingdom Come*. Vaudeville was providing stiff competition, however, and by the time of the Great Depression, the stage of the Opera House was deserted.

An exotic figure in Lexington's cultural community was the Lithuanian Yiddish poet, Israel Jacob Schwartz, who had earned a

177

respectable reputation in Yiddish literary circles before he and his family moved to Lexington in 1918. They opened the New York Wholesale Millinery Shop downtown, run mostly by Mrs. Schwartz. Meanwhile, the poet became absorbed in the beauty, folklore, and history of the state and wrote a volume of poetry entitled *Kentucky*, which was published in New York in 1925. His narrative poems deal with the struggle of immigrants seeking a new life in this strange but fascinating land. The Schwartzes departed from Lexington and their friends at the Ohavay Zion Synagogue in 1928, but he left a notable poetic legacy to the Bluegrass. He praised not only the natural beauty of the region but frequently described Lexington as it gradually expanded, including the crowded and dirty streets of the town's slums. Forgotten for years, Schwartz has been the subject of recent studies by Professor Joseph Jones at the University of Kentucky and Professor Gertrude Dubrovsky of Princeton University.

Adding to the literary activity in Lexington was the work of a number of historians who, after a gap of several generations following the publication of Perrin's *History of Fayette County* in 1882, were once again exploring the varied and rich history of the Bluegrass. Earliest of these was John Wilson Townsend who published *Kentucky in American Letters* in two volumes in 1913. William H. Townsend, local attorney and Lincoln scholar, published his colorful *Lincoln and His Wife's Hometown* in 1929, which gave a vivid and informative description of antebellum Lexington. At the University of Kentucky, professors William D. Funkhouser and William Webb issued their investigations of archeological explorations in the region in *Ancient Life in Kentucky* in 1928.

In the 1930's, J. Winston Coleman, Jr., engineer and homebuilder, began his productive career as explorer and recorder of Kentucky's historic heritage, both locally and statewide. Not only did he publish numerous books, pamphlets, and magazine articles, but he also toured the state, photographing historic structures that formed an integral part of Kentucky's past. Many of these buildings have long since disappeared, making his photographic record invaluable. Starting with his volumes on Masonry and stagecoaches in the mid-1930's,

Coleman published one of his most important works, *Slavery Times in Kentucky,* in 1940. *A Bibliography of Kentucky History,* published by the University of Kentucky Press in 1949, was a boon to both scholars and Kentucky book collectors. In recent decades he is probably best known for his editorial direction of the popular *Kentucky: A Pictorial History* (1971), a selection of his fine photographs in *Historic Kentucky* (1969), and *The Squire's Sketches of Lexington* (1972).

In 1937, Dr. Thomas D. Clark's *History of Kentucky* was published, which has deservedly been the most widely read history of the Commonwealth in this century. His dedication to building an outstanding history department at the University of Kentucky and enlarging and enriching its archival and library resources in southern and Kentucky history contributed to the academic stature of that institution. The most nationally prominent of Kentucky's historians, he has written significant works on the South as well as Kentucky.

Charles Staples' *The History of Pioneer Lexington* (1939) provided one of the best and most thorough accounts of that period. During the 1920-1940 period, Judge Samuel Wilson, a noted lawyer and history enthusiast, accumulated books and wrote on various subjects in Kentucky's history while encouraging all interested persons to join in the movement. His book and manuscript collection was left to the University of Kentucky — a major addition to its special collections. J. Winston Coleman, Jr., has donated his invaluable Kentuckiana collection to Transylvania University.

Recreational Activities

Racing fans faithfully attended the meets at the Association track and harness-racing at the Trotting Track. Horses brought here by train for the meets were unloaded at the stations on Water Street and South Broadway and walked up North Broadway to Fifth Street and over to the Association track, or south to the Trotting Track.

In 1933, the Kentucky Association, which had been operating since 1826, held its last meeting. As far back as 1920, Colonel E. R. Bradley had urged the Kentucky Jockey Club to build a new racetrack and threatened that if they took no action he would organize a group and do so. Hal Price Headley and Major Louis

An aerial view of Joyland Park, an amusement center located on the Paris Pike. It opened in the 1920's and was one of Lexington's most popular attractions for several decades.

A. Beard headed a committee of Bluegrass horsemen to evaluate the situation and make plans for a new track. It was their judgment that the property of the old Association track had deteriorated so badly "that reclamation is highly impractical." In addition, new housing had crowded around the racecourse and the access roads were in poor condition.

Determined to carry on the tradition of quality racing in the Bluegrass, this committee acquired a portion of Jack Keene's stud farm on which they constructed the Keeneland Race Course. This jewel of a track opened for its first meet in July 1936. It has remained a Bluegrass showplace, not only for its races, but as a site of one of the most prestigious and expensive yearling sales in the world.

For those seeking recreation other than at the racetrack or picnicking in Woodland Park, the Bluegrass Amusement Park on the Versailles Road near South Elkhorn Baptist Church presented a great variety of entertainment. Operated successfully for decades by the Kentucky Traction & Terminal Company, which ran special interurban cars to

the park, it was overshadowed when Joyland Park and its dance casino opened on the Paris Pike in May 1923. A year or two later Bluegrass Park closed. Joyland with its roller coaster, large swimming pool (the first public pool in the county), miniature train, and a score of carnival-like diversions, was a major attraction. In its first two decades many of the famous "Big Bands" played at the dance casino for Lexingtonians. The park gradually declined in popularity in the 1950's, and fire and neglect ended its existence in 1960, when it was replaced by a residential subdivision.

It was obvious, too, that sports, which only gradually began appearing in the post-Civil War period, were by now American pastimes that would expand beyond any prophetic sportsman's wildest dreams. The newspapers of the late 19th and early 20th centuries were generally indifferent to baseball, football, basketball, golf, etc. Horse racing was the major exception. By the 1920's, not only did the Lexington newspapers have special sports pages, and then a sports section, but certain sporting events became front-page news.

In late June 1921, international and national news was second in importance to the Jack Dempsey vs. George Carpentier heavyweight championship fight, slated for July 1. The Strand Theatre sold tickets to those wishing to hear a special telegraphic round-by-round report. Banner headlines on July 2 hailed Dempsey's victory. In 1923 Dempsey's win over Firpo was similarly featured. World Series baseball games were reported on the front page, as was the phenomenal contract of $120,000 paid by the New York Yankees to lure Babe Ruth away from the Boston Red Sox.

Enthusiasm for intercollegiate football in 1923 raised $200,000 among the University of Kentucky's fans and alumni to build a stadium on Stoll Field at Rose and Euclid avenues. Even the death of a UK football player from injuries suffered in a game did not check the crusade. Fred J. Murphy, the new UK football coach, was welcomed with a large banquet and front-page coverage. All Kentuckians shared in Centre College's delirium when its famed "Praying Colonels" defeated mighty Harvard 6-0 in October 1921, on the foe's home field.

Basketball's popularity was growing, although the fabulous years were yet ahead. The state high school basketball championship tournament, hosted by the University of Kentucky in 1925, included both girls' and boys' teams. Then, in May 1930, the newspaper reported that Adolph Rupp had accepted a two-year contract to coach basketball at the University, signalling a new era for the sport in Kentucky.

The popularity of golf was evidenced in the organization of the Lexington Country Club in 1907 by a group of Lexington businessmen. Located on the Paris Pike, the original frame clubhouse burned in 1925 but was immediately replaced. Lexington's first public golf course was the Picadome Golf Club, which was opened in May 1927, on Hal Price Headley's property on the Harrodsburg Road.

In 1928, Colonel E. R. Bradley took over the Ashland Country Club, which had leased property from him on the Richmond Road two years earlier to establish a golf course. Eventually, this became the Idle Hour Country Club.

This period also saw the continuation of the Bluegrass Fair and the Colored Fair, both of which drew large crowds to the Fairgrounds.

White Tavern hamburgers were popular in Lexington in the 1930's and 1940's. These small restaurants developed into the nationwide Jerrico, Inc., Lexington-based fast food chain. Photo courtesy of the University of Kentucky.

For the Colored Fair, special trains were run from Chicago, Indianapolis, and other midwest cities to hear such bands as Duke Ellington's.

Others enjoyed the Chautauqua programs, still operating at this late date on Stoll Field.

The Passing Scene

Singular daredevil exhibitions to catch the public's eye included Harry Gardiner, the "human fly," who scaled the First National Bank Building while a crowd on Cheapside and the courthouse lawn watched the ascent. In July 1928, Lexingtonians were fascinated for four days while "Shipwreck" Kelly, one of the few surviving sailors of the ill-fated *Titanic*, climbed the flagpole atop the Lafayette Hotel, and stood on a ten-inch disc for 100 hours, taking only liquid nourishment. Police soon had problems preventing curious viewers from interfering with traffic on Main Street. A large crowd gathered to cheer his descent and later attended his appearance at the Strand. After this excitement, some might have drifted into the Canary Cottage, one of Main Street's most popular restaurants, or tasted the fine fare at the Lafayette and Phoenix hotels.

Lexingtonians were doubtless amazed to read that John T. Hughes, the noted horseman, who died at age 84 in August 1924, had left a startling will dividing his property among his black housekeeper-mistress, Ellen Davis, their son, Robert Henry Hughes, and a faithful black manservant, plus leaving $100,000 to the Kentucky Female Orphan School in Midway. Relatives from every corner united to contest the will in a dramatic suit in May 1925. Attempts to prove Hughes of unsound mind when he wrote his will were fruitless against the testimony of Dr. J. C. Carrick, his physician and executor, and the jury upheld the will. Ellen Davis quickly sold her share of the farm to Harry Payne Whitney. Robert lived most of his life in Buffalo, New York, before returning to Lexington for his last years. After his death in June 1935, he left the residue of his estate, estimated to be worth between $50,000 and $100,000, for the establishment of a trust, which is still functioning. Administered by a Lexington bank, the income was to be used for scholarships for aspiring black and white college students.

One of the most interesting developments in church organizations in Lexington in this period was the formation of "Everybody's Church." The congregation was composed of individuals who wished to worship as a nonsectarian body. They secured the leadership of the Reverend J. Archer Gray, former pastor of Maxwell Street Presbyterian Church, an outstanding preacher and community leader. Their church was the Ben Ali Theatre where they held worship services every Sunday morning. Succeeding the Reverend Mr. Gray was the colorful and energetic Thomas "Scotty" Cowan, a gifted preacher and concerned citizen, who maintained the devotion and loyalty of this congregation to the community church concept. In 1958, the congregation vacated the Ben Ali and moved into the former Centenary Methodist Church building on the corner of North Broadway and Church Street. The congregation is now known as the First Community Church.

Two 20th century marvels also changed the life of Lexingtonians: the radio and the airplane. Radios were beginning to make their appearance in some Main Street stores, usually as a sideline item in an automobile accessory shop or sports equipment store. Such was the case with Barney Miller's, where radios, phonographs and television sets have long since replaced auto accessories.

Airplanes and Airfields

Aircraft had rapidly developed following the famous flight of the Wright brothers at Kitty Hawk in 1903, due partly to the military need for aircraft in the First World War. Many Lexingtonians had glimpsed an airplane prior to 1921, but in June of that year the town boasted of having its first privately-owned aircraft, appropriately named the "Daniel Boone." Under the control of pilot Jesse O. Creech, it was scheduled to leave Chicago at 8 a.m. speeding toward Lexington at 100 miles per hour and refueling at Indianapolis. A three-passenger British-type aircraft, it carried, in addition to the pilot, a pig for Mayor Bradley as a gift from Morris & Company meatpackers in Chicago, as a publicity stunt.

Creech landed safely, pig and all, on Lexington's first airfield, Halley Field, two miles from downtown on the Leestown Road. Creech made daily flights as the occasion demanded, scheduling them out of his office at the Lexington Aviation Company in the Bank of Commerce building. Operations were interrupted, however, when the "Daniel Boone," exhibited by Creech at the Montgomery County Fair, caught fire while taxiing for a take-off and burned, the pilot luckily escaping.

This ended the first pioneer airline operation. Flying circuses such as Roscoe Turner's used the field, occasionally called the "Meadowthorpe Field," for a few days of exhibition flying. Yet no action, private or public, was taken to establish a commercial operation until 1927, when the Lexington Board of Commerce leased Halley Field for three years and hired a manager who was head of the United Airplane Company. Five planes were to be stationed here, and a school for commercial flying was to be conducted. With "Lexington" painted on their undersides, the planes — using compasses, charts, and railroad tracks for guidance — were flown in from Dallas, Texas.

By January 1928, some commercial flights were operating out of this field. Ted Kincannon, the manager, became division superintendent of the Cincinnati to Chattanooga segment of the Dixie and Northern Airline which planned to put Lexington on its scheduled flight from Detroit to Miami. The planes were Ford Trimotors and passenger luggage was limited to thirty pounds.

Lexingtonians, as all Americans, had been thrilled by Charles A. Lindbergh's solo flight to Paris in May 1927, a feat that made him one of the country's most popular heroes of the decade. They were naturally excited when Lindbergh made an unpublicized visit by air to Lexington in March 1928, to visit Dr. Scott Breckinridge, brother of Henry Breckinridge, Lindbergh's legal advisor. Their excitement was dampened, however, by Lindbergh's comment that Lexington's airfield was too small at present to meet aviation needs. The "Lone Eagle" had difficulty himself in taking off, barely missing some trees at the end of the runway.

This incident stimulated a search for a better site for an airfield, and in 1930 property was leased on the James Blythe Anderson farm on the Newtown Pike, which received federal approval. The city agreed to purchase materials to build a hangar, and it was hoped federal funds would be available for development. By 1935, the field, named "Glengarry" for the farm on which it was located, appeared reasonably satisfactory, but hardly overburdened with traffic. In 1936 it was leased to the Lexington Air Taxi Service for $1 a year and an obligation to maintain the field. By 1937 air mail service was started on a trial basis.

Not until 1940, under the leadership and prodding of Mayor T. Ward Havely, was realistic planning for a suitable municipal airport begun. The federal Civil Aeronautics Administration engineers gave tentative approval to a site located on a 593-acre tract of the Van Meter property, opposite Keeneland, much to the dismay of Warren Wright who feared for the welfare of his farm and horses near the airfield. In January 1941, Delta Airlines expressed an interest in a Lexington stopover if a new field were built. The city and county jointly bought the property in March for $160,000. With a federal grant of $627,500, serious construction was started. Within a few

months, the United States had entered World War II and Lexington persuaded the federal government that the field was of military value. This produced the necessary federal funding to complete the first stages of development, including a usable runway.

On July 11, 1942, the first plane to land here was a B-25 bomber. The war delayed commercial operations, but Eastern Airlines received federal approval to use the Lexington field in 1943. There was considerable debate whether the field should be named after Mayor Havely or former Governor A. B. "Happy" Chandler, so a compromise was reached and the field was officially named Blue Grass Field in 1944. It would not become an airport facility worthy of its name for some time, however.

The Black Community

The black community, despite the terrible fear created by the Will Lockett riot, the lynching in nearby towns, and the ominous presence of the Ku Klux Klan, maintained a degree of identity and pride which carried it through these trials. It recognized the divisions that separated it from white Lexington, but also the bonds that united them. Despite obvious differentials of wage scales and, in most cases, physical facilities, the city black schools under the leadership of W. H. Fouse had much to be proud of in the quality of their teachers and the level of educational programs. It was noteworthy that the percentage of advanced degrees held by black teachers was higher than that among white teachers.

The recent war had united blacks and whites in a common cause, and, while celebrating at different parks, they made July Fourth a community holiday. Special films recording black soldiers in battle in France were shown at the St. Paul A.M.E. Church, documenting the role they had played in the war. In September 1920, the body of Sergeant Nathan Caulder, who had died in France, was brought home for burial in the No. 2 Cemetery on Seventh Street. The Negro American Legion Post No. 132 was named in his honor. Professor Fouse, speaking to the students at Transylvania, urged them to challenge the unexamined assumptions of the past, and to

The first commercial passenger plane to make a regularly scheduled stop at the new Blue Grass Field was a Delta DC-3, which flew into Lexington on October 13, 1946. The plane had a top speed of 212 miles per hour. Photo courtesy of Blue Grass Field.

recognize their common humanity and the need for "a kindly, tolerant, patient spirit, race toward race."

The black community enthusiastically supported the newly established community Welfare Fund, forerunner of the Community Chest and the United Way, which had combined a number of existing charity campaigns. In addition, appeals were made to support the NAACP and the black branch of the YMCA.

Black women spoke out, too. At a meeting of the Kentucky Club Women of Our State Confederation, a black women's organization, the speaker said, "The eyes of the world are upon us, the womanhood of the race, we who are holding the destiny of the future possibilities of the race within our grasp."

Dr. J. K. Polk, one of Lexington's Negro physicians and surgeons, opened a private infirmary in 1921. At its dedication he paid high tribute to Dr. J. E. Hunter and Dr. E. M. McKee, pioneers of their race in medicine and surgery. John W. Rowe, a graduate of Howard University, passed the Kentucky bar exam and established his law practice in an office in Polk's infirmary on Dewees Street.

Rising in prominence at this time was Robert Hogan who was later to become, according to the *Herald,* "one of Lexington's most respected businessmen and civic leaders." After working as a foreman for the Combs Lumber Company a number of years, he started his own construction firm, with some assistance from his former employer. He built numerous structures in Lexington, including Dunbar High School and the new Pleasant Green Baptist Church. His interest in civic affairs, especially public education, resulted in his appointment to many local and state committees. His most influential appointment was membership on the committee of the Southern Association of Colleges and Secondary Schools.

The black community voiced vigorous protest against the action of the Lexington Police Department in jailing Gertie Boulder, well-known Negro civic leader, on finding her unconscious on the street and assuming her to be drunk. She probably had suffered a heart attack, but no medical investigation was made and she died in jail. Mayor Yancey conducted a well-publicized and thorough investigation, which revealed incompetence more than calculated abuse. New regulations regarding the handling of unconscious persons by the police were established.

Blacks convicted of a capital crime and hanged in the county jailyard inevitably caused great distress in the black community. Notices in the paper signed by blacks condemning such criminals appeared to reflect concern that the whites might think the blacks condoned such crimes, or were less law-abiding than the whites.

The Ray Ross hanging in 1925 was the last in Fayette County. Police Chief J. J. Reagan successfully campaigned to have this public and brutal type of execution abolished.

The City Manager System

In 1932 Lexington inaugurated a city manager form of government. This was not achieved easily. The radical change in the city charter in 1912, which replaced the cumbersome Boards of Councilmen and Aldermen with a mayor and four commissioners, had not resulted in as much efficiency and nonpartisanship as its supporters had hoped.

Harry Giovannoli, editor of the *Leader,* began a campaign in 1923 to promote the manager plan through a series of editorials discussing its various aspects and benefits. By the late 1920's enough interested citizens, convinced that a city manager form of government would improve conditions in Lexington, formed a Charter League to persuade the electorate to vote for a manager plan and for a ticket of commissioners which stood behind it. On November 6, 1930, the voters approved the new plan and a year later voted in the Charter ticket.

In late November 1931, Paul Morton, a native of Louisville and an experienced city manager of Petersburg, Virginia, accepted the position as Lexington's first city manager. This new plan provided the manager with considerable independence and freedom of action. Morton, indifferent to the political toes he stepped on as he implemented his reform program, soon created a political backlash.

Determined to amend the city charter and reduce the power of the city manager, a so-called Home Town Party, headed by E. Reed Wilson as mayoral candidate, campaigned

vigorously on this issue in 1935 and swept the November elections.

Meanwhile, Richard P. Moloney, a new name on the political horizon, gradually attained leadership in local Democratic circles and increasingly on a state level.

The Great Depression

The Lexington press reported the great Wall Street panic and collapse of late October 1929, with remarkable calm. There appeared no undue alarm in the city. No bank officers leaped out of top-floor windows of the 15-story First National Bank Building, the city's tallest structure. No editorials predicted catastrophe. Kentucky and the Bluegrass were a world away from the frantic atmosphere of New York and Chicago. The Republican ticket for county offices won in November. Automobile sales in the spring of 1930 were actually above normal, but this was a deceptive barometer of overall economic conditions. Otherwise, why would the federal government allot $300,000 to Lexington in March 1930, to be spent on public works to reduce unemployment? This money was expended on street improvements and the building of the West High Street viaduct.

In November 1930, a general unemployment conference was held at City Hall with representatives from the Kiwanis, Rotary, Pyramid, and Altrusa clubs, along with other civic and industrial leaders. Mayor O'Brien appointed a ways and means committee to work with the retail community and the Lexington Board of Commerce to make plans to raise a fund for the indigent. Citizens urged city and county officials in December 1930, to establish an employment bureau, encourage construction, and create a fund to aid the unemployed.

In the spring of 1931, the Fayette National Bank closed its doors, dramatizing for Lexingtonians the growing financial crisis. As noted earlier, the First National Bank & Trust Company took over the defunct institution and moved its own headquarters into the tall bank building at that time.

As the depression deepened, 300 workers were sent out to canvass the city and county in search of jobs for the unemployed, a strategy successfully used in Rochester, New York. Salaries of every employee at the University of

Kentucky were cut in February 1932. In March, checks were entirely withheld until the trustees met in April, with rumors of a 50 percent cut causing general dismay. Across town at Transylvania, some faculty were dismissed and others took a reduction in salary. Public school salaries were reduced by five percent at the beginning of the 1932 school year.

Lawyers and doctors felt the pinch. The major partners of the Lexington Clinic reduced their salaries by 20 percent in 1931, and by July 1932, the staff was informed that no salaries could be guaranteed. Income depended on collections from the patients, but the staff exhibited remarkable loyalty by existing on a hand-to-mouth basis.

The city had managed to cut its operating expenses by $59,062 for the first ten months of 1932. The Fiscal Court, also seeking to trim costs, closed its Children's Home and placed 40 children in private homes. Each member of the Fiscal Court took a 10 percent salary reduction.

An historic tradition was revived when Lexington church women organized a soup kitchen, as they had in earlier depressions, although there now was no Gus Jaubert to prepare the steaming repast.

In November 1932, Fayette County gave Franklin D. Roosevelt a decisive majority in the election, even though the county had not been as traditional a Democratic stronghold as some of its central Bluegrass neighbors. This was evidenced by Fayette's majorities for McKinley in 1896 and 1900, and for Coolidge and Hoover in 1924 and 1928. The 1930's would also witness a large percentage of the Negro vote shifting to the Democratic party. Not only had the Hoover policies proved inadequate for the exigencies of the crisis, but Republican Governor Flem D. Sampson, elected in 1927, had become mired in controversy, especially over the free textbooks issue, and had lost popular support from his own party as well as the Democrats.

With the inauguration of Roosevelt on March 4, 1933 (the last time a U.S. President would be sworn into office on that date, a change resulting from the 20th Amendment),

A downtown Labor Day Parade in 1933, during the Great Depression era, attracted a large crowd. This view shows buildings and stores opposite the Fayette County Courthouse. Photo courtesy of the University of Kentucky.

185

The tap room of the Drake Hotel on West Short Street between Broadway and Mill was a popular gathering place during the post-Prohibition years. Photo courtesy of Kitty Portwood.

the New Deal was launched during the famous "Hundred Days." The new President immediately ordered a bank "holiday," though Kentucky had already closed its banks on instruction from Governor Ruby Laffoon three days earlier. Only after the Emergency Banking Act passed Congress on March 9 were the solvent banks reopened, and a week later all the Lexington banks were operating normally.

Federal relief funds soon began to pour into the states to relieve the empty or woefully inadequate state and municipal relief resources. By June 1933, one-fourth of the families in the county were receiving relief in some form. Even the YMCA had to close its doors due to heavy indebtedness and failure to secure necessary funds.

A boost to the local economy came from several sources. Swift & Company decided to build a meat processing plant on the Old Frankfort Pike. Work began on the Federal Narcotics Farm in July 1933, which also gave employment to some local residents. In that

same month the attractive, modest-sized Kentuckian Hotel opened on the corner of High Street and the Union Station viaduct. It was an interesting contrast. For many local residents the Great Depression was not a devastating or difficult time, and life seemed to maintain a normal equilibrium. But for many others it was a harsh and grueling experience. Because Lexington and Fayette County were not heavily industrialized, the impact of the depression was relatively less traumatic than in many other American cities.

Meanwhile, some of Lexington's unemployed young men joined one of the New Deal's most innovative programs — the Civilian Conservation Corps — initiated in May 1933. It was the purpose of this organization to enroll unemployed males between the ages of 17 and 28 in a semi-military fashion for work on roads, building trails, and reforestation. It proved not only to be a morale-booster for the participants engaged in constructive conservation programs but also improved their health and

186

made lasting contributions to the state and nation.

Lexington firms placed the Blue Eagle insignia in their windows in support of the National Industrial Recovery Act (NRA). Even though this measure eventually proved unworkable and was declared unconstitutional by the U.S. Supreme Court, it was at least an energetic attempt to stem the tide of the nation's worst economic disaster.

Harry Hopkins, President Roosevelt's right-hand man in dealing with relief programs, visited Lexington in August 1933 on his way to address a special session of the General Assembly, which had been called to assess the local relief problem. That there was one was indisputable. William Beehler, executive secretary of the Family Welfare Society, painted a grim picture in his description of Lexington's situation in September 1933.

> Unprecedented privation and hunger stalk through Lexington today, to the point where mere words are inadequate to describe the misery of the unemployed or the grave menace to the health and welfare of the community.

He pointed out that 1,500 Lexingtonians needed relief, with many families barely subsisting on $5 a week.

The *Leader* urged its readers to vote for a bond issue for public works, necessary at that time to match federal funds. The voters approved the issue on November 9. Within three weeks, 300 men were employed under the Civilian Works Administration, and soon that number swelled to 500.

On December 5, 1933, the Eighteenth Amendment was officially repealed and Americans could now soften the blows of the depression with their favorite alcoholic beverage, if they could afford it. However, not until March 18, 1934, was prohibition ended in Kentucky by state statute. Was it Prohibition's vengeful ghost that burned the James E. Pepper distillery on April 28, fueled by $4,500,000 of barreled whiskey, and $600,000 of bottled whiskey?

In 1934, new federal assistance was funneled into Kentucky through the Public Works Administration which financed such projects as sewers, a community health center,

community centers, and a new city jail. The new Federal Building on Barr Street was completed. In July a crowd packed Memorial Hall on the University of Kentucky campus to hear the indomitable Mrs. Eleanor Roosevelt. Many listened to her husband's "fireside chats" on Lexington's first commercial radio station, WLAP, owned by J. Lindsay and Gilmore N. Nunn, which had just begun operation.

By 1935, retail merchants reported an increase in sales and the worst of the depression seemed over. Yet one reporter estimated that 300 penniless, jobless, and homeless men of all ages — the hoboes— rolled into Lexington every day aboard trains from all directions. Some stopped temporarily in the city's "jungles," one of which was south of Virginia Avenue near the tracks of the Southern Railway. Others wandered through residential areas looking for handouts. Some panhandled passersby on the city streets, occasionally being arrested. Most just waited around the train yards to catch the next freight out of town.

By contrast, in this same year the handsome Keeneland Race Course was being built, and an exclusive subdivision on Eastin Road off the Paris Pike was being developed. The elaborate 30-room mansion at Spindletop Farm was being planned as was Warren Wright's new country home at Calumet.

For whites and blacks at the bottom of the economic ladder, some light on the horizon, some hope for better living conditions came closer to reality as federal funding for low cost housing and slum clearance resulted in new housing projects. The old Kentucky Association property became the site for the Bluegrass project for whites and Aspendale for blacks.

Construction in Lexington during 1936 showed a 34 percent increase. In 1937 Montgomery Ward bought the old Carty building at Main and Mill streets with its remarkable cast-iron facade, and tore it down to make way for a new store.

There were significant changes, too, in Lexington's newspaper ownership and editorial leadership. In 1916 the *Leader* had moved from its Upper Street site to a new plant on the corner of Market and Short streets. Harry Giovannoli, editor and manager from 1913 to

Keeneland Race Course has drawn large crowds throughout its history, even during the depression years of the 1930's when it was built. This photo, taken in the latter part of the 1930 decade, shows the track before it was extensively enlarged by combining the grandstand and clubhouse into one continuous structure. Photo courtesy of the Keeneland Library.

1927, was succeeded by Fred B. Wachs as general manager. In August 1937, John G. Stoll, editor and publisher of the *Leader*, bought the *Herald* from the Nunns, who had published the paper in the building on the southwest corner of Short and Walnut streets. After the purchase, both papers were printed at the *Leader* plant, and a combined paper, the *Herald-Leader*, was issued on Sundays.

In late January 1937, Lexington was transformed into a major relief center as the disastrous floods that swept through Louisville and Frankfort left 40,000 homeless. Thousands of refugees from the Falls City descended on Lexington by buses and trains to find temporary shelter here. Most frightening to local residents was the transfer of 1,300 prisoners from the flooded State Penitentiary at Frankfort to Lexington. Under heavy guard, 500 prisoners were packed in the former post office building at Main and Walnut, while others were sent to the U.S. Public Health

Service Hospital, the State Highway Garage, the city and county jails, Kentucky Village, and the city police station. Guards erected a barbed-wire barricade around the post office and mounted machine guns at strategic spots. Refugees were placed in homes, churches, and institutions, and Lexingtonians organized to feed them until they could return to their homes.

During this same year city public transportation underwent a major change with buses replacing the street railway that had carried citizens for over half a century. A few years earlier the interurban system had closed down.

Though Lexington listed 2,892 as unemployed in January 1938, *Forbes Business Magazine* cited the city as one of the bright spots in the nation and one of the more prosperous business centers. A massive federal grant made possible the construction of Charlotte Court, another large Negro public housing project on the Georgetown Road.

By 1940 Lexington had recovered from most of the effects of the depression. Population growth had been slowed somewhat, although Fayette County recorded an increase of 10,356 for a total of 78,899. Much of this was concentrated in the urban rather than rural areas, although the statutory city limits showed Lexington had a net gain of but 3,298 for a total of 49,034. Housing on the eve of Pearl Harbor had extended to Chinoe Road on the east, to Tahoma and Goodrich on the Nicholasville Road, to Lakewood and Montclair on Tates Creek, and to the north as far as Highlawn, and west toward Meadowthorpe, which was just in the planning stage. Adjacent to Charlotte Court was one of the newest black housing developments, started in 1940 by Ovan Haskins, an enterprising and energetic black real estate agent and developer.

Impact of World War II

With the beginning of World War II on September 1, 1939, when Hitler invaded Poland, the U.S. economy emerged from the Great Depression. The inexhaustible demands of England and France, and after June 1941, the Soviet Union, for tremendous quantities of war materials, converted the United States into the "arsenal of democracy." Most Americans from the outset of the war had never pretended to be neutral in thought and allegiance as President Wilson had advised in 1914. The nature and threat of Nazi Germany and Mussolini's Fascist Italy, and the growing menace of the militarily dominated Japanese government aroused a strong commitment among those nations confronting the Axis aggression.

But the deeply imbedded conviction that the United States had naively entered World War I from which little was achieved, compounded by the cynicism and disillusion expressed by the literary spokesmen of the "lost generation," and the trauma of the Great Depression, created little enthusiasm among Americans for involvement in another Great Crusade. It was believed America could best help the cause by delivering the necessary war supplies. The disaster of France's fall in June 1940, and the narrow escape of the British forces from Dunkirk, leaving Britain to face Hitler's onslaught alone, forced Americans unwillingly toward a reassessment of their stand.

The world situation soon began to affect Lexington and hundreds of other municipalities. In July 1940, a national defense trade school was established at Lafayette High School to train persons for industrial jobs necessary to national defense. Mayor Havely wrote aircraft manufacturers describing the area's assets for the establishment of an aircraft factory. Colonel Henry Breckinridge urged an audience at Henry Clay High School to support the move to provide more aid to the Allies. In October 1940, the 35-year-old Raymond F. McLain, Transylvania's new president, joined students, the younger faculty, and 10,853 other Fayette Countians in registering for the first peacetime draft in American history. Fayette County women began to collect clothing and other articles for "Bundles for Britain" as the Luftwaffe launched its flaming blitz on England.

The Lexington Telephone Company, in the interest of national defense, made plans to protect its plant against possible sabotage. Some Lexingtonians left town for jobs in defense plants in other cities.

The biggest news, however, was the Army's decision to construct a $3,000,000 depot at Avon, just east of Lexington, which was strategically located to Army installations in the Ohio River Valley. Fayette County officials took immediate steps to prevent the mushrooming of inadequate, unsanitary boarding houses, trailer camps, and cabins in the area, as had happened elsewhere. By late May 1942, the Lexington Signal Depot was in operation.

For a few weeks the attention of Lexingtonians was diverted from their concerns and fears of war by a sensational murder at the Lexington Country Club. In the early hours of Sunday, September 28, 1941, Tom Penney, an ex-convict, and Bobby Anderson, a Louisville nightclub owner of dubious reputation, were let into the clubhouse by Raymond Baxter, a greenskeeper, to look for money they thought was deposited there from the Saturday night's dance. Unfortunately, they aroused Mrs. Fred Miley, the club manager, and her attractive and talented daughter, Marion Miley, a nationally prominent golfer, who lived alone in the building. The two women were shot after

Scrap metal collection in front of Henry Clay High School on East Main Street during World War II. Metal was recycled for defense industries. The school building is now the headquarters of the Fayette County Public School system. Photo courtesy of Transylvania University.

putting up a struggle. Marion died immediately, but her mother, though mortally wounded, managed to stagger to a nearby dwelling for help. The three men were apprehended, convicted, and executed, but Lexington would not soon forget the bloody incident.

Lexingtonians were made acutely aware of possible U.S. involvement in the war in June 1941, six months before Pearl Harbor, by the organization of a Civilian Defense Commission to train volunteers to assist firemen and police in local emergencies. Already collections of scrap aluminum were being made. The Lexington Water Company properties were closed to public access as a precautionary measure.

By mid-1941, polls showed over 70 percent of the American people willing to help Britain, even at the risk of involvement in the war. This was a profound shift in public opinion and it now seemed only a matter of time before

incidents such as the German submarine attack on the U.S. destroyer *Greer* in the North Atlantic would precipitate war with Nazi Germany. It was a stunning surprise to be attacked by the Japanese at Pearl Harbor on December 7.

In retrospect, it seems that Lexingtonians were a bit over-cautious in making plans for a practice blackout two weeks after Pearl Harbor. Nevertheless, air raid wardens were appointed and air raid warning signals were installed downtown.

Meanwhile, the city was anticipating an economic upswing with the influx of several thousand defense workers to Avon. In April 1942, Fayette Countians dug into their pockets and savings to buy war bonds in the first of such campaigns. Residents purchased $343,000 worth in this first drive, but by the seventh drive, more than three years later, over $16,000,000 was subscribed, almost double the quota assigned, thanks to the cooperation of the banks and the strong commitment of this area to the war effort.

It was also in the spring of 1942 that the living patterns of all Americans were substantially affected by the elaborate rationing program. Some foods such as meat and sugar were rationed, as were tires and gasoline. Each person had his ration books and stamps. Many car owners, confronted with a limit of four gallons a week, unless their work or official position allowed larger allotments, put their cars on blocks in their garages, took off the tires, drained the radiators, and hung "for the duration" signs on them.

The Irving Air Chute Company built a new factory on the Versailles Road in 1942, moving from its previous location on West Main Street.

As the draft and defense industries cut into available manpower, women took up the slack. The famed "Rosie the Riveter" appeared on billboards across the country. Many entered war industries. The Hub Tool Company built a plant on Northeastern Avenue to manufacture precision tools for aircraft motor production, employing mostly women, one of the few defense plants in the United States to do so. More mundane duties, such as driving taxicabs and buses, were assumed by women. Many helped in the tobacco fields, weeding and harvesting the crop.

Male enrollment at Transylvania University plummeted and the school faced the real possibility of closing had not the Army Signal Corps rented part of the school's facilities to train radio operators. Later, 200 Air Force cadets were housed in the men's dormitory and trained in pre-flight courses. The University of Kentucky fared somewhat better with its large infantry ROTC unit and the addition of a Signal Corps ROTC. An Engineer Specialist School was added, the enrollees being housed at the Phoenix Hotel. Despite these programs, overall enrollment dropped almost 2,000 by 1944-45. The College of Agriculture and the Home Economics Department gave priority to increasing food production and teaching techniques for preserving large quantities of food.

Fayette County farmers increased production of vital agricultural products by 12 to 15 percent. Many residents dug up their back yards and planted "victory gardens" and raised chickens in their garages and basements.

In the fall of 1944, as Allied forces in France moved north and east toward the Siegfried Line and the Rhine River, Kentucky tobacco farmers, faced with a shortage of manpower to harvest their precious crop, found a novel, if controversial, solution. German prisoners of war, confined in various encampments about the country, were brought in. Over 600 were housed in the Kentucky militia armory on the Old Frankfort Pike and parceled out to work on the farms. There was even talk of using them in the redrying plants. The first outcry came from officials of Lexington's Central Labor Union who contended the labor shortage was not that acute. Then protests were heard from residents who lived in areas near where the prisoners were being confined. Despite such objections, the Germans were used without any major difficulties for the tobacco harvests of 1944 and 1945.

Death of President Roosevelt

On April 12, 1945, the nation was stunned by the death of President Roosevelt at Warm Springs, Georgia. Roosevelt had served as President for over twelve years, and many young Americans had never known any other chief executive. The loss of this familiar and notable leader was widely mourned. Stores in Lexington and throughout the country closed the afternoon of April 14 and memorial services were held.

Three weeks later they closed again, but for a happier occasion as news of victory in Europe was welcomed in a quiet and solemn manner, for the war still went on in the Pacific. A few months later came the momentous news that a new and incredibly powerful atomic bomb had been dropped on Hiroshima on August 6, and within three days another was detonated over Nagasaki. The capitulation of the Japanese followed shortly after. On August 15, 1945, Lexingtonians poured into the streets to celebrate enthusiastically the news of Japan's surrender and the end of this gigantic conflict in which 246 men from Fayette County had lost their lives.

Gleaming, new office buildings flank downtown Lexington's Vine Street in this photo looking west from Limestone Street in the spring of 1982.

Chapter IX

1945/1982

A City Transformed

In the postwar years, Lexington and Fayette County shared in the economic resurgence that characterized the nation as a whole, due to the pent-up consumer demand for goods and services. Transylvania and the University of Kentucky enjoyed an enrollment boom as hundreds of returning veterans took advantage of the "G. I. Bill of Rights" to acquire a college education many had never thought possible in the depression years of the 1930's.

Yet, the general pattern of life in this Bluegrass city in the years immediately following the war was a continuation of the pre-war era. Few could have predicted the tremendous changes of the next thirty-five years that would transform this community into one of the fastest growing cities in the United States. Not only would there develop an industrial and manufacturing complex larger in scope than the Chamber of Commerce had dreamed of, but the population would more than double, new housing and subdivisions would move relentlessly into the farmlands, the University of Kentucky and Transylvania would rebuild and expand their campuses and increase their enrollments, and the Albert B. Chandler Medical Center would be established on the UK campus which, along with numerous other hospitals and clinics, would make Lexington a major regional center for medical services. The entire character of downtown was profoundly changed as the heavily concentrated retail nucleus was atomized, spreading out into numerous malls and shopping centers ringing

the city, and was replaced by high-rise banks, office buildings, and hotels. The completion of the vast interstate highway system, with a strategic juncture at Lexington, accelerated the transformation.

The governmental structure that had administered city and county affairs for the past century and a half could not successfully cope with the complex of problems and diverse activities resulting from such expansion. The logical and inventive solution was a merged urban-county government. This did not come about without stress, however. While it caused dismay among some of the older, longtime residents, it energized others in the community. Some might have agreed with Gilbert King, a leader in the establishment of the city waterworks in the 1880's, who said

> The poet says: "There is a tide in the affairs of men, which taken at its flood leads on to fortune," and I believe that Lexington must now either advance, or take a permanent position in the rear of progress.

Lexington had by no means been a stagnant community, as the record shows. Population had grown from decade to decade, new businesses were opened, and more homes were built. With a county population of 100,746 in 1950, of which at least 75 percent was in the urban embrace of Lexington, the city was primarily a retail and wholesale trade and service center for the Bluegrass region and eastern Kentucky. Among the community's more notable assets were its prosperous tobacco industry and livestock markets, an expanding horse economy, two growing universities, and a countryside of exceptional beauty. Its way of life was generally pleasant, unhurried and traditional.

Lexingtonians in 1946 could boast of three radio stations, as WKLX and WLEX joined WLAP that year. Work began on a beltline highway from Georgetown Road to the Richmond Road that would eventually encircle the city. Piedmont Airlines joined Eastern and Delta in serving Blue Grass Field. The black community had a brand new theatre of its own when the Lyric was completed on the corner of Dewees and Third streets. An interracial baseball team, formed in 1945, was for a few years one of the top semi-professional teams in the state. Negro owned and operated, it was called The Hustlers, and played on a field near the Newtown Road before mixed crowds often numbering 2,000.

Both Harry Truman and Tom Dewey thought Lexington worth a visit in the hard-fought Presidential contest in 1948, and Fayette County cast its vote for the feisty Democrat who won such a stunning upset. Local politics were almost dull by comparison.

The city government attempted time and again to overcome the opposition of the anti-annexationists who were preventing a desperately needed expansion of the city limits. Soon, as many urbanites would be living outside as within the city limits, drawing heavily on certain city services, but paying only the lower county taxes. The failure to extend sewer services to the residential areas beyond the city led to dependence on thousands of septic tanks which drained into permeable limestone and created a sewage disposal problem of critical proportions.

This problem was dodged for years as Lexingtonians were preoccupied with other interests, such as their enthusiastic support for the winning University of Kentucky basketball and football teams of Adolph Rupp and Paul "Bear" Bryant. The spacious sports arena, Memorial Coliseum, dedicated on May 30, 1950, manifested the desire of Kentuckians to commemorate their servicemen, and to honor Rupp's sensational teams. In 1948 the UK team was chosen to represent the United States in the Olympics. Rupp's teams dominated the

Southeastern Conference and then moved on to win the National Collegiate Athletic Association (NCAA) championships in 1948, 1949, 1951 and 1958. Even the so-called "fix" scandals of 1951, which banned Kentucky from SEC play for a year, did not dampen the devotion of the crowds of students and fans that packed Memorial Coliseum for every basketball game, making the sport the most popular in the state. This tradition is continuing under Rupp's successor, Joe B. Hall.

For a few years, "Bear" Bryant kept UK's football teams in the same winning tradition as Rupp's basketball teams. With the brilliant "Babe" Parilli as quarterback, UK enjoyed winning seasons in 1949 and the early 1950's, playing in the Orange Bowl in 1950, the Sugar Bowl in 1951, and the Cotton Bowl in 1952. Bryant left UK in 1954 to become head football coach at Texas A & M, but was soon persuaded by President Frank Rose to coach at the University of Alabama. UK's football prowess has never regained the heights reached under Bryant.

The Bluegrass Industrial Revolution

Business activity in Lexington in the early 1950's showed only moderate growth. A new million-dollar Greyhound Bus Terminal, said to be one of the finest in the region, had been finished in 1948 on East Short and the Esplanade. In November 1949, the local telephone system introduced dial service. Technological advances of this nature were not achieved painlessly. One man wanted his old phone back. Another customer became hysterical while trying to use the new system and medical aid was summoned. Then there was a lady who reported her phone was dead. "Had she waited for the dial tone?" she was asked. "Yes," she replied plaintively, "I've been waiting for it since Sunday." Apparently no such traumatic experiences accompanied the introduction of television into Lexington with the establishment of WLEX-TV, Channel 18, in 1955.

Other business growth was evidenced by the opening in 1950 of Wolf Wile's new department store on Main Street, on the site of the old bus station. Stewart's moved into Wolf Wile's old store adjacent to the Union Station. New industries such as Archer & Smith, Big Run Coal & Clay Company, Kawneer, Marco

Wolf Wile's new department store building at Main and Quality streets was opened in 1950.

Products, and Standard Products located in Lexington at this time, some of them later closing or moving away. Brock-McVey expanded its warehouse and sales offices.

New building activity was reflected in the opening of the Central Baptist Hospital in 1954 and the new Shriners' Hospital a year later. The College of the Bible (now the Lexington Theological Seminary) dedicated its campus and buildings on South Limestone in 1950, and Lexington's first suburban hotel, the Campbell House, was completed in 1951.

This piecemeal construction was hardly the answer to Lexington's economic needs. One of the city's problems was the rather high level of seasonal unemployment due to the heavy dependence on the tobacco industry. A conviction that a new strategy was needed to reduce unemployment and enlarge the industrial base led to the formation in 1956 of the Lexington Industrial Foundation, a nonprofit organization headed by Caruthers A. Coleman, Sr., and later led by Floyd Fairman, vice-president of Kentucky Utilities, with the support of other business leaders. The Foundation bought a 139-acre tract of land north of Meadowthorpe and invested sizable

sums in providing sewers, water and gas supplies, storm water drainage, and access roads.

With this basic acreage and such essential services established, and with the added advantages of Lexington's strategic geographical location, ample supplies of investment capital and labor, good transportation systems, both highway and rail, dependable sources of coal and gas, acceptable levels of taxation, and a pleasant climate and attractive surroundings, the Foundation began to attract the attention of out-of-state companies. Soon, such major firms as Square D, manufacturer of electrical distribution equipment, Dixie Cup, and Mengel Company, a subsidiary of the Container Corporation of America, manufacturer of corrugated paper boxes and other products, were persuaded to purchase tracts on this site.

A "symbol" of the community's industrial expansion of the mid-years of the present century is the 180-foot tall "Dixie Cup" water tower of the James River-Dixie/Northern plant on Mercer Road.

It was fortuitous that at about the same time, the giant IBM corporation had decided to move its electric typewriter division here. As early as 1954, IBM had been scouting the area as a possible site. In 1956, favorable reports led IBM officials to make an in-depth investigation, including a study of the local schools and industrial plants, and to conduct interviews with UK President Donovan, a representative from the UK College of Engineering, and city officials. Members of the Chamber of Commerce and the Lexington Industrial Foundation urged IBM to locate here. A call from Governor A. B. Chandler to Thomas Watson, Sr., IBM president, apparently tipped the scales when Chandler made a tempting offer of a large tract of state land adjoining Eastern State Hospital at a reasonable price. The property had once been a part of the mental institution's extensive farming operations. Later, Marathon Industries purchased a 10-acre site adjacent to IBM to build a plant that would finish typewriter stands.

On the south end of town, R. J. Reynolds Tobacco Company purchased 283 acres on which to build twelve warehouses.

This impressive industrial growth within a brief period of two years was a stunning accomplishment, and marked the turning point in the transformation of Lexington into an expanding, dynamic metropolitan community.

IBM was the most significant single industry to settle in the city. Starting production in 1956, and bringing some 250 families from New York to Lexington, the plant began full-scale production in 1958, and by 1963 employed 3,494 men and women. By 1981, it employed about 6,000 persons, second only to the University of Kentucky which, with 10,000 employees, was Lexington's largest employer. Square D started operations in 1958 and by 1963 employed 1,156 persons. Not long afterward, it was joined by the Trane Corporation.

Among the larger existing manufacturing operations that formed a part of Lexington's greatly expanded industrial community were the Irving Air Chute Company, Inc., employing 1,100, the Standard Products Company, and the General Electric Company's Lexington Lamp and Kentucky Glass plants.

Employment in Lexington rose 260 percent between 1954 and 1963. Moreover, the city was fortunate in attracting what are generally termed as "clean" industries. There were no chemical, oil refining, or steel plants, so that the air remained relatively free of pollution and odor. And this continues to be the case in 1982.

Aerial view of IBM's electric typewriter plant on New Circle Road, Lexington's largest industrial facility. IBM was one of a number of national firms to locate new manufacturing operations in the city during the community's "industrial revolution" of the 1950's and 1960's. Photo courtesy of IBM.

A typical scene during the buying season at one of Lexington's many tobacco warehouses. More than $164 million of burley was sold in the Lexington market in the 1981-82 sales season. Photo courtesy of Lexington Herald-Leader Company.

The industrial structure is well diversified among the manufacturing of food and associated items, tobacco stemming and redrying, electrical and non-electrical machinery, apparel and related goods, lumber and wood materials, printing and related industries, stone, clay, glass, and fabricated metal products. The value of Lexington's manufacturing output in 1950 was approximately $39 million compared to its combined retail and wholesale trade of $319 million. But with the influx of new industry, value added by manufacturing between 1954 and 1963 leaped to $143 million. By 1977, 216 local manufacturers raised that figure to $801 million. The impact on the wholesale, retail, and service industries was enormous.

Lexington's work force is distributed among manufacturing, wholesale and retail trade, construction, federal, state and local government, and services, the latter rapidly expanding as the population grows.

Between 1955 and 1962, more than 9,000 people moved into Lexington and Fayette County, of whom two-thirds came from out of state and the remaining one-third from the central Bluegrass and eastern Kentucky. The demand for housing, schools, and expanded city services became intense.

In 1950, Lexington's population, still cramped within its statutory limits, was 55,534 and the whole of Fayette County's was 100,746. By 1960, these figures had grown to 62,810 and 131,906, respectively. The phenomenal increase came in the next decade. The city in 1970 had a population of 108,137 and the county 174,323, a fantastic 32 percent gain that placed Lexington among the fastest growing communities in the nation. By 1980, the merged government had eliminated city and county differentials, and the population of the county, including the city, totaled 204,165, a 17 percent ten-year increase. Of this total, 13 percent were blacks. At present, Lexington has

At the Keeneland annual summer sales in 1982, this colt by Nijinsky II was sold for $4.25 million, a world record sum for a publicly-auctioned Thoroughbred yearling. Photo courtesy of the Thoroughbred Record.

a median age of about 28, but the community is growing older more quickly than the rest of Kentucky.

Meanwhile, the number of dwellings multiplied at an impressive rate. In 1950, there was a total of 27,905. This rose to 59,528 in 1970 and to more than 76,000 by 1980.

Tobacco and Horse Industries

Lexington's traditional tobacco industry prospered during the postwar period despite growing concern over increasing evidence linking smoking to cancer and heart disease. Over the past 40 years the city had become one of the largest burley tobacco markets in the world. During the 1981-82 marketing season, tobacco processors paid $164,459,095 for 90,693,299 pounds of burley grown by Kentucky farmers. The impact on Lexington's economy of such heavy sales activity has been significant since many tobacco farmers buy a large volume of goods in the community.

In addition, the city's importance as a tobacco center is enhanced by the fact that the headquarters of the Burley Tobacco Growers Cooperative Association, organized in 1921, is located here. This organization administers the tobacco price support program in five states.

The breeding and sale of race horses was another traditional industry to fare well in the postwar era. The Keeneland annual sales, joined in recent years by Thoroughbred vendues sponsored by Fasig-Tipton and other marketing groups, were attracting horse buyers from all over the world. New records in prices paid for these magnificent "individuals," as many horsemen are wont to call their charges, were established every year. At the Keeneland annual summer sales in 1982, a colt by Nijinsky II, (son of Northern Dancer, one of the great sires of this century) was auctioned off at $4.25 million, a world record sum for a Thoroughbred yearling. Revenues from Standardbred sales also continued to increase. More than 900 yearlings brought a total of $31 million at the 1981 annual auctions of Tattersalls and the Kentucky Standardbred Sales Company.

The Bursting School System

The difficulties of dual city-county divisions — instead of a single governmental unit — dealing with Lexington's fast-growing population were especially critical and frustrating for the public schools. When Dr. Noah Turpen was appointed county school superintendent in 1949, he saw the crises appearing on the horizon and supported the recommendation of consultants that the two school systems be merged. However, a different salary schedule, different tax rates, different fiscal years, and "more subtly, a perceived difference in quality of programs by a majority of the city school staff," blocked merger. Turpen acted to improve the county schools, closing a number of the older, smaller facilities, building Clay's Mill and Yates elementary schools, remodeling the existing Lafayette High School buildings to add a junior high school, and beginning construction of Glendover Elementary School.

The segregation barrier in higher education mandated by the 1904 Day Law had already been challenged successfully. As early as 1941, Negroes had applied futilely for admission to the University of Kentucky. However, when Lyman Johnson, a 42-year-old Louisville schoolteacher and Navy veteran, was refused admission to the University's graduate school in 1949, he brought suit in Federal District Court. Judge H. Church Ford ordered the University of Kentucky to admit Negroes to its graduate school and Colleges of Law, Engineering, and Pharmacy because comparable programs were not offered at Kentucky State College at Frankfort. After a heated debate, the UK trustees accepted President Donovan's recommendation to forego appealing the court's decision. In the summer of 1949, Johnson and twenty-nine other blacks registered and attended classes at the University of Kentucky. Some threats were heard and a few crosses burned on campus, but there were no acts of violence.

Within five years, the U. S. Supreme Court handed down a landmark decision in the *Brown v. Board of Education* case of 1954, which reversed the 1896 "separate but equal" doctrine as applied to laws requiring segregation. At the time, Fayette County was operating only one black school — Douglas, grades 1 through 12. When Dr. James B. Kincheloe succeeded Turpen as county school superintendent in 1957, he faced both the integration problem and the massive wave of pupil enrollment increases caused by the postwar "baby boom" and the influx of new families accompanying industrial expansion.

In 1950, the county schools enrolled 5,900 pupils, 10 percent of whom were blacks, and the city had 6,100 enrollees, of whom 34 percent were blacks. By 1960, the county enrollment had exploded to 13,000 and the city's had grown to 8,300. During Kincheloe's four-year term, Bryan Station Senior High, and James Lane Allen, Mary Todd, and Leestown

elementary schools were opened, yet numbers outpaced facilities.

Additional large sums of money were needed desperately in both the city and county to handle this crisis. Incredibly, the electorate stubbornly defeated proposed tax increases in 1959 and 1960 despite the large number of families whose own children would have benefited from the higher levies. Both the city and county school boards were forced to take emergency measures. The entire kindergarten program was scuttled, and students were jammed into remodeled existing buildings, church buildings, and even Hamilton Hall, a former Transylvania girls' dormitory.

When Dr. Guy Potts replaced Kincheloe as county superintendent in June 1961, he persuaded the County Board of Education to attempt another public vote on tax increases. A well-coordinated and highly-publicized campaign turned the tide and the voters approved the increase in the spring of 1962. From 1962 to 1967, eleven new schools were opened in addition to Stonewall and Meadowthorpe whose construction had begun before the vote. The Federal Civil Rights Act of 1964 increased pressure to implement the desegregation decision of ten years earlier. Fayette County under Dr. Potts' leadership moved to respond to the mandate. The inadequate Douglas High School was temporarily closed, and then for a time converted into an integrated elementary school. By 1966 there was a sufficient distribution of black students in the county schools to receive federal approval.

The city school system presented a more difficult problem because retaining a neighborhood school policy only preserved segregated schools. Nor did the freedom of choice policy, used as an experimental device for several years, produce any significant change. Black students accounted for about 40 percent of the city's enrollment. There were not enough school buses, and school revenues were inadequate. Merger of the two systems was the only answer, and the Kentucky Court of Appeals mandated merger in July 1967. Dr. Potts now headed a combined Fayette County School system. A new Henry Clay High School was built. Dunbar Senior High was closed and the entire black student body was divided among the four other high schools, a decision which caused deep resentment in the black community as Dunbar had been a source of pride for many years.

In the process, a suit was initiated by a black citizens' group in 1971 charging the Fayette County School Board with violating the 1964 Civil Rights Act and the 14th Amendment, thus placing the matter in Judge Mac Swinford's U. S. District Court. This resulted in the creation of a new desegregation plan which Judge Swinford approved, and which was sustained by the U. S. Sixth Circuit Court. Fayette County schools were now considered to be in compliance with federal law as of the fall of 1972.

Under this plan, Carver, Constitution, Jefferson Davis, and Dunbar schools were closed and approximately 4,500 pupils were reassigned. Despite objections, occasional incidents of conflict, and the recognition of still existing racial prejudice in both white and black groups, Fayette County did not experience the mass confrontations and violence seen in some communities elsewhere in the nation.

The merged school system under able leadership has brought Fayette County public education to a level of quality unprecedented in

its history and more commensurate with the citizens' expectations.

The historic Sayre School and the recently established Lexington School continue the tradition of excellent private education.

Unprecedented Campus Growth

Lexington's institutions of higher learning were also expanding. Transylvania, under the energetic leadership of Frank Rose, who left in 1957 to become the president of the University of Alabama, and Irvin Lunger, whose 18-year term was the longest in the school's history, experienced unprecedented growth. Not only did its student body double, and then triple, in numbers and the quality of programs and faculty improve, but the physical campus was literally rebuilt between 1954 and 1970. Old Morrison, which had had its exterior restored to its original design in the 1960's, suffered a devastating fire in 1969, but remained sufficiently intact to enable restoration of its classic appearance, while the interior was completely remodeled and modernized. Under President William W. Kelly, Transylvania celebrated its bicentennial in 1980-81 with an impressive display of Matthew Jouett portraits

Happy students heading for cars and homes at the end of the class day at Henry Clay Senior High School on Fontaine Road, one of more than a dozen new schools built in the city since 1962. Photo courtesy of Lexington-Herald Leader Company.

and silverware crafted by 19th century central Bluegrass silversmiths, as well as fairs, lectures, and a grand ball. A remarkably successful capital funds campaign, led by businessman William T. Young, provided the school with the first substantial endowment in its long history.

The University of Kentucky expanded prodigiously under the forceful leadership of President John W. Oswald, who succeeded Frank G. Dickey in 1963. The opening of the Chandler Medical Center, anchored by new Colleges of Medicine, Dentistry and Nursing, profoundly affected the scope and character of the university. Under Dean William R. Willard's leadership, an outstanding faculty was recruited. Though there was dissatisfaction over salary differentials between medical and dental schools' faculties and the faculties of the other colleges of the university, the goals and quality of the university were raised. Oswald's policies were designed to bring the University of Kentucky into the forefront of southern universities. Much overhauling, reorganization, and tension resulted, a situation Dr. Otis Singletary faced when he succeeded Oswald in 1968. The demonstrations and violence associated with student anti-Viet Nam war protests and the problems of drugs and general student unrest Singletary likewise inherited. The post-Watergate and post-Kent State period proved to be more tranquil. The university, with an enrollment of over 20,000 on the Lexington campus, has achieved notable progress since 1950, including the building of many fine, new facilities, such as the 58,000-seat Commonwealth Stadium for football.

While the University of Kentucky is the largest single employer in Lexington, thus forming a major component of the local economy, and the public shares enthusiastically in the school's sports and cultural events, there has not been as much interaction between city and university planning as might have been anticipated. Though the merged government, as part of the new Lexington Center, supported the construction of a giant sports arena named for the University's most famous coach, which has provided additional exposure for its basketball teams, the two communities operate independently of each other in many respects.

However, the presence of the University of Kentucky and the smaller Transylvania

University continues to enhance the cultural dimension of life in Lexington.

The Civil Rights Movement

The Supreme Court's school desegregation decision of 1954 also accelerated the civil rights movement in the areas of voting and equal access to public transportation and public facilities. The rise of Martin Luther King, Jr., and the bus boycott in Montgomery, Alabama, dramatized that change. The issue was highlighted in the memorable "March on Washington" in the summer of 1963 and the enactment of the Civil Rights Act of 1964. In Lexington, educational barriers were the first to fall, and by the mid-1950's the University of Kentucky was admitting black undergraduates as well as graduate students. The National Association for the Advancement of Colored People (NAACP) organized a Lexington chapter in 1945 and within a year had raised a bi-racial membership of over 300. The local chapter of the Congress of Racial Equality (CORE) was organized in the 1950's and claimed more than 100 members by the end of the decade.

Following Martin Luther King's example of nonviolent demonstration against discrimination in public facilities, a number of blacks, mostly students, were organized by CORE and the NAACP with some assistance from white Transylvania and UK students, and engaged in a series of sit-ins in 1960 at Main Street lunch counters. Lamont Jones, who led the first attempt to integrate eating establishments, later recalled that there was little overt violence, but some of the demonstrators suffered indignities such as having water or coffee spilled on them or finding counters chained off. This problem was dramatized when on October 18, 1961, five Negro members of the Boston Celtics, in town to play an exhibition basketball game with the St. Louis Hawks at Memorial Coliseum, were refused service at the Phoenix Hotel coffee shop. They departed on the next plane. This left only the white players of the Celtics to perform, among whom was Frank Ramsey, a former UK star.

The sit-ins and boycotts eventually proved effective. By the mid-1960's, most of the discriminatory policies of theaters and restaurants, and maintenance of separate facilities at the Greyhound Bus Terminal were abolished. An unexpected result was the disastrous effect on the Lyric Theater which lost patronage and was obliged to close down because its exclusively black clientele was now able to go to any theater they wished without experiencing discriminatory seating policies.

Pressure was placed on employers engaging in discriminatory hiring practices. The Lexington *Herald* and *Leader* were criticized for their reluctance to report these and other civil rights events and issues. It was said this policy was based on a belief that publicizing conflict only engendered more. One of the largest demonstrations occurred in 1963 when approximately 250 blacks and some whites marched from both the Pleasant Green and Greater Liberty Baptist churches. Singing as they went, they met on Main Street and picketed the newspapers.

In 1963, the Lexington Commission on Human Rights — an outgrowth of the Committee on Religion and Human Rights of the late 1950's — was established by local ordinance, and three years later was given enforcement powers in the areas of housing, employment, and public accommodations.

A ten-year campaign to abolish the column in the *Leader* headed, "Colored Notes," which had been published for decades, finally resulted in its demise in 1967. There was sharp disagreement in the black community itself over this issue since many readers believed the "Notes" gave them more identity and coverage than they would otherwise receive.

For the black community, 1963 was a landmark year as Harry Sykes was elected Lexington's first black city commissioner. A tall, amiable, and popular figure, this former member of the famed Harlem Globetrotters basketball team was reelected three times. He ran unsuccessfully for mayor against Foster Pettit in 1971.

Carl Lynem, a Lexington insurance man, was the first black to be elected to the School Board. One of the most promising leaders in the black community, Lynem died tragically in an automobile accident. After his death, he was replaced by the Reverend H. H. Greene, another active and familiar community leader.

The most violent outburst by blacks in Lexington — during an era which saw

In 1963, Harry Sykes became the first black to be elected as a city commissioner. Photo courtesy of Lexington Herald-Leader Company.

explosive riots in Watts and Newark — was sparked by the news that Martin Luther King had been assassinated in Memphis. Most of the acts of arson and vandalism were committed by teenagers. Harry Sykes did much to calm the situation by walking the streets for several nights and talking to the people, and a number of other black leaders also counseled moderation.

A group of ministers and other concerned citizens called a mass meeting at Second Presbyterian Church to consider priorities for actions recommended by a separate meeting of black leaders. Though over 700 persons attended, little of consequence resulted.

On September 4, 1968, the drugstore of Zirl Palmer in the Georgetown Plaza was bombed by men reported to be members of the Ku Klux Klan, seriously injuring Palmer. He had been operating the only black pharmacy in Lexington since 1951. Active in many community organizations, Palmer was later appointed to the University of Kentucky Board of Trustees, the first black to serve in that capacity.

In the 1960's, Sykes provided the leadership in organizing a branch of the Urban League, long advocated by such men as Dr. T. B. Biggerstaff. Sykes served as its first president and assisted in having it accepted as a United Way agency. Under its present executive director, Porter Peeples, it continues to seek wider participation of blacks in the economic sector of Lexington.

Under the Economic Opportunity Act of 1964, the organization known as Community Action Lexington-Fayette County (CALF) was formed to focus on the problems of the low-income population. Since 1964 the agency has developed and administered a wide variety of programs. These include Project Head Start, which is designed to enhance the educational and social competence of three to five-year-old children, day care, and transportation for elderly persons for medical and other essential purposes. An outreach and referral program has been operated to maintain contact with people in the lower socio-economic level. The extent and variety of CALF's programs have fluctuated with the amount of federal, state, and local funding.

One of the most unusual projects funded by CALF has been the Micro-City Government, started in 1970, whose purpose is to help young people work together to develop their talents and improve their community. Led by Ronald Berry since its inception, this para-governmental body has assisted school dropouts, young people with drug and delinquency problems, and others who need counseling, tutoring, or jobs. It also has operated free lunch programs for children.

Another source of federal government aid for the low and moderate income population since 1976 has been the Community Development Block Grant Program. Monies from this fund have been used to renovate Black and Williams, Carver, and Dunbar community centers; to finance the Pralltown development program; to fund housing rehabilitation, historic preservation, public improvements such as ramps for the handicapped, and downtown redevelopment studies.

Trains filled the downtown air with excitement, noise and pollution before removal of the railroad tracks on Water Street and conversion of this artery into a modern boulevard, Vine Street, in the late 1960's. Photo courtesy L&N Railroad archives.

Downtown and Suburban Development

Downtown was faced with the challenge of upgrading its appearance and retail appeal, and of providing easy access and adequate parking. The railroad tracks that ran through the heart of town were a major obstacle to such improvements. During the heyday of rail transportation, a downtown depot and trackage had been essential to moving the city's passenger and freight traffic, but now the tracks thwarted the expansion of modern-day enterprises along Vine and Water streets and impeded the movement of automobiles and pedestrians.

With the institution of a federal urban renewal program in the 1960's, Lexington had the opportunity to rebuild some of the downtown sector. The program made possible razing, rehabilitation, and new construction on a scope broader than ever envisioned because of the availability of matching federal funds, which provided financial resources that had not been previously available. Fred Fugazzi, who had already served one term as mayor from 1952 to 1956 and fought courageously to pass the city payroll tax so essential for badly needed revenue, was reelected mayor for the 1964-68 period. Though the Union Station had been torn down in 1960, previous administrations had regarded the removal of the railroad tracks as an impossibility. But Fugazzi was determined to accomplish this, for on their removal depended the implementation of a significant urban renewal program.

With $9,500,000 made available in the proposed urban renewal budget (of which $4,058,000 was from the federal government and the remainder from the city), successful negotiations were conducted with the railroads to remove the downtown trackage. Lexington was one of the few cities in the United States engaged in urban renewal to undertake such a task, which resulted in routing the L & N and C & O trains around Lexington by connections with the old Beltline railroad tracks. Fugazzi, who was then serving as City Commissioner, played a leading role in track removal ceremonies on December 18, 1968, which were attended by approximately 1,000 persons.

In the summer of 1966, the Lexington Urban Renewal and Community Development Agency began its operations in the area bounded by Midland, Main, Patterson, and High streets. Of the 268 structures involved, 68 percent were to be rehabilitated and 37 percent razed. Some 55 businesses, 44 families, and 71 individuals were affected. The largest manufacturing structure to be torn down was the historic Lexington Roller Mills at Broadway and Vine streets.

The way was now clear for the submission of plans by the city and private developers for a major restructuring of downtown Lexington. Included in such plans would be the fulfillment of Lexington's long postponed goal of a municipal center or auditorium.

A new investment in downtown Lexington paralleling urban renewal activity was the $3 million expansion of Stewart's that included a four-story addition and a multi-level parking facility. A new financial institution, the Bank of Lexington, opened for business in 1966 on East Main, and eventually built one of the structures in the urban renewal area on the northeast corner of Vine and Limestone streets. Also significant to downtown was the announcement in 1963 that Garvice D. Kincaid, an increasingly influential financial figure in Lexington's economy, had decided to move the headquarters of Kentucky Central Life Insurance Company, the state's oldest life insurer, founded in 1902, of which he was the chief executive officer, from suburban Louisville to the former Lafayette Hotel, remodeled at a cost of several million dollars.

On the outskirts of town, enhancing Lexington's image as a progressive community, was the establishment of Spindletop Research Center in 1960 on the Ironworks Road, attractively situated on part of the Spindletop estate. Within a decade, the Council of State Governments decided to move from Chicago and locate its headquarters, library, and editorial staff in Lexington on a site close by the Research Center, which now houses the State Center for Energy Research.

In the same vicinity, near the Lexington-Cincinnati interstate highway, the Kentucky state government created a major tourist attraction — the Kentucky Horse Park. The large increase in tourists wishing to visit the private horse farms had created such problems as to force the closing of many of these farms to visitors. Yet, most tourists traveling to the Bluegrass came, in large part,

City Commissioner Fred Fugazzi who, as mayor in 1964, envisioned removal of the railroad tracks from downtown Lexington, participated in track removal ceremonies on December 17, 1968. Traffic Engineer Joseph Heidenreich, who aided Fugazzi in the project, is at right. Photo courtesy of Lexington Herald-Leader Company.

to see the horses and the famous farms that bred them. To solve this problem, the idea of developing a special horse park within the Kentucky state park system was conceived by Representative William Kenton of Lexington and received the endorsement of Governor Wendell Ford and the General Assembly in 1972. Being central to the horse industry, Fayette County was chosen as the site, and between 1972 and 1976 some 1,000 acres were purchased for this purpose, the larger portion being bought from the Walnut Hall Stud farm. An elaborate complex of new buildings, renovated structures, and a seven-acre ornamental lake were built at a cost of nearly $27 million.

The statue of Man o' War was moved to the main entrance, and the remains of the famed jockey, Isaac Murphy, were reinterred close by. The park was opened with great fanfare in September 1978, by hosting for the first time in the United States the World Championship Three-Day Event. Prince Philip of Great Britain, an official of the equestrian

organization sponsoring the event, came to Lexington for the occasion, thus adding a royal flavor.

Though not yet attracting the volume of patrons hoped for, the Kentucky Horse Park has benefited Lexington because of the uniqueness and quality of the facility and the income derived from the increased number of tourists.

"Urban sprawl," as it has been called, was a phenomenon of the post-war era not only in Lexington but all over the nation. As America's love affair with the automobile grew more intense and as home ownership was made easier by the federal government's FHA and VA mortgage programs, residential and commercial developments spread farther and farther into the countryside. In Fayette County, new homes sprouted up almost overnight in such areas as Southland, Gainesway, Lansdowne, Eastland and Meadowthorpe. Between 1950 and 1980, motor vehicle registrations in the county rose nearly five-fold, from 31,410 to 147,403. This movement, in turn, precipitated the collapse of

Turfland Mall and Harrod Hills, both in the southern part of the city off Harrodsburg Road, were typical of shopping centers and residential subdivisions built in the 1960-80 period to accommodate Lexington's rapid growth.

the privately-owned local transportation system in 1973 and its replacement by a privately-managed, tax-supported operation, LexTran. In just sixteen years, 1956 to 1972, the local bus system had lost 36 percent of its fare-paying passengers.

Historic Preservation

As promising as urban renewal appeared to be for reviving and restructuring downtown Lexington, it also posed a serious threat to the preservation of historically significant buildings that formed part of Lexington's heritage. Despite its rich history, Lexington had been as casual, if not indifferent, toward the preservation of its architectural past as many other American communities. Razing deteriorated historic structures and replacing them with parking lots, or removing them as a matter of convenience to avoid expensive upkeep, occurred in such a piecemeal and haphazard fashion that residents were hardly conscious of the ominous pattern that was emerging.

What triggered organized resistance to the unexamined and unchallenged continuation of this practice was the demolition of the Colonel Thomas Hart-John Bradford-Laura Clay house on the southwest corner of Mill and Second streets in March, 1955. The Hunt-Morgan house across the street was threatened with the same fate, but a group of concerned citizens organized the Foundation for the Preservation of Historic Lexington and Fayette County, soon renamed the Blue Grass Trust for Historic Preservation, in April, 1955. Their first act was to purchase the Hunt-Morgan house, saving it from destruction, and over the years gradually restoring it to its original architectural distinctiveness.

In succeeding years, the Blue Grass Trust has expanded its membership, bolstered its finances through dues and fund-raising events, initiated a program of identifying historically and architecturally significant buildings in Lexington with "BGT" plaques, and established a revolving fund for the purchase of historically valuable buildings and their resale with deed restrictions.

The most dramatic confrontation between the Blue Grass Trust, supported by other concerned preservationists, and the urban

The Western Suburb in the West Short Street area, one of several historic districts in the city where building renovation continues.

renewal program occurred in 1971. Plans for the new Citizens Union Bank building and other structures required the razing of three blocks of historic houses on the north side of West High Street between Limestone Street and Broadway, including the Adam Rankin house, one of the oldest houses in Lexington. Though planners at one time said the houses could be saved, they later argued that it was not feasible. Despite attempts to save the houses by court injunctions, demonstrations, and all-night vigils, the bulldozers won out. Only the Rankin house was saved when it was moved by the Blue Grass Trust to South Mill Street.

The concern for preservation stimulated the organization of numerous other citizens' groups, which focused their energy and attention not only on the preservation of buildings and areas but also on those aspects of the community contributing to the quality of life in these areas. Neighborhood associations, such as the Northside Association established in 1961, and others such as the Bell Court, Woodward Heights, and Western Suburb (Short Street) associations have worked actively toward these goals.

The Bluegrass Land and Nature Trust was formed to alert local residents to the various threats to the natural environment of the region.

Interest was reawakened in saving the decaying Mary Todd Lincoln house on West Main Street, which was endangered by the expanding downtown building program. Thanks to the enthusiastic leadership of Mrs. Beulah Nunn, wife of former Governor Louie Nunn, and a Federal grant, a movement was started in 1971 to collect additional funds to make plans for the restoration of this structure. Dedicated in June 1977, after thorough restoration, the house has become a major downtown tourist attraction.

Another important restoration project undertaken during this period was that of Henry Clay's law office on North Mill Street.

In preparation for celebrating the local and national bicentennials and to support the community's growing concern for historic preservation, the Lexington-Fayette County Historic Commission was created by joint action of the City and County in 1973. Its purpose is to "maintain surveillance of historic areas and buildings ... to prevent buildings and areas from being demolished with no advance warning and to submit recommendations on all matters relating to the preservation, conservation, and enhancement of historic buildings and areas."

Once used as an academy of Transylvania, the partially renovated Gratz Kitchen on Market Street now houses the Historic Commission, which has published important works on Lexington's history and architecture, conducted extensive surveys of city and county structures and sites, and publicized its aims, resources, and programs. Starting in May 1974, and for several years thereafter, the Commission planned celebrations for the Bicentennial that featured horse racing on Vine Street, arts and crafts exhibits, parades, entertainment, and street dancing.

Though a number of older buildings have been restored, it is perhaps too soon to say whether the combined efforts of the aforementioned organizations have stemmed the tide of casual or indifferent destruction of important city landmarks. The pressure for modernization and profit and the tendency toward architectural mediocrity and monotony are formidable. However, there is evidence of a greater awareness among some developers of the need to preserve Lexington's special features, architectural and otherwise, and this could bring the forces of expansion and conservation into better balance.

The Underwood Interlude

In the onward thrust of Lexington's expansion and change, two notable events occurred in the 1970-74 period that had a substantial impact on that progress. One was the election of Thomas R. Underwood Jr., Ray Boggs, and Paul Fowler to the City Commission in 1969. The other was the approval of a merged Lexington-Fayette Urban County Government in 1972 and its installation in January 1974.

Underwood, a practicing attorney, was the son of Thomas R. Underwood, Sr., who had been a U. S. Congressman and Senator and editor of the *Herald.* Young Underwood had served several terms as a city commissioner under Mayors Fugazzi and Charles Wylie. The popular outcry against a 1968-69 sewer service charge, which was instituted to fund a bond issue for enlargement of the city's sewage treatment facilities, provided Underwood with an ideal election platform. Frequently a minority voice in actions taken by the City Commission, he created a three-man bloc called the "People's Ticket" which ran its 1969 campaign on the promise to remove the sewer service charge. The voters gave the Underwood trio a winning majority, leaving Mayor Charles Wylie and Harry Sykes, the other members of the Commission, as a constant minority.

The two years that Underwood, Boggs, and Fowler controlled the Commission were among the most controversial in the city's history. Though the actions of this bloc in deferring a decision on the civic center, firing the architectural firm employed to draw the plans, and initiating a 5 percent rental tax on hotel and motel rooms drew critical response, the first dramatic controversy erupted with the initiation of a 55-year, later 57-year, mandatory retirement age ordinance for police and firemen, and a reduction in the health department budget. Two thousand signatures were secured on a petition protesting the retirement policy and the Commission chambers became an arena of intense confrontations between Underwood and his critics. These sessions created a field day for the press, and Lexington newspaper readers avidly followed the activities of the city government.

Another tense situation was precipitated by the public library budget. In contrast to the city's "Athens of the West" image, the public library had long been low on the city's and county's budgetary totem poles. Dr. Irvin Lunger, president of Transylvania and chairman of the library's Board of Trustees, had pressed for a long overdue program of expansion and adequate financing. The City Commission, under his urging, had supplemented the library appropriation in 1969 by $95,000, for a total of $249,975. When the Underwood budget provided only $166,610 for the library, Lunger responded by stating that such inadequate financing would necessitate discontinuing bookmobile service, closing the library on Saturdays and Sundays, and greatly reducing book purchases. A stalemate existed for several months until an agreement was reached in June 1970, on a $206,000 appropriation and provision for a graduated scale of increases over the next few years.

Meanwhile, opponents of the early retirement ordinance successfully secured a court order supporting their petition, forcing it on the ballot of the next general election. Opponents were also successful in amending the proposal to set the retirement age at 68 and it was passed by the voters.

Rumblings from the Kentucky State Water Pollution Control Commission were heard in the summer of 1970, threatening to ban further sewer tap-ons unless progress was seen in the construction of the West Hickman Creek Treatment Plant. This problem was solved in part when the trunk lines to the filtration lagoons were completed, the pollution of the creek reduced, and the completion of the plant scheduled for 1972. Later, the state banned all future sewer tap-ons to Lexington's main sewage treatment plant, although Judge Henry Meigs granted a temporary injunction in May 1971. In July, the city advertised for bids for the construction of an expansion to the main plant.

The *Herald* complimented Underwood for his condemnation of the smoky and polluting city incinerator and the purchase of a sanitary landfill.

At the end of 1970, a small celebration was held by Underwood, Boggs, and Fowler to burn the 1971 sewer tax bills at a public bonfire. At that same time, the authorization to

City government actions and deliberations have taken place at this site since 1928. City Hall's original facade, with a handsome, columned portico, was covered over with the present facade when the structure was substantially enlarged in 1963.

issue $2 million in bonds to buy the Tates Creek Country Club for a public recreational facility was resented by some of the black residents of St. Martin's Village who had been asking for a park for fourteen years. The Commission majority responded by creating the Whitney Young, Jr., Park in that area after the untimely death of this distinguished national black leader and Kentucky native.

Underwood's troubles were not over, however. In February 1971, he was indicted by the Fayette County Grand Jury on five counts of soliciting and accepting a bribe, but a jury acquitted him of these charges in a trial a few months later.

In the summer of 1971, as crime increased in the Blue Grass public housing area, the commissioners hired a private security force to supplement the regular police force and patrol that section of the city. The City Commission also moved to upgrade the housing code and place pressure on the owners of substandard housing to upgrade or tear down those structures.

The controversial Underwood administration made the 1971 election an especially lively one. As early as January of that year, Foster Pettit indicated his willingness to run as a mayoral candidate, and in June he officially launched his campaign. Pettit, a native Lexingtonian and practicing attorney, had been elected three times to the State House of Representatives, where he had been voted the "most valuable member of the House" by the Capital Press Corps. Harry Sykes also filed to run as mayor.

Gradually, Pettit developed an anti-Underwood ticket consisting of Dr. J. Farra Van Meter, a well-known and highly respected surgeon, Richard Vimont, William Hoskins, and Scott Yellman. They ran on a platform supporting adequate sewage disposal, reduction of the city payroll, restoration of the merit system, and the merger of city and county governments.

In the primary election on September 18, Pettit and Sykes won the two mayoral candidate positions by 10,586 and 5,983 votes, respectively, while Underwood received 3,959 votes. Boggs and Fowler were among the eight candidates for the City Commission. In the November election, Pettit and his ticket were elected, with Boggs and Fowler trailing the other candidates by a wide margin.

The Underwood interlude was ended. Though Underwood's supporters claimed a sizable number of accomplishments for his administration, many of them, such as the Reservoir Park (later renamed Jacobson Park after E. E. Jacobson, late general manager of the Lexington Water Company), had been started earlier and had come to fruition during the Underwood regime. Many of these acclaimed accomplishments were projects beneficial in themselves, such as keeping the buses rolling, that were not special or significant to this administration alone. Underwood did appoint Helen McQuinn as Lexington's first ombudsman. The promise to remove the sewer service charge had been kept, but at a substantial cost to the city's resources. Ultimately, Underwood lost much of the support of those who had voted for him in 1969.

The Merger Movement

For decades many Lexingtonians, both city officials and the average citizen, had become increasingly frustrated by the cumbersome overlapping and division of city and county powers and responsibilities. The health departments had been combined and merger of

other county and city services such as schools, police, and firemen seemed not only logical but essential. However, such were the forces of tradition and anti-annexationist sentiment that not until the very size and character of Lexington and Fayette County changed was merger possible. By 1970, Lexington's population of over 100,000 qualified it as a first-class city, and the General Assembly would be constitutionally obligated to so designate it.

Many community leaders were doubtful that a first-class city form of government would serve Lexington effectively. In addition, a sizable number of new residents, many of whom were from out of state, were not wedded to the county government structure. William E. Lyons, a professor in the political science department at the University of Kentucky, who was to become a key figure in the merger movement, pointed out to Lexingtonians that experiments in consolidated city-county governments elsewhere offered another option. Years earlier, Penrose Ecton, well-known Lexington civic leader, had promoted the same idea. A pivotal leader in moving Lexington in the direction of merger was Judge Bart N. Peak, who had served as general secretary of the YMCA at the University of Kentucky for thirty-seven years before entering politics. He was elected to the General Assembly in 1952 and served as Fayette County Judge from 1958 to 1966. His study of merged governments in other cities persuaded him of its viability for this community. While serving again in the legislature in 1970, he co-sponsored with William McCann, a Lexington lawyer, the bill that permitted merged governments in Kentucky. This apparently paved the way for a merger in Lexington of city and county governments.

Citizens interested in following the merger route secured the required number of signatures by November 1970, to establish a representative commission composed of individuals appointed by the city and the county to study the aspects of merger. County Judge Robert Stephens, sympathetic to merger, persuaded the Fiscal Court to approve the appointment of county representatives. Underwood's lack of enthusiasm for merger by the city was manifest in the delay in appointing members to the commission, a number of whom were frequently absent from the meetings, which slowed progress.

When Foster Pettit took office in January 1971, new momentum was given the charter-making process. The city provided financing and more supportive individuals were appointed to the commission. Hammering out the details was an arduous task, but by the summer of 1972 the charter was ready to be placed on the November ballot. Polls taken in 1971-72 indicated a strong preference for merger, which was evidenced by the decisive 70 percent majority approving the charter.

By law, the charter could not go into effect until January 1, 1974, when the term of the incumbent county judge expired. However, the city and county proceeded with their plan to merge the fire and police departments prior to that date, and in early 1973 this consolidation was achieved. The thirteen months provided time to prepare for the complicated task of implementing the charter provisions and testing its constitutionality in the state courts.

Under the charter, the city manager role was replaced by a strong mayor assisted by a chief administrative officer. The four-member City Commission was replaced by a fifteen-member Urban County Council consisting of twelve district representatives and three at-large representatives.

The problem remained of how to deal with the constitutional officers such as the county attorney, sheriff, jailer, court clerk, and property evaluation officer. In the proposed merged government, the sheriff became chief tax collector, and the county jailer the chief detention officer for the combined city-county jail facilities. The assessments in the county would be conducted by the property evaluation officer.

The most important constitutional officer, the county judge, likewise had to be retained under the Kentucky Constitution, but the merged government reduced his power to an essentially judicial one. Under the charter, his executive and administrative authorities were assumed by the mayor. Even the important judicial functions, however, were removed from the county judge by the Judicial Reform Act, which was approved by the voters of Kentucky in November 1975.

Since the Fiscal Court would be stripped of its statutory legislative and executive authority by the urban-county government, it was provided that the three county

Foster Pettit (right) and James G. Amato, the first two mayors to serve under a merged city-county government. The merger was implemented by Pettit during his term of office that ended in 1977. Photo courtesy of the Lexington Herald-Leader Company.

commissioners would receive no compensation for performing their limited duties.

The merger commission was fortunate in securing the services of Dr. Malcolm Jewell, a professor of political science at the University of Kentucky whose expertise was legislative representation, to undertake the complicated task of designating the districts.

By mid-September 1973, Fayette Circuit Judge George Barker approved the constitutionality of most of the charter, though certain non-crucial provisions were ruled invalid. Thanks to the cooperation of the Kentucky Court of Appeals, the case was heard in early December and a decision was rendered on December 28, 1973, upholding the basic provisions of the charter, thus enabling its inauguration on January 1, 1974.

Complications of an unexpected nature had developed from the November 6 election. Representatives for the Urban County Council were elected without difficulty, but an incredibly close race between Pettit and Municipal Court Judge James Amato resulted in an apparent victory for the latter by 112 votes. However, when it was discovered that a voting machine error in the Aylesford precinct had reversed the voters' preference there, the courts were forced to decide. Not until January 15, 1974, did the Kentucky Court of Appeals rule in Pettit's favor, thus reelecting him as mayor by the razor-thin margin of 54 votes. It was a testimony to the character of both these candidates that bitterness and divisiveness did not result from this situation. Though the Council's work was temporarily delayed, the full operation of the newly merged government soon was underway.

It was to take two to three years, however, to complete the many changes required by the charter, including the time-consuming task of recruiting first-rate personnel for such positions as the chief administrative officer. A novel five-year capital improvements program was difficult to design, and the new civil service classification was another complicated task.

The sewage treatment plant expansion and the necessity for providing sewers in areas of greatest health hazard also caused difficulties. Residents in areas expecting immediate full urban services harassed the councilmen. Some of those dissatisfied with the merged government attempted to have it repealed but failed.

Another major reform in Kentucky developing at about the same time as the installation of the merged government in Lexington and Fayette County was the restructuring of the judicial system. This long overdue action was the result of dedicated effort by the Kentucky Citizens for Judicial Improvement, Inc., headed by Amato as executive director. This organization not only successfully guided the Judicial Reform Amendment through the General Assembly, but educated and persuaded a notoriously tradition-bound electorate to approve the amendment on November 4, 1975.

By this amendment, the historic and cumbersome judicial structure of County Courts, Quarterly Courts, Circuit Courts, Police Courts, Magistrate Courts, and the Court of Appeals was replaced with a simplified system headed by a State Supreme Court, under which were the Court of Appeals, Circuit Courts, and District Courts.

When Pettit completed his term as mayor in 1977, he could look back over the challenging years of growth and the implementation of a new government with considerable satisfaction. Certainly, his support of and leadership in the Lexington-Fayette County Urban government was a major achievement. Another was the successful completion of the impressive $60 million Lexington Center complex, the western terminus of a new downtown Lexington and the nucleus for future development.

In April 1972, the Lexington Center Corporation was created by city and county officials, together with the Lexington-Fayette County Tourist, Recreational, and Convention Commission, to plan, finance, and develop a convention center, exhibition hall, a sports center and arena, and a theater. The plans would later include a 375-400 room hotel. The board of directors of the Lexington Center Corporation, with Jake Graves, head of the Second National Bank, as president, included Linda Carey, Margaret Cravens, William Hoskins, William Jackson, Bruce Glenn, Dewitt Hisle, and Doc T. Ferrell. Thomas C. Minter was appointed as executive director.

From the numerous plans submitted by teams of competing architects, builders, and investors, the directors contracted with Ellerle Architectural Associates of Bloomington, Minnesota, to design the complex, and chose Huber, Hunt, and Nichols of Indianapolis as construction managers. Garvice Kincaid, along with other bankers and financial leaders, conducted the complicated negotiations necessary to sell the bond issues and complete other financial arrangements to underwrite the construction. On June 22, 1974, ground was broken for this monumental project. A year later, as the city celebrated its bicentennial, a stone brought from Lexington, Massachusetts, by horse and wagon was inserted into the structure.

Restored Opera House Dedication

Work on restoring the Opera House, the theatre component of the Lexington Center complex, was begun. George Carey and William T. Young, co-chairmen of the Opera House Fund, successfully raised large sums of money from private sources to assist in the remarkable restoration and improvement of the Opera House and its surroundings.

In the space of five years, 1976-81, the arts in Lexington were richly blessed with a restored Opera House and a new University of Kentucky Center for the Arts. In the top photo by Tony Leonard, Dr. George Zack leads the Lexington Philharmonic in an Opera House concert. The bottom photo (courtesy of the University of Kentucky) shows spectators at a Center for the Arts' exhibit of the nationally-famous Armand Hammer collection of paintings.

Dancers on stage at the restored Opera House. Photo courtesy of Host Communications.

The restored Opera House was dedicated on May 7, 1976, and a full season of concerts and theatrical events began in the fall. Lexingtonians could take pride in having preserved this distinctive, historic structure, successfully linking the best of the old with the cultural needs of the present.

In October 1976, the Lexington Center opened with a Central Kentucky Exposition, and a concert by Lawrence Welk and his orchestra. A month later, a cheering sell-out crowd of 23,000 basketball fans filled Rupp Arena to watch their beloved University of Kentucky Wildcats defeat the University of Wisconsin, while the fabled coach, Adolph Rupp, despite failing health, occupied a special seat to savor the moment.

The Hyatt Regency Hotel enjoyed a booming business almost from the beginning. Soon, specialty shops began to fill the retail space in the new Lexington Center Mall.

The most controversial aspect in the construction of the Lexington Center was the Council's decision to raze a large section of the South Hill area to provide parking lots. The displacement of many families and the levelling of their homes caused a considerable amount of anger, dismay, and hardship among those affected, though municipal authorities attempted to find new homes for the displaced.

There were, of course, continuing problems that confronted Mayor Pettit and the Urban-County Government, including waste management, housing for low-income families, sewers yet to be built in some sections of the city, and a new main library building. A dramatic issue was the attempt to unionize municipal employees, especially police and firemen.

In August 1974, the firemen pressed the Council to recognize Local 526 of the Professional Firefighters Union for the purpose of collective bargaining. Mayor Pettit opposed the demand, and picketing and "sick-ins" by the firemen resulted.

University of Kentucky basketball coach Adolph Rupp at the dedication on December 11, 1976, of the arena named in his honor in downtown Lexington. The chair was presented to him by the school's athletic department. Photo courtesy of University of Kentucky.

The downtown renaissance of the 1970's and 1980's began with construction of a Hyatt Regency Hotel (left) and the Lexington Center and Rupp Arena, as seen from Triangle Park, which was completed in the summer of 1982.

The following month the Metro police backed the firemen in their demands and expressed an interest in unionization themselves. Two hundred firemen participated in a protest march before City Hall to demand that their request for a collective bargaining organization be recognized. When this request was refused, they went on strike September 24, 1974. Three days later, the firemen met with an Urban-County Government reconciliation committee, and on October 4 they ended their strike as the Council agreed to recognize a "legitimate employee organization."

Pettit's administration supervised the renovation of Main Street, the erection of a modern jail, the modernization of the city transit service, and the completion of adequate sewage treatment facilities. Also during this era, the large, modern Blue Grass Field airport terminal was opened. Pettit's administration, and that of his successor, benefited from the program of revenue sharing that was enacted into law by Congress in 1972. This program has allowed the local government to provide and improve services for Lexington without an increase in taxes. Annual revenue sharing appropriations have risen to approximately $6 million since 1977. The funds have been used for the "home fleet" plan for police (which allows patrolmen continuous use of police vehicles, on and off duty), competitive salaries and benefits for employees of the Urban-County government, improvement of the city's cars and trucks, and planning for new services.

A row of small stores, restaurants and liquor bars on South Broadway was torn down as part of the city's urban renewal program. This land is now the site of Triangle Park. Some of the structures dated back to the early 1800's. Photo courtesy of Transylvania University.

'Threshold of Greatness'

Joseph C. Graves Jr., a prominent Lexington businessman and developer, had also been active in civic and political affairs. He had served effectively as both state representative and senator from Lexington, as well as being a city commissioner. In 1977, he entered the race for mayor against James Amato, who defeated him in the November election. When he took office, Amato expressed his belief that Lexington was on "the threshold of greatness." It was his intent to move Lexington toward that goal by implementing solutions to tenacious problems that had in the past become bogged down in study committees.

To solve the ever-increasing traffic congestion on Nicholasville Road, he worked with the state to install a reversible lane system. Plans were made and construction initiated to replace three deteriorating bridges at the western edge of the downtown area on Jefferson, West High and West Main streets. A lengthy debate over cable TV was resolved by granting Telecable, Inc., a franchise. Mayor Amato also made progress on plans for an overpass over the Southern Railway crossing on South Broadway, a major traffic bottleneck for years.

Since 1928, there has been a planning and zoning commission whose membership and assigned powers and responsibilities have changed over the years. This commission has drawn up comprehensive plans at various times for the orderly growth of the county and the city. That those plans were sometimes followed only haphazardly was due to the perpetual struggle between the private developers and the officials, with the developers frequently overriding the objections or doubts of the government, which led to some unfortunate results. One such example was the way in which the earliest section of New Circle Road, between Russell Cave and Richmond roads, became cluttered with commercial enterprises of all kinds, with a maze of access roads feeding into the main artery.

In 1958, the City-County Planning Commission adopted a plan to divide the county into Urban and Rural Service Areas. This would confine the more concentrated commercial, manufacturing, and residential development to the Urban Service Area, which provides essential city services. The aim of establishing an Urban Service Area was, in part, to prevent leap-frog development and to protect, as far as possible, the vulnerable agricultural and horse farm areas.

In 1961, William Qualls was appointed director of the City-County Planning Commission. During his twelve-year administration, funding from federal and city sources, plus contributions from the Chamber of Commerce, enabled him to expand his staff. This made possible the research for, and publication of, a series of comprehensive studies on all aspects of Lexington and Fayette County, each of which was oriented to a specific program. These studies provided concrete guides for governmental action, such as paving the way for urban renewal and selecting the site for the Lexington Center. The city-county park plan was expanded from the original 100 acres to about 2,000 acres.

Qualls also conducted an active public education program which included communicating with neighborhood groups to improve local areas, and newspaper columns which reached a larger audience, informing the citizens of contemporary planning and the need for comprehensive future guidelines. Indeed, the quality of his staff and the comprehensive plan drawn up in 1965, with its projections for 1980, are best proved by the fact that, by the latter year, most of the projections had become realities.

On January 1, 1974, the Lexington-Fayette County Urban Planning Commission was created under the merger charter and assigned the task of creating a growth plan for the next two decades.

Mayor Amato was conscious of the tension existing between private developers and city planning and zoning officials and encouraged its resolution by urging private enterprise to undertake greater initiative in the thoughtful planning of development. He established the Lexington Economic Development Commission, whose scope was extended to a citywide perspective. Amato's philosophy was to avoid either dictating or vetoing their plans, unless obvious city welfare issues were involved. Triangle Park, under the leadership of Alex Campbell, is an example of an important downtown improvement, designed and financed by private donations, which traditionally would have been a tax-supported city project.

Though by no means unique to Lexington, it is noteworthy that a substantial proportion of Lexington's recent downtown building expansion, as well as some projects in the suburbs, have been initiated by individuals from small Kentucky towns. Garvice Kincaid was born in a small village in Lee County before his family moved to Richmond. After graduating from the University of Kentucky, he remained on campus to earn a law degree and made Lexington his home. He found that investing in real estate and making money in a variety of enterprises was more interesting and profitable than law practice. Eventually he moved into finance, banking, and insurance. In 1945, at the age of thirty-three, he acquired the Central Exchange Bank, renaming it the Central Bank and Trust Company. His most successful venture was obtaining control of Kentucky Central Life Insurance Company in 1959. A year later he received a national Horatio Alger Award. The extent of his multiple enterprises was impressive. They included banks, finance companies, and radio and television stations throughout the south. Kincaid died in 1975,

Mayor Scotty Baesler with three business and civic leaders at the dedication of Triangle Park in the summer of 1982. From left: W. E. Burnett, Jr., Lexington Economic Development Commission; Alex Campbell, Triangle Foundation; Mayor Baesler; and W. L. Rouse, Jr., Lexington Chamber of Commerce. Photo courtesy of Charles Bertram.

A typical springtime paddock scene at Keeneland Race Course. Photo by Bill Straus.

but the $25 million, 22-story Kincaid Towers (officially the headquarters of Kentucky Central), erected after his death, stands as a memorial to him.

Donald and Dudley Webb were born and raised in the Whitesburg, Kentucky, area, and graduated from Georgetown College and the University of Kentucky Law School. They both eventually settled in Lexington to practice law, and gradually moved into real estate and development. Since 1974, they have played a key role in $150 million of new construction in Lexington, culminating in the $60 million Vine Center.

Wallace Wilkinson, born on a farm in Casey County, has likewise made a successful career in Lexington, starting with his expanding textbook business and moving into many different enterprises. His latest project, which has aroused some controversy, is a proposed 50-story World Coal Center to be built on the site of the Phoenix Hotel, which was razed in 1982. Wilkinson says his criteria for a project are "it should be fun, it should be beneficial to the community, and it should be profitable."

In 1982, the year when Scotty Baesler succeeded Amato as mayor, Main and Vine Streets remained in the throes of change. The empty store fronts which once housed Stewart's, Meyer's, Embry's and Ben Snyder's stared bleakly on the passersby. The vast levelled areas, where the Phoenix Hotel and the *Herald-Leader* buildings had stood, awaited development. Other businesses like Barney Miller's, Wolf Wile's, Lowenthal's, Graves Cox, Skuller's, and Villeminot's hung on tenaciously in hopes that the anticipated turn-around in the long Main Street retail decline would come soon enough to enable them to survive.

One can glimpse the future more accurately, perhaps, by walking from the Lexington Center eastward along Vine Street. Over the pedestrians' heads loom the Hyatt Regency, Vine Center and the Kincaid Towers — then one moves past the new Citizens Union Bank Building, the First Federal Savings & Loan Association, the Bank of Lexington, and the Merrill Lynch Plaza. Farther down Vine Street, one can see the new Kentucky Utilities Building, the Christ Church Housing Center, the Bluegrass Commerce Center, and the giant, gleaming *Herald-Leader* plant at Midland Avenue. Turning, one proceeds westward along Main Street where the new Second National Bank Building and the earlier First Security National Bank building stand as soaring symbols of progress.

Plans for further development are announced faster than the average citizen can comprehend them; gallerias, condominiums, the restoration of the old houses and the building of new town houses on West Short Street are part of the resurgence. It is a blueprint for a transformed downtown Lexington, both in its physical appearance and style of life. On the outskirts, headquarters of major corporations have been constructed, such as the Island Creek Coal Corporation, Jerrico, Inc., and the Ashland Oil Company. Other new suburban facilities include the Marriott Resort Hotel and Griffin Gate complex on Newtown Road, Corporate and Southcreek office centers on Harrodsburg Road, and vast quantities of new retail space in Fayette Mall, North Park, South Park, Turfland and Lexington malls. In the past decade, construction completed or on the drawing board in the downtown area alone has amounted to more than $400 million.

Within the context of this multiple construction downtown, the burgeoning subdivisions, the proliferation of malls and smaller shopping centers, and the vitality of the horse industry, and the livestock and tobacco markets, emerges an increasingly creative and

This house on South Mill Street, built by John W. Scott in 1886, is one of several Victorian houses on this street, another area of renovation activity.

vigorous cultural dimension. The Lexington Philharmonic continues to prosper, guided for the past ten years by its dynamic director, George Zack, with strong community support under the leadership of Caruthers A. Coleman, Sr., and the Women's Guild. The Central Kentucky Youth Symphony, the Chamber Music Society, and the Lexington Singers also continue their successful careers. The Central Kentucky Concert and Lecture Series has been a mainstay for decades in providing thousands

A major suburban development of the early 1980's was the construction of a new Marriott Hotel and golf course, along with a fashionable residential subdivision — Griffin Gate — in the northwestern part of the county.

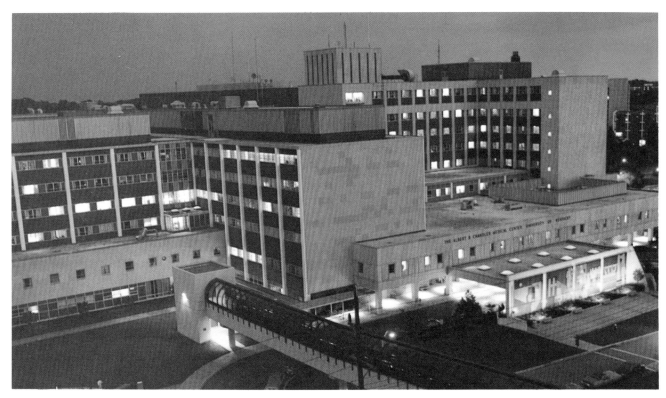

The Albert B. Chandler Medical Center, which opened on the University of Kentucky campus in April, 1962, has greatly enhanced Lexington's stature as a regional center of medical services. Photo courtesy of the University of Kentucky.

University of Kentucky basketball teams have played to capacity crowds since the opening of the 23,000-seat Rupp Arena in downtown Lexington in 1976, one of the largest basketball facilities in the nation. Photo by Bill Straus.

of patrons with the finest programs for the least expense, especially in the ample space of Memorial Coliseum. The opening of the new University of Kentucky Center for the Arts in 1981 is a splendid addition to Lexington's cultural facilities.

Numerous modest art galleries now are operating in various locations about town, though Lexington itself needs a municipal museum and gallery. The Lexington Living Arts and Science Center continues its educational role. The renovation of the old YWCA building, to be known as ArtsPlace, will provide a major center for artistic activities of all kinds.

Lexingtonians no longer have to drive to Cincinnati or Louisville to see Broadway shows, now that the restored Opera House brings them here. The vitality of the drama programs at the University of Kentucky and Transylvania, and the increasing number of local theatrical groups, of which the Studio Players is the oldest and best known, offer a wide variety of theatrical fare. There are also Lexington ballet and modern dance groups and an excellent Children's Theatre of long standing.

Over the past three or four decades, the association with Lexington of such outstanding individuals as Victor Hammer, internationally known artist, type designer, and printer, and John Jacob Niles, an extraordinary composer, performer, collector, and preserver of the rich Appalachian musical heritage, have enriched Lexington's cultural prestige. Adding to that lustre are former Lexingtonians who are pursuing their careers elsewhere, including Elizabeth Hardwick and A. B. Guthrie, Jr., who are among America's foremost novelists, and Dr. William Lipscomb, Lexington's second Nobel Prize winner. It is also noteworthy that the present governor of Kentucky, John Y. Brown, Jr., is a native Lexingtonian.

Finally, the enduring strengths of a community are not what it manufactures, builds, and grows, essential as these are to the prosperity and functioning of the city. It is, rather, the distinctiveness of its way of life, the values it offers, the cultural and creative activities it fosters, and the unique individuals it produces or who are attracted to it because of what the city is or may become. By that measure, Lexington has been, and continues to be, a unique and vibrant community.

The former Lafayette Hotel building, which was erected in 1920 and used as a hotel until 1962, was purchased in 1982 by the city government for a municipal office building. Photo courtesy of the University of Kentucky.

Aerial view of downtown Lexington and the western environs in the spring of 1982. Photo by Lloyd Beard.

Nearby downtown Lexington skyscrapers serve as the backdrop as horses and their drivers cross the finish line at the historic Red Mile pacing and trotting track on South Broadway.

Epilogue

The distinctiveness of any community is determined by its geographical attributes, the men and women who have lived there, and the events in which they have participated through the years. Looking back over Lexington's history as this community moves into its third century, long-established residents as well as large numbers of recent arrivals may well ask: what is distinctive about Lexington and Fayette County?

There seems little doubt that Lexington's early decades were remarkable. Not only did its population and economy grow rapidly, but the town attracted a significant number of distinguished individuals, of whom Henry Clay was indisputably the most famous. No Lexingtonian since has occupied the position of national prominence that Clay held for so many years. In addition, Transylvania University brought to its campus and the town an exceptional array of promising young men whose later careers in medicine, law, business, and political life were notable.

Lexington was a community, surrounded by a fertile and beautiful countryside, that achieved distinction in many areas. Yet, in the decades before the Civil War, the town's predominance in Kentucky began to wane. Louisville and Cincinnati surpassed her in size and economic productivity. Transylvania University declined. The void left by Henry Clay's death was never filled, and the career of Clay's most promising successor, John C. Breckinridge, was cut short by the Civil War.

In the post-Civil War years, Lexington, cherishing the achievements of its past, proud of its fine homes and genteel style of life, and enjoying a moderately expanding economy, even during periods of national depression, appeared content. Lexingtonians were apprehensive when they saw wealthy non-Kentuckians purchase the traditional and familiar horse farms, but their fears were calmed when it became apparent that the new owners not only improved these farms in size, wealth, and appearance, but preserved the Bluegrass pattern of life.

Race relations, while marked by segregation and numerous restrictions and handicaps on the rights of black citizens, became relatively stable by the turn of the century, and the blacks created a viable community of their own.

Oldtime residents recall the Lexington of the early 20th century as a community that "had class." One lady remembered that when she moved to Lexington in 1906 it was "the sweetest little burg of a southern aristocratic town." Many residents shared her view. But that complacency over the years created a degree of smugness that resulted in indifference to political reform, and a lethargy in meeting such community needs as the waterworks in the 1880's, and, later, an adequate sewage disposal system, storm drainage for downtown, an acceptable air terminal, a good public library, and housing for the low-income populations, to name a few.

Though Lexington and Fayette County established the first local planning and zoning commission in 1928, the Great Depression and World War II intervened to prevent any significant implementation of the commission's recommendations.

In the nearly forty years since World War II, Lexington has undergone a major transformation in size, in the character of its population, and in its economic base. The horse farms and tobacco industry remain familiar features of the historic scene, but there is now no longer a downtown nucleus, surrounded by residents who work and buy their goods in the central area. The void created by the decline of

Photo by Clyde T. Burke.

the inner city retail and manufacturing center is being filled by high-rise banks, hotels, and office buildings. The momentum behind this energetic construction program has been provided by Urban Renewal and developers, with the encouragement and support of the Urban-County government.

The question that continues to haunt many Lexingtonians who enjoy living and working in this city is whether the distinctive character of the community is being destroyed in the very process of expansion.

One gazes out over the sprawling subdivisions, neatly landscaped and bespeaking affluence, to the famed horse farms, bounded by miles of plank fences, luxurious stables, and imposing mansions. On the rolling green pastures expensive horses peacefully graze. This is part of what makes Lexington distinctive, it is said, and although even Arabian oil money is being invested in the farms, it is hoped the character of the Bluegrass will be preserved, as it was a century earlier. But the horse farms themselves are endangered by Lexington's growth, although the adoption of the Urban Service Area plan may have reduced that threat.

New Lexingtonians, scattered throughout the broad suburbs and often driving to work on roads that never intersect downtown, may be less aware of the inner heart of Lexington's unique character, reflected most obviously in the architectural creations of previous generations. Many have never seen or walked through Gratz Park, or the Carnegie Library,

or paused before the Hunt-Morgan house to read the historical plaques describing its most famous residents. They may not have appreciated the graceful statues in the James Lane Allen memorial fountain or looked up at the stately columned Old Morrison on the Transylvania campus. Necessary to an appreciation of this dimension of Lexington's heritage is not only some degree of architectural insight but also a sense and knowledge of the history which brings life and meaning to these mute structures.

As in all cities, the quality of Lexington's life has been inherited in part from those who preceded us. If those who now enthusiastically proclaim this community's virtues, which make it "a pleasant place in which to live," remain ignorant of the historical roots from which the city has emerged, then an important element of the distinctiveness of the city will be lost. The preservationists' crusade to save significant structures of a previous era from thoughtless destruction is not alone an antiquarian's obsession with conserving what is old; it is also an effort to keep alive the meaningful implications of what earlier Lexingtonians have achieved.

Linkage between the special past and the living present must be maintained. The new should be built in some proportion to the old, and skillfully related to it architecturally and functionally.

What we are and where we have been will determine where we are going and what we

shall be. The early 19th century leaders in Lexington had some vision of what they wished their town to be, and did remarkably well in fulfilling that goal. Will Lexington in its third century produce leadership similarly cognizant of the total community in all its aspects: the human needs as well as physical growth; cultural creativity as well as economic expansion; and a shared sense of purpose in a burgeoning urban environment?

The Lexingtonian of today might well raise the question: what does he/she wish the Lexington of tomorrow to be, and what relation will it bear to the historic traditions and achievements of the past? Despite the presence of the University of Kentucky and Transylvania, and the variety of cultural centers and activities, is Lexington eventually to be known only as the basketball capital of the region? Or the horse-breeding capital of the world? Or a pleasant place to attend the horse races? Or a convention center?

Is it unreasonable to hope that new generations of Lexingtonians will be sufficiently sensitive to the fundamental continuity of life that they will inform themselves of their city's past so that their outlook and plans for its future will be more wisely balanced?

Perspective is crucial. Developers and city planners, the influential and wealthy leaders, as well as the bulk of the residents, should have some consensus of what they wish Lexington to be. Distinction is a mercurial quality, and may easily slip through our fingers. The heart of the

Bluegrass in the century ahead will be markedly different from what it has been. Like other American cities, Lexington must confront the challenge of maintaining its identity in a society becoming increasingly homogenized by the mass media and technology.

Part of a city's uniqueness is a sense of community, which is difficult to preserve in a large city. The essence of such a feeling is hard to define. Perhaps it can be understood by a simple illustration. Imbedded in the sidewalk on the northeast corner of Main and Limestone streets, which for many years was one of the busiest intersections in downtown Lexington, is a bronze plaque dedicated to the memory of a dog. "Smiley Pete" was a friendly black and white animal of mixed parentage, who in the 1940's and 1950's made his home in the area. Fed by nearby restaurant owners and friends, patted by passersby, spoken to by rich and poor alike, and beribboned on holidays by unknown admirers, "Smiley Pete" was a symbol of that sense of community. I suspect few towns would have bothered to place a plaque on a busy sidewalk for a dog. Yet, it remains emblematic of this sense of a shared and common experience, part of the city's tradition.

As the towering new structures are thrust ever higher along Vine and Main streets and the subdivisions push deeper into the countryside, one may hope that Lexingtonians will preserve some sense of community, of caring for one another, and of cherishing their special past.

225

Map of Lexington's Growth

Source: Lexington-Fayette County Urban Government, Division of Planning

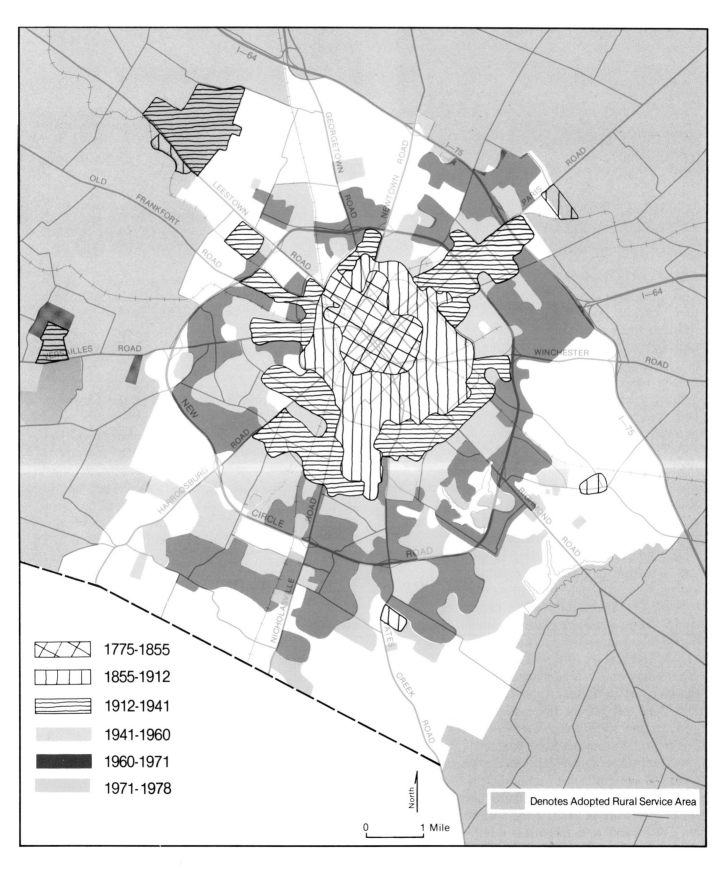

1775-1855
1855-1912
1912-1941
1941-1960
1960-1971
1971-1978

Denotes Adopted Rural Service Area

North

0   1 Mile

Notes on Sources

Since the text of this book is not documented by footnotes, it is hoped that a listing of the major sources used for each chapter will be of some service to the reader. It may also prove useful to those wishing to extend their reading in a particular field.

CHAPTER I

The two best, most recent, and available general histories of Kentucky which provide the broad background for local history are Thomas D. Clark, *A History of Kentucky* (revised edition, Lexington, 1960) and Steven B. Channing, *Kentucky* (New York, 1977). Clark treats Kentucky's history in a most readable and topical fashion in his *Kentucky: Land of Contrast* (New York, 1968). The two histories of Lexington are both written by George W. Ranck. In 1872, Ranck published his *History of Lexington: Its Early Annals and Recent Progress* and ten years later rewrote and updated the history for William H. Perrin, ed., *History of Fayette County, Kentucky* (Chicago, 1882). The first third of Perrin's volume was written by Dr. Robert Peter and contains additional information, both physical and historical, about the county. The only other recent overview of Lexington's past is J. Winston Coleman, Jr., *The Squire's Sketches of Lexington* (Lexington, 1975) which provides a most informative chronological outline of Lexington's past.

Carolyn Wooley, *The Founding of Lexington, 1775-1776* (Lexington, 1975) is an invaluable source of information on the naming of Lexington and the location of McConnell's Spring. Also informative for the pioneer period are Charles R. Staples, *The History of Pioneer Lexington, 1779-1806* (Lexington, 1939) and Bettye Lee Mastin, *Lexington, 1779* (Lexington, 1979). The best history of the Episcopal Diocese of Lexington is Frances Keller Swinford and Rebecca Smith Lee, *The Great Elm Tree* (Lexington, 1969). Other sources for this period include J. W. Coleman, Jr. *John Bradford, Esq.* (Lexington, 1950), Richard C. Wade, *The Urban Frontier: The Rise of the Western Cities, 1790-1830* (Cambridge, Mass., 1959), and John D. Wright, Jr., *Transylvania: Tutor to the West* (Lexington, 1980). *The Register of the Kentucky Historical Society* and the *Filson Club History Quarterly* are rich periodical sources of information. For this period some of the more useful articles were Willard Rouse Jillson, "A Sketch of Thomas Parvin — First Printer in Kentucky," *The Register* (October, 1936); Robert Stuart Sanders, "Walnut Hill Presbyterian Church," *The Register* (April, 1953); and Edna T. Whitley, "George Beck: An Eighteenth Century Painter," *The Register* (January, 1969).

The newspapers are a main source of information from the beginnings of the *Kentucky Gazette* in 1787 to the present-day *Lexington Herald* and *Lexington Leader.* There have been an impressive number of newspapers in Lexington during the past 200 years, but many stayed in business only a short time. In the limited time available for research for this project, it is obvious that all of these could not be examined. Those providing the better sources of information on local events were used. References to these are made in the text.

CHAPTER II

One of the richest collections of personal reminiscences for this period is William A. Leavy, "A Memoir of Lexington and Its Vicinity," which was printed in *The Register*, Vols. 40, 41, 42. Other useful sources for the 1800-1840 era are F. Garvin Davenport, *Antebellum Kentucky* (Oxford, Ohio, 1943); J. W. Coleman, Jr. pamphlet, *Lexington: The Athens of the West* (Lexington, 1981); and Bettie Kerr, "Lexington, Kentucky, 1780-1840, 'The Athens of the West'" (an unpublished manuscript, 1977). Another informative collection of reminiscences is that of Samuel D. McCullough, "Reminiscences of Lexington," *The Register* (January, 1929). James A. Ramage, *John Wesley Hunt* (Lexington, 1974) is the only biographical study of the merchant, and fills a major gap. Many more such studies are needed of outstanding businessmen. Also useful were John Robert Shaw, *The Life and Adventures of John Robert Shaw* (Lexington, 1807), and Glyndon Van Deusen, *The Life of Henry Clay* (Boston, 1937). Lexington's first printed directory was published as part of *Charless' Kentucky, Tennessee, and Ohio Almanac, for the Year 1806,* (Lexington, 1805). The second directory is part of *Worsley & Smith's Kentucky Almanac, and Farmer's Calendar for the Year, 1819* (Lexington, 1818). John D. Wright, Jr., *Transylvania: Tutor to the West* (Lexington, 1980). J. W. Coleman, Jr., *Masonry in the Bluegrass, 1788-1933* (Lexington, 1933). Use was also made of West T. Hill, Jr., *The Theatre in Early Kentucky, 1790-1820* (Lexington, 1971); Joy Carden, *Music in Lexington Before 1840* (Lexington, 1980); William Barrow Floyd, *Jouett-Bush-Frazer: Early Kentucky Artists* (Lexington, 1968) and his "Early Kentucky Artists," in *Lexington: As It Was* (Lexington, 1981); J. W. Coleman, Jr., "Lexington as Seen by Travellers, 1810-1835," *The Filson Club History Quarterly* (July, 1955); Huntley Dupre, "The French in Early Kentucky," *The Filson Club History Quarterly* (April, 1941); Edgar Erskine Hume, "Lafayette in Kentucky," *The Register* (January, 1936); Nancy D. Baird, "Asiatic Cholera's First Visit to Kentucky: A Study in Panic and Fear," *The Filson Club History Quarterly* (July, 1974); and William H. Townsend, *Lincoln and the Bluegrass* (Lexington, 1955). The most valuable recent volume on horses and horse farms for the general reader is Mary E. Wharton, et al., *The Horse World of the Bluegrass* (Lexington, 1980).

CHAPTER III

The most informative and readable account of the stagecoach era in the Bluegrass is J. Winston Coleman, Jr., *Stage-Coach Days in the Bluegrass* (Louisville, 1935). Another rich source of reminiscences for this period is Frances L. S. Dugan and Jacqueline Bull, eds., *Bluegrass Craftsman: Being the Reminiscences of Ebenezer Hiram Stedman, Papermaker, 1808-1885*

(Lexington, 1959). Thomas D. Clark, "The Lexington and Ohio Railroad," *The Register* (January, 1933). David Hume, "The Lexington and Ohio Railroad," (an unpublished manuscript, 1981). Robert M. Ireland, *The County Courts in Antebellum Kentucky* (Lexington, 1972). Joseph M. Heidenreich, selections from the Minute Books of the Town Trustees. John B. Clark, Jr., "The Fire Problem in Kentucky, 1778-1865, *The Register* (April, 1953). J. W. Coleman, Jr., *Famous Kentucky Duels* (Lexington, 1969). Wade, *Urban Frontier,* cited earlier, also provided pertinent information for this chapter. On turnpikes, see Turner W. Allen, "The Turnpike System in Kentucky: A Review of the State Road Policy in the Nineteenth Century," *The Filson Club History Quarterly* (July, 1954). Clay Lancaster, *Vestiges of the Venerable City* (Lexington, 1978), provides an invaluable and authoritative source on Lexington's architects and architecture by its foremost architectural historian. Also see, J. W. Coleman, Jr., "Early Lexington Architects and Their Work," *The Filson Club* (July, 1968). Wallace Turner, "A Rising Social Consciousness in Kentucky During the 1850's," *The Filson Club History Quarterly* (January, 1962). Ray N. Cooley, "Religious Ministry at the Lexington, Kentucky, State Asylum, 1844-1869," *The Register* (April, 1972). William Clayton Bower, *Central Christian Church, Lexington, Kentucky* (St. Louis, 1962). Historical material on the origin and development of Pleasant Green and First Baptist churches was generously supplied by the respective churches. Swinford and Lee, *The Great Elm Tree,* previously cited. Also see Frank Masters, *A History of the Baptists in Kentucky* (Louisville, 1953).

CHAPTER IV

Alexis de Tocqueville, *Democracy in America* is available in a variety of editions. The most informative volume on slavery in Kentucky is J. Winston Coleman, Jr., *Slavery Times in Kentucky* (Chapel Hill, 1940). The best general study of the urban slave in the South in Richard C. Wade, *Slavery in the Cities: The South 1820-1860* (New York, 1964). Of special interest is Loris Points, "Free Negroes in Lexington, Kentucky: 1830-1840," (unpublished manuscript, 1968). J. W. Coleman, Jr., "Lexington's Slave Dealers and Their Southern Trade," *The Filson Club History Quarterly* (January, 1938). See also Townsend, *Lincoln and the Bluegrass,* already cited. Of great value in the 1845-1865 period is the diary of the Reverend William Pratt in the special collections of the University of Kentucky. The best study of Cassius Marcellus Clay is David L. Smiley, *Lion of White Hall* (reprint by Peter Smith, Gloucester, Mass., 1969). Wallace B. Turner, "Abolitionism in Kentucky," *The Register* (October, 1971). Allen J. Share, *Cities in the Commonwealth* (Lexington, 1982). See also Lancaster, *Vestiges of the Venerable City,* previously cited. Also previously cited, Van Deusen, *Henry Clay.* E. Merton Coulter, "The Downfall of the Whig Party in Kentucky," *The Register* (May 1925). For the return of the cholera in 1849 see Nancy D. Baird, "Asiatic Cholera: Kentucky's First Public Health Instructor," *The Filson Club History Quarterly* (October, 1974). Frank H. Heck, *Proud Kentuckian: John C. Breckinridge, 1821-1875* (Lexington, 1976). E. Merton Coulter, *The Civil War and Readjustment in Kentucky* (Chapel Hill, 1926). Lowell H. Harrison, *The Civil War in Kentucky* (Lexington, 1975). J. W. Coleman, Jr., *Lexington During the Civil War* (Lexington, 1938). John David Smith and William

Cooper, Jr., eds., *Window on the War: Frances Dallam Peter's Lexington Civil War Diary* (Lexington, 1976). Richard H. Collins, "Civil War Annals: 1861-65," edited by Hambleton Tapp, *The Filson Club History Quarterly* (July, 1961). John D. Smith, "The Recruitment of Negro Soldiers in Kentucky, 1863-1865," *The Register* (October, 1974). Hambleton Tapp, "Robert J. Breckinridge During the Civil War," *The Filson Club History Quarterly* (April, 1937).

CHAPTER V

James Lane Allen, *Flute and Violin and Other Kentucky Tales* (New York, 1891). The best account of the complex political and social situation in Kentucky in the decades after the Civil War is Hambleton Tapp and James E. Klotter, *Kentucky: Decades of Discord, 1865-1900* (Frankfort, Ky., 1977). A complete series of brief biographies of all of Lexington's mayors was compiled during the administration of Mayor Foster Pettit who generously made them available to the author for this work. The major sources for the information on the black migration into Lexington and the creation of new housing patterns are Herbert A. Thomas, Jr., "Victims of Circumstance: Negroes in a Southern Town, 1865-1880," *The Register* (July, 1973), and John Kellogg, "The Formation of Black Residential Areas in Lexington, Kentucky, 1865-1887," *The Journal of Southern History* (February, 1982). On the Negro testimony and suffrage issues see Victor B. Howard, "The Kentucky Press and the Negro Testimony Controversy, 1866-1872," *The Register* (January, 1973) and his "Negro Politics and the Suffrage Question in Kentucky, 1866-1872," *The Register* (April, 1974). Also valuable are the records of the city ordinances and the Minutes of the Board of Aldermen. Material may also be found in the columns of the *Gazette,* the *Daily Press,* and the *Transcript.* James Lane Allen, "County Court Day," from *The Blue-Grass Region of Kentucky and Other Kentucky Articles* (New York, 1892) reprinted in Thomas D. Clark, *Bluegrass Cavalcade* (Lexington, 1956). For a delightful and informative account of the construction of the Lexington waterworks and the politics involved in it, see Frances L. S. Dugan, *Rainfall Harvest* (Lexington, 1953). Useful in evaluating the census figures of 1870 and 1880 and the significant population trends in this era is Thomas R. Ford, "Kentucky in the 1880's: An Exploration in Historical Demography," *The Kentucky Review* (April, 1982). *A History of the Police and Fire Departments* (Lexington, 1914). Jack Womack, "The Urbanization of Lexington, Ky., from 1880 to 1890: A Study of Wasted Potential." (unpublished manuscript, 1975). Wright, *Transylvania,* previously cited. James F. Hopkins, *The University of Kentucky: Origins and Early Years* (Lexington, 1951). Frank L. McVey, *The Gates Open Slowly: A History of Education in Kentucky* (Lexington, 1949).

CHAPTER VI

The material dealing with horses and horse farms is derived to a large extent from Mary E. Wharton, et al., *The Horse World of the Bluegrass* (Lexington, 1980). For information on William (Billy) Francis Klair, see Nancy Graves, "William F. Klair," (an unpublished manuscript on microfilm in the special collections of the University of Kentucky) and James Joshua Mott, Jr., "City Manager Government in Lexington, Kentucky, 1947," (an unpublished master's thesis, University of Kentucky, 1947). Information on Klair was also provided from notes of Bettye Lee Mastin. Robert Rives was most gracious in sharing his knowledge and recollections of Klair and politics in Lexington in the early decades. On the closing of the turnpikes, see Allen, "The Turnpike System in Kentucky," previously cited. The most recent account of the famed Belle Breezing is J. Winston Coleman, Jr. *Belle Breezing: A Famous Lexington Bawd* (Lexington, 1980). Information on doctors and medical practice in this era is scarce but some useful facts were derived from Carl Fortune, M. D., *The First Fifty Years: A History of the Lexington Clinic, 1920-1970* (Lexington, 1971), updated in his *The Lexington Clinic, 1920-1980* (Lexington, 1981). The material on the public schools was provided by Burtis Franklin, a teacher for many years in the county schools and former director of pupil personnel for the merged Fayette County school system. Again, considerable information was derived from the columns of the *Lexington Herald* and the *Lexington Leader.* Some special articles written for the 50th anniversary edition of the *Leader* in 1938 were useful.

CHAPTER VII

On Laura Clay, see Paul E. Fuller, *Laura Clay and the Women's Rights Movement* (Lexington, 1975). Also see Helen Deiss Irvin, *Women in Kentucky* (Lexington, 1979). Material on Isaac Burns Murphy was generously made available by Betty E. Borries, whose manuscript, based on research by the late Frank Borries and Mrs. Borries, on the famed jockey, is the most thorough available. On Hathaway, see "Isaac Scott Hathaway: Lexington Sculptor," in *Historic Fayette County* (April, 1978). W. D. Johnson, *Prominent Negro Men and Women in Kentucky* (Lexington, 1897). On the W. C. P. Breckinridge scandal, see Paul E. Fuller, "Congressman Breckinridge and the Ladies, or Sex, Politics, and Morality in the Gilded Age," *Adena* (Spring, 1977). Charles Chilton Moore, *Behind the Bars: 31498* (Lexington, 1899). On Judge James H. Mulligan, see E. I. Thompson, "The Mulligans of Maxwell Place," in *Lexington: As It Was* (Lexington, 1981). On the conflicting stories relating to the John Hunt Morgan statue, see Burton Milward, "The Unveiling of the Morgan Statue," in *Lexington: As It Was* (Lexington, 1981). Valuable insight and information were gained from personal interviews with Mrs. Mary Powell Phelps Norment, Mrs. Graham Kerr, Mrs. Laura Wendell Moore, Miss Marion Hogan, Mr. Robert Jewell, Mr. Robert Rives, and Mr. Maurice Strider, among others. J. Winston Coleman, Jr., *The Squire's Memoirs* previously cited, also provided useful details.

There is a substantial amount of material, including photographs, on the Barrow Unit in the special collections of the University of Kentucky, including the interesting letters of Edward Jones, an enlisted man, who served with the unit.

CHAPTER VIII

Most of the material on the Will Lockett riot and the impact of prohibition on Lexington may be found in newspaper accounts in the *Herald* and the *Leader.* On Mrs. Cecil Cantrill, see the informative article by Bettye Lee Mastin in the *Herald,* November 3, 1981. The city directories are useful sources of information on businesses and the location of specific individuals and homes which over the years give a clue to changing housing patterns. Coleman, *Squire's Sketches of Lexington,* previously cited, is useful throughout this,

and all periods of the city's history. Of special interest is "A Promotive Survey of Lexington, Kentucky," prepared for the Board of Commerce by the General Organization Company, Chicago (July, 1923). Information on Lexington's mayors is derived from Mayor Pettit's file, previously cited. Material on the public schools is based on Franklin's research, previously cited. Information on Israel Jacob Schwartz may be found in Gertrude Dubrovsky, "Kentucky's Yiddish Poet," *Courier-Journal,* September 14, 1975, and Joseph R. Jones, "I. J. Schwartz in Lexington," *The Kentucky Review* (September, 1981). For voting patterns in Lexington and Fayette County in recent decades see Malcolm E. Jewell, *Kentucky Votes* (3 vols., Lexington 1963). Also of interest is the *Historical and Pictorial Review of the Police and Fire Departments of the City of Lexington* (June, 1929). The U.S. Census reports of the decades from 1920 through 1980 provide valuable information on population, manufacturing, employment, housing, etc. Though the Miley murder was covered in great detail in the local press at the time, the incident was recently retold in an article by Don Edwards in the *Leader,* July 16, 1981.

For information on Transylvania and the University of Kentucky during this period and the impact of World War II on these institutions see Wright, *Transylvania,* and Charles Gano Talbert, *The University of Kentucky: The Maturing Years* (Lexington, 1965).

CHAPTER IX

Because of the lack of extensive studies on Lexington in this period, the newspaper sources provide the major amount of information. Also useful are the special articles written for the annual Bluegrass Review, appearing in the Sunday edition of the *Herald-Leader* in the early months of each year for more than thirty years. Use was also made of the official records of the city, city directories, and U.S. Census data. Especially valuable in the study of the expansion of manufacturing in Lexington in this period was Dietrich M. Zimmer, *The Current Manufacturing Industries of Metropolitan Lexington* (Department of Geography, University of Kentucky, 1965). Material on the school system was derived from Franklin's research, previously cited. On the University of Kentucky in this period, see Talbert, *The University of Kentucky: The Maturing Years,* previously cited. A valuable source on recent black history in Lexington is contained in the 80 tapes of oral interviews with a great variety of blacks conducted by the Urban League which are housed in the special collections of the University of Kentucky. Material on CALF, Micro-City, the Planning Commission, the Blue Grass Trust, the Lexington-Fayette County Historic Commission, and the Kentucky-American Water Company was made available by these organizations. Information on the Underwood, Pettit, and Amato years, in addition to the newspapers, was provided, in part, by these gentlemen through correspondence, written records, and oral interviews.

The best account of the merger movement is William E. Lyons, *The Politics of City-County Merger: The Lexington-Fayette County Experience* (Lexington, 1977). On the judicial reform movement, see the final project report of the Kentucky Citizens for Judicial Improvement, Inc. (Lexington, 1976). The *1980 Comprehensive Plan: Growth Planning System* (Lexington, 1980) prepared by the Lexington-Fayette Urban County Planning Commission is a useful and informative document.

Index

Lexington's Mayors: 1832-1982

1832-34	Charlton Hunt	1866	David W. Standeford	1924-28	Hogan Yancey
1835-36	James E. Davis	1867	Jerry T. Frazer	1928-32	James J. O'Brien
1837-38	James G. McKinney	1868	Joseph G. Chinn	1932-34	William Thomas Congleton
1839-40	Charles H. Wickliffe	1869-80	Jerry T. Frazer	1934-35	Charles R. Thompson
1841	Daniel Bradford	1880-87	Claudius M. Johnson, Jr.	1936-40	E. Reed Wilson
1842-45	James Logue	1888-91	Charles W. Foushee	1940-43	T. Ward Havely
1846	Thomas Ross	1892-93	J. Hull Davidson	1943-47	R. Mack Oldham
1847	John Henry	1894-95	Henry T. Duncan	1948-52	Thomas G. Mooney
1848-49	George Payne Jouett	1896-99	Joseph Bullock Simrall	1952-56	Fred Fugazzi
1849-50	Orlando F. Payne	1900-03	Henry T. Duncan	1956-60	Shelby C. Kinkead
1851-53	Edward W. Dowden	1904-07	Thomas A. Combs	1960-64	Richard J. Colbert
1854	Thomas Hart Pindell	1907-08	R. B. Waddy	1964-68	Fred Fugazzi
1855-58	William Swift	1908-12	John Skain	1968-72	Charles Wylie
1859	Thomas B. Monroe, Jr.	1912-16	J. Ernest Cassidy	1972-77	Foster Pettit
1860-61	Benjamin F. Graves	1916-19	James C. Rogers	1978-81	James Amato
1862	Caleb Thomas Worley	1919	William H. McCorkle	1982-	H. Scott Baesler
1863-65	Joseph Wingate, Jr.	1920-24	Thomas Clark Bradley		